EVERYTHING YOU WANT IS ON THE OTHER SIDE OF HARD

EVERYTHING YOU WANT IS ON THE OTHER SIDE OF HARD

KEN RIDEOUT

CENTURY

CENTURY

UK | USA | Canada | Ireland | Australia
India | New Zealand | South Africa

Century is part of the Penguin Random House group of companies whose addresses can be found at global.penguinrandomhouse.com

Penguin Random House UK,
One Embassy Gardens, 8 Viaduct Gardens, London SW11 7BW

penguin.co.uk

First published in the US by Scribner, an imprint of Simon & Schuster 2026
First published in the UK by Century 2026
001

Copyright © Kenneth B. Rideout, 2026

The moral right of the author has been asserted

Penguin Random House values and supports copyright. Copyright fuels creativity, encourages diverse voices, promotes freedom of expression and supports a vibrant culture. Thank you for purchasing an authorised edition of this book and for respecting intellectual property laws by not reproducing, scanning or distributing any part of it by any means without permission. You are supporting authors and enabling Penguin Random House to continue to publish books for everyone. No part of this book may be used or reproduced in any manner for the purpose of training artificial intelligence technologies or systems. In accordance with Article 4(3) of the DSM Directive 2019/790, Penguin Random House expressly reserves this work from the text and data mining exception.

Printed and bound in Great Britain by Clays Ltd, Elcograf S.p.A.

The authorised representative in the EEA is Penguin Random House Ireland, Morrison Chambers, 32 Nassau Street, Dublin D02 YH68

A CIP catalogue record for this book is available from the British Library

ISBN: 978–1–529–95603–0 (hardback)
ISBN: 978–1–529–95604–7 (trade paperback)

Penguin Random House is committed to a sustainable future for our business, our readers and our planet. This book is made from Forest Stewardship Council® certified paper.

For my wife, Shelby.
For my children: Tensae, Jack, Luke, and Cameron.
And for everyone trying to get better.

CONTENTS

PROLOGUE: BLOOD AND DIRT	1
1. YOU THINK YOU'RE BETTER THAN US?	9
2. LOOK AT YOU FUCKING LOSERS	35
3. PERCS OF THE JOB	69
4. FULLY LOADED	89
5. JOYKILLERS	109
6. RUNNING THROUGH HELL	129
7. A NEW LIFE	145
8. WIN OR DIE TRYING	153
9. ESCAPE FROM NEW YORK	165
10. MARATHON MAN	185
11. NEXT WE TAKE BERLIN	203
12. ONWARD, UPWARD, INWARD	225
13. THE HARDEST RACE IN THE WORLD	245
14. SHOWDOWN IN CHICAGO	273

Success is how high you bounce when you hit bottom.
—General George S. Patton

PROLOGUE

BLOOD AND DIRT

I HIT THE DIRT HARD AND BY THE TIME I CAME UP, I WAS ALREADY DRIPPPING blood. Several times while training for Ironman, I've crashed my bike and jumped right back up—there was so much adrenaline flowing that I didn't feel pain in the moment. This fall was the opposite. My exhausted body exploded in pain, and my elbow was quickly drenched in blood.

I was two days into the Gobi March, a brutally difficult six-stage, 155-mile ultramarathon through the steppes, sand dunes, and rock valleys of Central Mongolia. I'd journeyed sixty-five hundred miles from my home in Nashville, and I was here to win. On the first stage of twenty-one miles, I'd gone out super hard. I knew it wasn't sustainable for the entire stage, but I thought for sure that if I went out at a crazy pace, I'd ditch my competition and buy myself enough space to get strategic. I was quickly stunned by how fast some of the other runners were. Not only had a few stayed with me, two of the guys—a Swiss and an Israeli—had left me behind with four or five miles left. Then an Italian guy passed me with maybe two miles to go. I came in fourth, around ten minutes behind the leader.

That first finish had me seriously questioning myself. I'd made a boneheaded mistake, traveling more than twenty-four hours from Nashville to Ulaanbaatar less than a day before the race start. I hadn't even considered how the jet lag and sleep deprivation would affect me. And I'd been arrogant. I thought I could just show up, fake my way through my first ultramarathon, and destroy everyone. Forget about winning, now I was going to have to destroy myself just to make it to the top three.

I knew I needed a different strategy for the second day. The Gobi March had drawn elite, savvy ultrarunners from around the globe who'd been preparing for this race for years, and I wasn't going to be able to just drop them like regular marathoners. For the second stage of twenty-eight miles, I decided to just run at a comfortable pace and not worry about anyone else. I focused on managing the distance and didn't allow myself to think about others. If they wanted to go out hard and blow up, they were welcome to. I just had to put my head down and run my best race and maybe—just maybe—I'd chip away at that ten-minute lead.

Day two started with single track and jeep trails that meandered through rolling, mountainous terrain. None of it was smooth turf or sure-footing. Hugo Reinhold, the Swiss guy, and David Dano, the Israeli, raced out in front of me early on, but they never got out of my sight. I wasn't even consciously trying to focus on them. I was just chatting with this British guy and running my race. Around ten miles, the British guy peeled off and I started closing distance to the leaders. I wasn't even trying to catch them. I wasn't speeding up; they were just slowing down. They'd gone hard on the first day, too, and it must have taken more out of them than it had me.

Very slowly, I started gaining on them. Then I caught up with them and we shared a few words—no trash talk, just checking in with each other. Then, without really trying, I slowly pulled away. I wasn't looking at them, I wasn't thinking about them. I was focused on running my race and nothing else existed.

Finally, I allowed myself a discreet peek over my shoulder. They were ten yards back. Then they were twenty yards back. We were probably twenty miles into the second stage when I realized I could no longer see them. At that time, we were running through rolling pasture and open fields with good visibility. At a minimum, they had to be five minutes behind me, maybe even ten. I started to feel good. Time to turn up the heat. I might blow this whole thing open right here, right now.

As much as my spirits were lifted by eking out some breathing room, I was still deep in the hurt locker and ready for the day to end. I didn't have a map so I didn't know exactly where I was, and since I was in the lead, there were no footprints in the dust to follow. I knew the rough distances of the stages and the distance between aid stations, but we were out here for a primal, even savage experience, and sometimes the distances were off. The sky was so vast, open, and empty, I felt as if I were the only person on some distant planet.

When you're depleted after a couple of days of hard running, seeing something that may indicate your suffering is over is almost like seeing a mirage. At the slightest hint that your ordeal is about to end, you immediately project all your hopes and dreams onto that illusion. I crested a rise and saw a little circle of yurts, and my heart soared. *This is definitely the village where this stage ends. My day is done. I won the stage and may have taken the lead. I'm fucking back, baby.*

Seeing those yurts on the horizon lit a fire under my ass and I started running harder, doing everything I could to bring my time down. When I finally rolled up, I realized what I thought was the end point was a deserted Mongolian shepherd village. The yurts had been left behind by nomads who'd taken their sheep, goats, or cattle somewhere else this time of year. I couldn't see another village from here so that meant, what, another four miles? Maybe five? That distance was incomprehensible.

My mood instantly tanked. I'd carried a twenty-pound pack almost fifty miles in these last two days, the first time I'd run with a pack. Between the travel and the exertion, I was incredibly fatigued. I was in the lead and didn't want to waste a second doing anything unnecessary, so I hadn't been eating enough. At first it was because I didn't want to break stride, but as my energy plummeted from lack of calories, it became impossible to muster up the willpower necessary to even reach for a gel pack. I was so dehydrated that my vision had started to blur. And I was so depleted that I couldn't even think straight. *How many miles are left? How many minutes per mile? How much time in total?* I kept sending those requests for information, and my brain kept coming up with nothing. I kept running.

Nothing felt stable. My reflexes were so slow, it was like I was underwater. My forward momentum was the only thing keeping me upright. But my body was so fatigued by this point that all the stabilizer muscles in my ankles and feet were lagging. The signals weren't getting to my brain fast enough, and everything felt squishy.

You got to fucking pay attention here because your brain's not working. I still couldn't see the next village. The day had suddenly become incredibly long, and I couldn't conceptualize that, eventually, it would end. *Hold fast, buddy. This could go really bad really fast.* I kept hammering out of instinct alone.

Around twenty-five miles with maybe only three miles to go, I started descending a small hill. From a distance, the tall grass made the terrain look smooth, but it was anything but. It was hybrid desert pasture, full of rocks and roots and tiny coarse bushes grabbing at your feet. It would have been terrible to run on if I was a fresh, fleet-footed twenty-year-old, but I was fifty-one, totally beat to shit, and still trying to outrun guys half my age.

My pack plagued me with each step. Twenty pounds doesn't sound like a lot, but I was only 170, which meant I had an extra 10 percent of body weight resting above my center of gravity. With that added weight, even the slightest misstep made me feel like I was about to careen out of control. I was catching myself constantly, just trying to manage getting down the hill, but each footstep felt more unstable than the last. Then my foot slipped just a little more than I could account for, I lost my stability, and that heavy pack drove me into the dirt hard.

I went ass over teakettle, tumbling and flipping and flopping down the hill, just a ball of dust. I felt something pop. *Dear God, let that not be a ligament or tendon I need to run.* I was ready to crawl the rest of the way in to finish the stage if I had to, but a torn hamstring or Achilles tendon would end my race.

When I finally stopped falling, I sat up. My sunglasses had fallen off, there was dirt in my teeth, and everything hurt. I jumped up, determined to finish. My elbow was bleeding pretty badly but

I could stand without any issue. The pop I'd felt was the strap of my backpack breaking. I grabbed hold of the broken strap and, somehow, I started running again.

My pack flopped awkwardly on my back like it was an animal fighting to get free. I could feel the blood dripping down my arm, but I could not give a shit. My skin would heal. My backpack wouldn't. And it would be impossible to run another hundred miles with it flopping around.

I couldn't believe it. I'd come all the way to Mongolia, and now I wasn't going to be able to finish this race because of a stupid equipment failure? All my buried insecurity came roaring to the surface. *No one's going to believe this really broke. They're going to think I was just hurt and tired and frustrated and ripped it myself to give myself an out so I could quit.*

I hobbled as fast as I could, fighting the flopping backpack with each step. I'd killed myself to bury the leaders from the first stage and now, inch by painful inch, I could feel that lead slipping away.

Finally, finally, *finally*, I saw what was unmistakably the finish for the second stage. As I shuffled across the finish line, I could see the race organizers' eyes widen at the blood smeared on my face and dripping off my arm. I'd done it. I'd won the stage.

Yeah, I'd prevailed, but I'd completely ruined myself in the process. I was dehydrated and starved for calories and utterly exhausted. The cut on my elbow that had been so alarming was just a flesh wound. But what other damage had I done in the fall? I knew I'd be feeling every bit of it in the morning. But the deal-breaker was the backpack. There was no way to fix it. And replacing it was out of the question. We were out in the middle of nowhere. We'd had to bring in everything we needed for the race. The race organizer had supplied each runner with an exhaustive list of everything from a waterproof bag to a whistle to lip balm with sunscreen. I had one backpack, and it was busted. If I had to drop, there wasn't even a way home. We'd landed in Ulaanbaatar, a major city with all the modern comforts available, but then they'd bussed us hours outside of the city to no-man's-land to start the race. I'd have to ride with the organizers from stage to stage till the race ended five days later. The thought of that futile caravan of shame made my skin crawl. I'd come here to win.

Was this it? Was this my last day? Had I been so intent on winning the stage that I'd tanked the entire race?

I'd overcome so much in my life to be out here, running one of the toughest races in the world with elite runners from around the globe. I'd been at the bottom so many times in so many different ways: the lonely, unloved little kid, full of anxiety and despair and desperate dreams; the lost, raging hockey thug, drawn into bar fight after coked-up bar fight; the dopesick Wall Street trader, strung out on Percocet and Subutex. All of this I'd endured and eventually overcome. There *had* to be a way forward . . .

CHAPTER ONE

YOU THINK YOU'RE BETTER THAN US?

I WAS BORN IN 1971 IN SOMERVILLE, A BOMBED-OUT BLUE-COLLAR SUBURB of Boston. Somerville had flourished in the first half of the 1900s: first brickmaking and railyards, then meatpacking and grocery distribution, then the booming auto industry in the 1940s. The Irish had poured in and Somerville became known for its "triple-deckers": cheap three-family houses—soulless utilitarian shitholes, really—crammed in side by side to accommodate all those working families. Then the Ford Motor plant in Assembly Square closed in 1958. The grocery distributor Finast took over the building, but when they finally fled in 1976, Assembly Square emptied out and the city began to eat itself. When I was growing up, the community was in aggressive decline, working-class families fighting tooth and nail not to fall any further. In Somerville, no one dreamed of being an astronaut or the president. The fantasy was hitting the numbers, scoring a sanitation department job with a pension, or getting on disability.

My family was poor, Irish, and Catholic so we fit right in. I was named Ken after my father, but my family called me Kenny. My mother had me when she was nineteen and my father twenty—two dumb kids with no idea what they were doing. My brother Keith was born just eleven months later—Irish twins, as they say. Though we both had my father's brown eyes, I was dark and Keith was blond, the first indication of the different paths we'd take. My parents divorced right after Keith was born, so he and I went to live with my mother and her parents.

My grandfather was a truck driver, but he still had some pride. He always had a Cadillac and each day he drove it down to the trucking yard before his shift. Good guy, worked hard, we all loved him. I was in first grade when he died at forty-two of a massive heart attack. I was at T-ball and they came to get me off the field, including my grandmother, who was almost frozen with shock. Grandpa left her the house, a run-down two-family home in inner-city Somerville. It was a dump—clapboard siding with peeling paint, sagging shingle roof, no yard. The top floor was us kids, my mother, and whatever guy was hanging around her. Downstairs, it was my grandmother and her lifelong heroin addict son, Barney.

Barney'd had a hard run of it. Even as a little kid I could tell that. One of his legs was shorter than the other, so he walked with a crutch. My dad said that Barney got thrown down the stairs in junior high, but deep down I knew that probably wasn't true. Barney wasn't a bad guy, just a dead-end punk rock burnout—slightly overweight in a Ramones T-shirt, black leather jacket, and ripped jeans, his face constantly shiny with sweat. When he wasn't whacked out of his skull or coming down, he had a level of kindness to him. But if he was jonesing or going into withdrawals, Barney would run you over.

I was real little the first time I saw him shooting up. I wandered into his room unannounced and he was sitting on the edge of his waterbed, injecting something into his arm. He screamed at me and I ran out. I loved Barney, but I learned early on that I couldn't trust him. Before he was anything else, Barney was a junkie. And high or low, chaos constantly surrounded him. There were always junkies coming and going from the house. And then there were the people coming by to beat up Barney and his junkie friends for running scams or stealing shit. It was disgusting, the worst type of environment for kids. It must have been constant heartbreak for my grandma to watch her son living that way.

My grandmother had my mother when she was eighteen, so she was barely in her forties. I'd started calling her Granny as a goof because she looked nothing like a granny. It stuck. She was short and stocky, tough as hell, shanty Irish, constantly dropping f-bombs. She could down a "double six-pack" of whatever was on sale in one sitting: "Run down to Kappy's—they got double six-packs of Meister Bräu for $3.99." Granny called our tiny, rickety stoop "the piazza," as if it were some gorgeous marble balcony overlooking the town square and she were a grande dame. Our dumpy old living room was the parlor, but in her thick Boston accent, it became "the pahlah." She had a bottomless heart and couldn't say no to anyone, so people were always taking advantage of her. In our house, she was the one person who was unconditionally kind to me.

Granny had grown up in the Depression, so she could make a meal out of nothing. My mother never met a government program she didn't love. We got regular food stamps and WIC—

a government assistance program for women, infants, and children that was limited to flour, milk, sugar, and other staples. With the WIC, my mother would buy a head of cabbage and a piece of fatback—a rectangular block of solid white oily fat cut from the back of a pig. My grandmother would then boil that in a pot with shredded cabbage. She'd take a pack of hot dogs my mother got with the food stamps, chop 'em all up, and throw 'em in the pot. She called it Hot Dog Soup. We ate it all the time—a whole meal in one pot. I remember it tasting incredible, but maybe it's because I loved her so much. Tough as she was, Granny was always sweet to everyone, she always did the right thing, and she always had compassion for me. I remember looking up at her and wondering, *How are you even related to these other people?*

Even from my earliest memories, my mother was perpetually overwhelmed, always smoking weed or popping pills. At times, my mother would be present and try to be a good mom, but most of the time, she seemed to have zero interest in being a mother. At this stage, her only goal in life seemed to be getting a free ride—scoring a bigger welfare check, another hundred bucks in food stamps, and Section 8 housing. My mother would apply for every possible handout. Even as a child, that blew my mind. I couldn't believe she was taking all this free shit—didn't she have any pride? And then she'd send me to the store to get eggs or bread with the food stamps. It looked like fake money from a board game. I'd be mortified walking in, stuffing those shameful "food coupons" into the bottom of my pocket. I'd wait till the last second to pull them out to hand them to the cashier. And then the asshole behind the counter would always hold them up to the light to read them so everyone would know.

We were poor but we weren't the worst off. There was a whole shifting hierarchy in the neighborhood, people always jostling and fighting to look better than Patrick down the street. Lurking barely below the surface was poisonous self-loathing—*maybe we don't have shit, but at least we're not those other people and you can never take that away from us.* Nobody cares more about status than people with no status. We owned our house, my grandfather had worked, and we were fairly neat and clean. We weren't doing as good as our mailman neighbor with a wife and kids and a real job with a pension and all that, but we weren't the bottom rung. But I had cousins and family on my mother's side who kept me terrified of what awaited us if things got worse.

Not many people in Somerville had money for entertainment, so weekends people would just go visit friends or family the next town over. My mother was the kind of poor who, although she got every kind of public assistance available and was constantly on my dad for more child support, somehow always had a nice car. She and Granny would load us up in her blue four-door Cadillac DeVille sedan to go visit her family in the Cambridge projects. Sometimes even Barney would come along. It'd be burned-out cars and snarling dogs chained up in a courtyard that was just layers of tar and crushed stone, not a hedge or a single blade of grass to be seen. It was like someone had just plopped down these square Lego buildings in the middle of concrete nowhere. There were packs of kids running around with dirty faces and scabby knees, snot running out of their noses, some only eight years old and already jumping other kids to steal their bikes or shoes.

Of all the busted, dangerous places we visited, the worst was the Mystic River projects. It was built like an outdoor prison—no wonder so many people there wound up going away, it probably felt like home. That neighborhood looked absolutely war-torn—where hope goes to die. This was my mother's dream—to get Section 8 housing, rent out our apartment, and get paid to live in the degenerate squalor of the Mystic River projects.

I can't remember any part of my childhood where I wasn't getting hit. I was constantly getting whacked around—occasionally by Barney but more frequently by my mother. She had this one boyfriend, Jimmy Pandolfo, a weaselly scumbag with a big porno mustache and a messed-up old blue Camaro, who loved slapping us kids and my mother around. My grandmother hated this guy, called him "that fucking loser Pandolfo." She disliked my father, but she *really* hated Jimmy.

One time he had me with him while he was trying to plow the snow at his mom's house on a steep hill in a borrowed Jeep. I was scared we were going to roll over and I started crying. He slapped me across the face and told me to toughen up. My father got wind of it, came over, and beat the snot out of him. I remember watching Jimmy Pandolfo crying for mercy, cowering on the floor, not even trying to fight back. Pathetic.

When I was eight, my mother got remarried to a guy several years younger than her and the abuse continued. My stepfather was a naive young former marine from some backwater in Alabama who'd just moved to Boston. He was a redneck southerner living in blue-collar Boston, and that put a target on his back. He was working these manual-labor jobs with guys from the inner city, so he was always getting in scraps. But as tough as he talked to me and Keith, any time there was a dustup my stepfather was always getting the wrong end of it.

One day, Keith and I watched him get into a shouting match with someone in traffic while we were in the back seat. The other guy got out of his car. My stepfather got out of his car. The other guy punched him in the face. Without a word, my stepfather got back in the car. We drove away. Keith and I glanced at each other as if to say "what a pussy."

He was always coming home banged up like that—sometimes two black eyes and a broken nose from "walking into a ladder." But you can bet that every beating he took, he made sure there was a little something extra left over for us.

My mother popped out another kid, my half brother whom I'll call Matt. Then she just lay around the house, smoked weed, and complained constantly about her migraines. My stepfather was constantly on my case. Keith and I had been getting smacked since we were babies, but my stepfather preferred the belt. My mother tried to stick up for us in the beginning, at least when she wasn't doing the hitting. Eventually, she got sick of trying and just looked the other way. Getting regularly slapped around by every adult in our house was the most painful, destabilizing feeling. I felt neglected and unloved and on edge, like the world could spin out of control at any moment.

My stepfather had a motorcycle, a 1970s Honda street bike. As little boys, we were enamored with the motorbike and always asking to go for rides. Here's where you'd hope that my mother would have enough common sense to say, "No, you can't take an eight-year-old kid riding around Boston on a street bike." But my stepfather decided it was a good idea for us to go for a tool around town. We put on our helmets, and I got on the back of the motorcycle and put my hands in the front pockets of his leather jacket, holding on super tight. Then I remember waking up in the hospital. My hand was in a cast, elevated in some weird sling so I wouldn't roll over on it. I later found out it was broken.

I only remember what was told to me. I guess a car had pulled out of a side street in front of us. We T-boned the car at full speed, no brakes. The front wheel turned sideways and before he got launched over the car, my stepfather got stabbed hard enough in the guts by the handlebars that he was taken to the hospital with internal injuries. I don't remember any of it, but the ambulance driver told my mother they found me sitting on the curb on the side of the street with my helmet still on. When they took the helmet off, it was obvious that I was either in shock or had a severe concussion, because I was completely out of it, with no memory of the next twelve hours.

When we went home, my stepfather was still in the hospital. After several days, he finally came home, too. For the next year, the twisted-up useless motorcycle lingered in our front yard like a silent accusation.

—

One night, the house caught fire. It didn't burn down, but the damaged structure needed to be renovated. So my mother's new husband loaded the family—a seven-year-old and an eight-year-old, a newborn baby, and my mom, who'd just given birth—into the car and we bombed down to his bumblefuck hometown of Sheffield, Alabama, right outside of Muscle Shoals.

I remember lying in bed alone, crying, the night before we were to leave. My mother happened to notice and asked me what was the matter. *Are you kidding me?* I thought. She was taking us away from our father and our family and our friends and everything we knew. Alabama might as well have been Argentina as far as we were concerned, we were little kids. My mother would have been twenty-seven then, so my stepfather was twenty-three. To them, it was some grand adventure, maybe even a new beginning. Reality: it was white-trash hell on earth.

Sheffield wasn't some inner-city ghetto or lonely rural wasteland. It was just a busted little town with nothing going for it—no community, no jobs, no reason to exist. Maybe Somerville had lost its hope as a city, but Sheffield had never had it. We lived in one of the crappier houses in one of the crappier neighborhoods, a dingy swaybacked old wooden structure propped up on four concrete blocks. It was the color of a chain-smoker's teeth and it looked like it couldn't wait to fall down.

In that miserable year I wish I could forget, there's one incident that stands out. We had no supervision, so one night while my parents were partying, I wandered out of the house. I ended up walking more than a mile to the high school football game. A bunch of other little kids I knew from the neighborhood and from my school were at the game, all hanging out together. When they saw me, they weren't like, "Oh, there's the kid from Boston, how interesting." One little kid said something and pointed, then they all came over in a group.

"Fuck you, Yankee."

I don't think I said anything. What do you say to that?

They threw me on the ground. One of the kids from my second-grade class—a kid whom I thought was a complete pussy—stood over me.

"What are you gonna do? You can't do anything about it."

He was right. I wasn't afraid to fight this kid, I knew I could probably win. But there was a whole bunch of them, and I knew they'd beat my ass. I just lay there on the ground and didn't say anything and prayed for it to end.

When they left, I stood up and brushed myself off. A wave of shame crashed over me. I should have jumped up and attacked this asshole and instead I was like *please let this go away*. Like a baby. How could I sleep that night? How could I go to bed knowing I was a coward and a quitter and a loser?

I swore to myself that I'd never allow myself to be bullied again, I'd fight till the death and never surrender. It'd be better to get beaten to death than ever feel like that again. That's how empty I felt. I was eight years old.

When I look back, it seems like an unimportant incident. Most people were shoved and bullied as kids. But in me it planted a transformative vow. I swore to myself that I'd never tap out, never give up. I'd never allow myself to feel like that again.

One of my greatest fears as a child was our living room floor in Somerville. Our house wasn't filthy or disgusting when I was growing up, it was just barely restrained chaos. Shit could pop off at any minute—doors slamming, people screaming, people throwing dishes or bottles, my stepfather asking me whether I wanted the belt now or one hour after dinner. Counting out the strokes, like "move your fucking hands and take your punishment."

But it wasn't even my stepfather's belt that was my nightmare—it was the living room carpet. It was this gross dogshit-gold color, but not a shag rug. It had a weird pattern of some kind on it, like a paisley, but it was such a tight weave, it was almost abrasive. If someone dragged you across it, it'd strip the skin right off you. Under that carpet, the floor sagged badly. Remember, we lived on the top floor of a two-story house of the shoddiest construction. The doors were made of Masonite so thin, it may as well have been cardboard. If you punched a hole in a door, it'd completely disintegrate. Any time someone would jump around or make sudden movements in the house, it felt like you might fall through the sagging floor into the apartment downstairs. My throat starts to close just thinking about it. My entire childhood, I had this mounting fear that something horrible was going to happen to our house, that this hole was going to open up in the middle of our living room and swallow me up.

My father lived only one town over, in Malden, but it seemed like he was worlds away. He benefited from the instability at home, because whenever I saw him for hockey or the occasional weekend visit, it felt like an escape, a reprieve from the constant assault of abuse.

Ice time was hard to come by in Boston because everyone played hockey. The younger you were, the earlier your games were. It wouldn't be uncommon for my father and a carload of buddies to pick me up at five thirty in the morning for a six o'clock game. Sometimes there'd be three of us up front with no one in the back, my father and a friend propping their tall glasses of beer on the dash of my father's Buick LeSabre. Other times it'd be me and my dad up front with a whole peanut gallery of three or four guys crammed into the back seat. No seat belts, of course, while everyone in the car was drinking and had been drinking all night.

No one found this even remotely out of order. It was business as usual. And it wasn't just my father, all the dads in our neighborhood were like this.

It gave me the weirdest feeling, riding to hockey with my dad and his pals. They all loved hockey and I was good at hockey, so they loved me. That felt so good it hurt—being one of the guys, belonging, and having them all rally around me on the way to the rink. But I also knew I didn't belong. They were adults and I was a little kid, and even our sacred hockey could only bridge that divide temporarily. And the drinking and swearing in front of a little kid in the very early morning . . . I knew it was inappropriate before I even knew the word.

My father leaned into his role as Keith's and my savior, always shit-talking my mother and stepfather, which only made me feel worse about the situation. He was proud of his job at the Finast grocery distribution center, proud that he kicked back in a triple-decker attic apartment. There was a little living room facing out toward the street. Then you had to walk through his bedroom, with an old comforter pulled over a double bed, to get to the eat-in kitchen with a TV, a metal bookshelf with no books on it, and a love seat. That dingy gold love seat folded out into a bed—but not even a queen-size, just a full. The whole place had a distinct attic-y smell, like shredded newspaper insulation, tar-paper roofing tiles, and mildew.

Keith and I visited my father a couple of weekends each month. Keith hated him. Every time he came to pick us up, it'd be a battle between them.

"I'm not going."

"Get in the car, Keith."

"I said I'm not going."

"Get in the car," my father would say, "you're fucking going."

Keith would plant his feet and lower his head like a dog about to fight. My father would try to force him into the back of his black Buick, Keith would scream and flail around like my father was kidnapping him, and my father would start dishing out hard slaps . . . it was embarrassing. My father would eventually get him in the car because Keith was just a little kid, maybe seven or eight, but it was an ugly process. Not because Keith was particularly strong or a good fighter but because nothing held him back. Like a wounded rat in a corner, he was ready to fight to the death.

Every time we visited, I knew that when it came time to go to bed, my father would point us to the foldout love seat. The entire evening I'd pray to God that I wouldn't piss the bed. But my prayers didn't work. Every single morning, my father would lose his mind upon seeing that I'd wet the bed again, screaming at me and belittling me. I hated every second of it. It got so bad that I'd try to stay awake the entire night to avoid pissing the bed. The way my father reacted, you'd think I'd stood up on that hard, thin mattress in the middle of the night and hosed down the entire bed on purpose.

One night, driving home from a hockey game, he said, "So, Kenny, I was talking to Eddie O'Brien's dad tonight."

"Yeah?"

"He said the same thing happens to Eddie occasionally. You know, about the bed."

I felt hot shame creep up the back of my neck like a fever coming on. *You told someone else at the hockey game, someone outside of our family, that I pissed the bed? You are supposed to protect me.*

Did he actually tell my friend's father that I pissed the bed? I don't know. But in the moment, the possibility was incredibly hurtful to me. I knew that I was a little kid and that parents were supposed to take care of little kids. But I was quickly learning that no one really had my back.

My father tried to intervene a couple of times in the violence we were enduring at home, but nothing ever changed. After a while, I gave up the fantasy that he'd come save me. I felt so vulnerable. I remember thinking, *I know one day this will be over. I know one day this will end. God, just get me to the finish line.* I still don't know whether I was dreaming of safety or suicide.

Even through all that, I knew that one day I'd be a father. My kids would feel unconditionally loved and supported. I'd be at their football and hockey games, cheering them on and rooting for them even if they were losing, especially if they were losing. They'd have every single thing they needed, not just good food paid for with actual money and decent clothes, but new skates and sticks and pads when they needed them, even new sneakers, not the discount garbage we got but Nikes or Reeboks. They'd never have to live through the shit I did—the junkies squabbling on our porch, the claustrophobic smell of overflowing ashtrays, and a quarter inch of warm Schlitz in the bottom of a can, the destabilizing knowledge that any adult could smack you across the face at any time for any reason and you couldn't do anything about it.

I knew I'd have kids, and I knew I had to get out of Somerville. If anyone in our house was ever going to do anything, it had to be me, that much was clear. It wasn't going to be Keith. He seemed like a lost cause, even from the earliest days. He was chubby and he sucked at sports, so he was insecure. But he was defiant, so he'd get into fights all the time—battles he rarely won. Keith took more beatings than anyone I've ever seen. We hated each other, but I don't think he hated me as much as I hated him. Every time I turned around, he was fighting one of my friends. I felt like I had to defend him, but how could you defend someone who was so completely out of line? Looking back, I know exactly why he turned out the way he did, and I know it wasn't his fault. He'd certainly suffered trauma, abuse, and neglect, and may have been suffering from clinical mental health issues that my parents didn't have the wherewithal to get diagnosed and treated. But as a kid, I didn't understand Keith and I couldn't understand Keith, so I made him my enemy. We were oil and water, from the very beginning.

I was the good kid. We were allowed to run wild in the streets until dark, but I never got in trouble. I always came home when I was called. All I did was play sports and get good enough grades and follow the rules. Granny had told me I was special, and I believed her. She made no attempt to hide her affection for me—she'd tell all the grandkids and everyone else in the family all the time that I was her favorite grandkid. She'd call me the golden child in front of everyone and wink at me, like we were in on something together.

"You think you're better than us?" my mother or stepfather would taunt me.

I didn't just think it, I knew it. They knew it, too. Better than this dead-end shithole, anyway.

Hockey was the only thing I was proud of, and I knew it'd be my ticket out. It was my father's only dream for me. My mother couldn't have cared less about hockey, but my dad had us on skates before we could walk. Keith only played a season or two before he quit and refused to ever play again, but from the earliest age, I played constantly, year-round. Hockey was one of the only ways I ever got any praise from my father. Unless, of course, we lost a game. Then he'd scream at me the entire way home, and I'd cry the entire way home. It was insane: he'd be yelling at me about every little nuance when, even as a little kid, I knew he knew very little about this game he loved so much.

Still, I loved hockey. I identified as a hockey player. It's all I ever knew, all I ever did, and all I ever wanted to be. No one around me ever thought to tell me it was an unrealistic dream, that maybe I should have a backup plan in case I wasn't a first-round NHL draft pick at nineteen. I practiced for hours by myself in our driveway, pretending to be the Bruins enforcer Terry O'Reilly, firing slap shot after slap shot into the gray chain-link fence until it was completely deformed and twisted out of shape.

—

One summer when I was in third or fourth grade, my parents sent us to a sleep-away camp in Poland, Maine, called Agassiz Village—a welfare camp. This was the late seventies, when the racial tensions that had simmered in Boston for many years were finally boiling over. The Racial Imbalance Act of 1965 had made segregation of public schools illegal in Massachusetts, the first legislation of its kind. City and school officials protested and obstructed the law till 1974, when Judge W. Arthur Garrity Jr. implemented a forced busing plan to desegregate predominantly white and Black schools—but only poor, inner-city public schools. Judge Garrity's kids weren't affected. Neither were the children of Massachusetts senator Ted Kennedy.

People lost their minds. Parents protested, kids skipped school en masse, and attendance plummeted. From September 1974 to the fall of 1976, there were at least forty riots in Boston, several race-related stabbings, and probably hundreds if not thousands of minor hate crimes.

Agassiz Village was dedicated to helping "underserved and at-risk youth." The majority were Black kids from inner-city Boston. My brother and I were white Irish kids from a white Irish neighborhood. It felt like we were being shipped off to Vietnam.

My mother packed lunches for Keith and me—a bologna and American cheese sandwich on white bread with a can of soda wrapped in tinfoil to keep it cold. Then she and my stepfather loaded us in the back seat of my stepfather's Camaro to drive us to our doom. The pickup for this camp was on the Boston Common in downtown Boston. We lived right outside of the city, but the trip was still like journeying from a quiet little neighborhood in Queens to 1970s Times Square. Our eyes were peeled wide open that whole ride, the thought taking hold that *Oh shit, we're in for it now.*

I'd never been to camp even for one night, and now we were going away for two weeks? It was madness. I was so uncomfortable, so scared, I'd rather have gone to jail. *Just send me straight to the electric chair.* When we got down there, sure enough, it was all rough Black kids. Two weeks alone at welfare summer camp with my maniac brother and a bunch of older, tougher kids who already hate my guts—how could things get worse?

That day my brother Keith was seeing everything I was seeing. But he had a plan. The second the car stopped, he yanked the door open, jumped out, and took off running across Boston Common. Like that, he was gone. My parents started looking for him but they couldn't find him. They were looking everywhere. Finally, he'd been gone so long that the buses were leaving. My mother squatted down next to me.

"All right, Kenny, just get on the bus. We'll find your brother and we'll deal with this later."

What do you know, things *could* always get worse.

The minute we got off the bus after a harrowing three-hour ride, one of those older city kids came up to me.

"Yo, let me get those Cons."

I had a brand-new pair of white-on-white leather Converse All Stars, just like the ones that Larry Bird wore. We'd bought them at the Converse outlet mall, so they were defects. You couldn't see that there was anything wrong with them, but in my heart I knew they were defective. But they were mine, and no one was taking them away from me.

"Not gonna happen."

The other kid looked at me, nodded and said, "I'm gonna get 'em," then walked away.

I had my clothes for the trip packed in my hockey bag. For the rest of the trip, any time that those All Stars weren't on my feet, they were buried in the bottom of my hockey bag. The bag zipped up and there was a tiny lock for the zipper. I carried the keys with me every day. At night, I slept with them hidden inside my pillowcase. They never got my All Stars.

The people running the camp had different themes for every two-week session. Luckily, while I was there, the theme was the Olympics, so it was all sports. At that stage of my life, I was much further along physically than the other kids. My parents had no other dreams for me so sports was everything. I'd been skating, jumping, shooting, and tackling from the moment I could walk.

I was dominating at the camp, just winning everything. The cabin could be a gauntlet after lights-out, but the other kids quickly figured out that there were easier targets.

On maybe the third day, I was called to a cabin that belonged to the camp leader, this older Black dude named Jeff, very fit and put together, like he'd been in the military. My mother was there with my brother. Keith was freaking out, screaming . . . he didn't want to be there. My mother looked like she'd had it. He'd clearly been giving her the business the entire ride up.

"Listen, Kenny," Jeff said, "you've been doing great. But you know your brother doesn't want to be here."

"If you want to go, let's just go," my mother said. "I'll take you both, and we'll just go home."

My parents had dumped me in this hostile environment even after my brother had abandoned me. Now that I'd figured it out and was actually succeeding, they were going to yank me out because Keith was weak?

"I'm gonna stay."

"Kenny, are you sure?" Jeff said.

I didn't need these people to save me.

"Yeah. You guys can leave. I'm going to stick it out."

I didn't envy Jeff's position. He was a good guy, firm but kind and fair. It couldn't have been an easy decision to make. He could see how messed up it was—two kids from an abusive home, one of whom was normal, even resilient, and the other emotionally damaged. But Jeff and my mom decided to make my brother stay.

Every day for the remainder of the two weeks, I had to watch Keith saying crazy shit and acting like a maniac and starting fights and getting his butt whipped. And he had to watch me winning virtually every event and having praise heaped on me by the camp counselors. I felt obligated to defend him, and sometimes I did, but we weren't friendly. I never checked in on him. I never asked whether he was okay.

It was a horrible situation. Keith was my brother, my blood. We should have gone to that camp together and drawn strength from each other. But we were so different. My parents never did anything to try to mend our broken relationship. They should have told us, "You guys stick together, no matter what happens." But without intending to, Keith made camp a nightmare for me, and, likewise, I unintentionally made camp a nightmare for him. And we hated each other for it.

On the last day, as the camp was winding down, the counselors handed out prizes. I won like ten prizes, including camper of the year. Jeff, the camp leader, pulled me aside after the whole ceremony.

"You should be really proud of yourself, Kenny. You're going to do really well in life. Don't let them drag you down."

It felt so good to hear that from an adult. For the first time in my life, I realized that I didn't have to let my family define who I was. I was going to be my own person.

When I was in sixth grade, I got a paper route. The papers came first thing in the morning, so I'd get up at five to fold and deliver newspapers in the heat, rain, snow—all kinds of weather—while the rest of my family slept. It'd be pitch-black and I'd be up and waiting in the dark by myself like a psychopath. A guy in a crappy little Datsun pickup would deliver a huge bundle of newspapers strapped together. I'd run out and lug it inside in the cold, cut the plastic strap, and it'd snap open. I'd have to fold and rubber band this entire bale of papers. By the time I was done, my hands would be black with ink.

They gave all the paperboys a huge round canvas bag with a strap so we could throw it over our shoulders. But when it was full, that bag was as big around as a rain barrel and so heavy it'd choke you and drag you off the back of your bike. I had a bike Granny had bought for me that I loved, the cheapest decent BMX they had: a Huffy with plastic mag wheels instead of spokes, all done up in Hulk Hogan colors, light blue and bright yellow. As the money from the paper route came in, I'd upgraded it with pegs on the back, then valve stem caps that looked like dice, other little things. I'd wrestle that big bag of papers up onto the crossbar, then climb into the seat and pull the strap over my head onto my neck. I'd have to kick my legs way out to the sides, but I could still pedal—barely. I'd ride carefully a couple of blocks over to where my route began, then bike slowly up and down the streets, flinging papers onto porches while steering with one hand, freezing and cursing and praying for the sun to come up.

Looking back now, I can't even believe I did this. It was such fucking hard work. To get up so early to do this before school . . . who even taught me how to set the alarm clock? I was maybe twelve years old—how did I get all this shit done? But I did.

One night, I did something wrong—left a dish out in the kitchen or didn't put the milk away or something. When I woke up the next morning, I found my stepfather had locked my bike up with a heavy padlock so I wouldn't be able to use my bike to deliver the papers. I'd have to walk, which would add at least an hour to my morning routine. Of all the horrible things to do to a kid. Somehow,

I got a pair of tweezers and a safety pin and fiddled with the lock until it popped open. *Fuck you, you can't stop me.* I got on my bike, delivered my papers, came home, and locked it up again. Dumbass would never even know.

—

Maybe a year later, I fell in love with sneakers. The new Nike Cortez was blowing up everywhere and I just had to have a pair. They were impossible to get, sold out nearly everywhere. But I had the money from the paper route, so I was the first kid in seventh grade to get a pair. The Cortez was a white leather sneaker with that trademark Nike Swoosh on the side in red. The first day I wore them to school, everyone noticed.

"Aw, man, those are so cool."

"Those are wicked, Kenny."

But some kids were so jealous, they had to try to drag me down.

"Look at this idiot. Thinks he's better than everyone."

They were right—I did want to differentiate myself from the dirty-ass kids from my neighborhood, my family, my home. But their insults struck at the heart of my insecurity. If you had shitty things, they'd tease you for being poor. If you owned anything nice, they hated you more. These Somerville kids were like crabs in a bucket—you'd try to get out and they'd just pull you back down into the muck.

And the adults—maybe they were adults, but they weren't grown-ups. They behaved like kids who no longer had to follow rules. At Trum Field, the baseball park a couple of blocks from my house, I watched one of my uncle's friends, Jerry Shea, get beaten to a bloody pulp. I finally had to be the one to step in, holding an aluminum bat, and say, "Okay, he's had enough." I was twelve or thirteen. It felt like no one was in charge, all the adults were drunk or stoned or high and acting like animals.

—

Finally, my family's luck seemed to break. It no longer felt like we were about to run out of money at any second. Nicer things started showing up at our house. One day when I came home from school, there was a massive wood-grain VCR sitting on top of our dusty old console TV. The next day, there were movies, too: *Stripes*, *Animal House*, *Gorky Park*. They looked like they were store copies from a rental place but somehow, they were ours. We got a new dining set. We'd never had new furniture of any kind. Every single piece of furniture in our house had been there from the minute I was born, and it'd been old and falling apart then. But this dining set was brand-new—the finish on the wood gleamed like it was glistening wet.

One day I came home to discover a matching leather sofa and love seat set. It was green, the color of a twenty-dollar bill if you squinted at it a little bit so the colors blurred. It blew my mind. I remember just putting my book bag down, taking a deep breath, and sitting down on the sofa, then lying back into its soft cushions, then rolling around in it like a dog, huffing the clean chemical scent of the new fabric. It had finally happened—we were rich! God, it felt so good.

The Christmas of my eighth-grade year, we got every single thing we asked for. It was magical. There were a ton of gifts but two really stuck out. I got Rollerblade-type skates before most people in my neighborhood even knew they existed. I was an excellent skater from years of hockey, and I had the skates on my feet in minutes, whizzing around the house, then out onto the street and around the corner to nearby Trum Field. I loved those skates and for the next few years I rode them everywhere. Keith got a real off-road gas-powered dirt bike with the knobby tires and everything. It was insane, we'd never gotten gifts like this in our lives. I wanted to ask what had changed, but I was scared to break the magic spell.

Later that day, my stepfather and Barney loaded us boys in my mother's car with the bike in the trunk and drove to an empty field a few towns over. We got the bike out. Keith had no clue how to ride so we were all trying to figure out how to teach him. I must have read in an encyclopedia or something about how you had to shift gears, and I was super nervous about that. I knew you had to pull in the clutch with your hand and then step down on the shifter to put it in gear. My stepfather had ridden motorcycles before so he was giving a big speech about when to put in the clutch, where the gears were located, and so on.

"When do you have to downshift into first gear?" I asked him.

He just looked at me and laughed, then jabbed Barney in the ribs with an elbow.

"Ha, little shit thinks you need to downshift into first."

"Okay, what do you call it?"

"You *shift* into first, you numbskull."

We got Keith on the bike. He was revving the engine while smiling nervously and it sounded awesome. He squeezed the clutch, kicked it into first gear, revved it, then just let go of the clutch completely.

In slow motion, I watched the bike leap forward. Keith's eyes widened in panic. As the bike roared forward, the front wheels peeled off the ground, then lifted higher and higher in the air till I swore the bike was going over. But it never did. The last thing I saw before that little 50cc bike whipped past me was my wild brother's face, split wide in a grin, absolutely consumed with joy. We took turns riding Keith's bike around that tiny muddy field for hours, till it got so dark we couldn't see.

—

A couple of months later, my stepfather finally got pinched with one of my mother's cousins, a career criminal from the projects. They'd been stealing credit cards, buying electronics with them, then selling them around town at a discount. It all became clear—the extravagant gifts, the new furniture, and the rental VCR tapes we owned. The idiots had been using the stolen cards to gas up their cars and that's how they finally got caught. My stepfather was convinced he was smart enough to get off, so why waste their money on a lawyer? He got sentenced to three years.

As bad as it'd been living under the same roof with that tyrant, it was somehow worse when he went away. My father lived in the next town over, so I never thought of this guy as my dad. But he was my stepdad, he'd lived with me and my mom from when I was eight, so it was still traumatizing when he got locked up.

The authorities never took possession of the money-green sofa and love seat set, but I wish they had. It felt like proof that my family was shit, that we'd always be shit. The only breaks we'd get would be from criminal enterprises. Even then, the good times wouldn't last long.

CHAPTER TWO

LOOK AT YOU FUCKING LOSERS

MY SOPHOMORE YEAR OF HIGH SCHOOL, MY STEPDAD WAS RELEASED FROM prison. My mom was all jazzed up about it. I'd been dreading it. Traumatic as it was to see him get locked up, the fact was, he was much less of an embarrassment inside than outside. To have him back and hanging around the house again . . . man, they could have just kept him.

I came home from school one day and my mom was like, "Hey, Kenny, your stepfather got a job."

"Cool," I said, registering the least amount of emotion possible. I couldn't wait to put my mother and her husband in the rearview.

"He's going to be a janitor."

Okay, not great. But no reason to panic yet.

"Where?"

"Somerville Public Schools."

Now I'm panicking.

"Which school?"

"Somerville High."

"Please tell me you're kidding. Please tell me that you're joking with me."

Not gonna lie, I burst into tears. Maybe in more affluent towns, kids would be willing to give something like that a pass, but in Somerville a setup like that was too juicy not to be used as an instrument of torture. Something like that put the stink of shit on a kid that was impossible to shake.

"Oh, stop it right now. Don't be so selfish. You should be proud of Kenneth."

Yeah, I was Kenny, my dad was Ken, and my stepdad was Kenneth. I was already tied to this buffoon by my mother and by my first name. And now my nincompoop ex-con stepfather was going to be the janitor at my fucking high school, mopping up barf in the hallways and piss in the bathrooms? When I think back on it now, I can't believe I survived it emotionally.

By tenth grade, I'd done everything I could to distance myself from my dysfunctional family. They didn't put effort into anything, so I got good grades and excelled at every sport my school offered. They didn't take much pride in their physical appearance, so I stayed in the best possible shape, always had clean clothes, and always looked presentable. They always had the cheapest, shittiest everything. My dad always contributed to anything sports related, but with the money from my paper route, I made sure I had all the best gear. All my athletic equipment was top-notch—I had primo skates and cleats. I had the two-tone Jordache jeans—regular denim on one side and acid wash on the other. I had them in black, too.

But sneakers were the ultimate status symbol. I kept every pair I had spotless, like they'd just come out of the box. When I rocked my first pair of Air Jordans, I stuck out like I was wearing a Gucci jacket. I felt like a champion. The Air Jordans were so expensive and so cool that I was kind of reluctant to wear them and mess them up. I was so desperate to be cool, to send these other kids the message that I wasn't poor. But kids are intuitive. Over time, what shone through for them was my desperation. I became the insecure idiot trying to overcompensate with all the cool clothes. There was no way out.

I started dating a girl at my school—my first girlfriend, Debbie. She was a senior and a cheerleader for the football team. She was kind and well-liked, loved animals, just a good person through and through. She was the perfect antidote to the chaos and bile at home. Losing my virginity made me feel a bit like my unhappy childhood was in the rearview, that I was finally a man in control of my own life.

Debbie drove a gigantic "woody" station wagon that took leaded gasoline and had rumble seats in the back. We'd pile in it with a bunch of our friends till the muffler was dragging on the ground. I loved it when I was driving and another kid was pulled up behind us at a stoplight.

"Watch this," I'd call out, "I'm going to smokescreen these motherfuckers."

When the light turned green, I'd punch the gas. That old beast of a station wagon would throw up a cloud of smoke so thick and black that it left the kids in the car behind us coughing.

Hockey was still at the center of my life, but other things began to creep in. I started drinking with a teammate, Ray Sullivan. Ray was one of my best friends. Great guy, very funny, very soft-spoken and passive, adored by everyone who knew him. He never got in fights, never raised his voice, just kind of snuck through life with zero confidence. Something had broken Ray's sense of self, but I never asked him about it.

Ray would steal vodka out of his father's bottle, then fill it back up with water. The nights before games, our coach would call each of us at home to make sure we were in bed. As soon as that call came, Ray and I would go out and get bombed. I'd watch for the headlights of his father's massive black seventies Ford LTD, then slip out of my house, unnoticed.

"Sully."

I always came up to him on the driver's side.

"Rideout."

"Move over."

"What? Why?"

"Gimme the fucking keys, bro, you ain't driving."

"Kenny, I dunno," he said, already sliding over to the passenger side, "if anything happens to the car, my father's gonna kill me."

I'd mash the accelerator to the floor and peel out, the massive LTD fishtailing all the way up the block, Sully and I howling like hyenas. My parents had to know what was going on, but they couldn't give a shit. We'd go to Bruins games or just raise hell in Somerville, acting like fools. Night after night, Sully got blackout drunk. As sweet as he was sober, he was a raving lunatic when he was in his cups. I'd never seen a kid drink like Ray.

―

Fighting was unavoidable in Somerville, especially with Keith constantly acting the fool. I knew kids who loved to fight, kids who lived for it, kids who had to fight kids from other high schools on the weekend because they'd already whipped everyone else at Somerville High. I hated fighting and hoped to never fight again. But if I had to fight, I wanted to win. One day, scared shitless, I forced myself to walk into the Somerville Boxing Club to learn how to fight.

This was no pristine, shiny, shopping mall of a gym. It didn't cater to bankers and Realtors and soccer moms. This was not a nerd gym, it was a bad-motherfucker gym. Norman Stone was training the current heavyweight champion of the world, Johnny Ruiz, there.

The minute I walked in, the smell hit me: decades of sour sweat, wet athletic tape, and Icy Hot. The legendary Somerville Boxing Club was just a beat-up old warehouse. The heavy bags were heavily duct-taped. The gloves were falling apart. A mixture of inner-city Blacks, Hispanics, and whites with taped wrists and drenched sweat suits pounded it out on heavy bags, speed bags, and mitts. There were no tourists. These guys were athletes or fighters or thugs.

There was a very old Italian guy named Tony sitting down in an open office, a Cus D'Amato type—serious, no-nonsense, nothing particularly kind or welcoming about him.

"Hey, I'm interested in a membership," I mumbled to him.

"You ever box before?"

"No."

"You have your own gloves and headgear?"

"No."

"You don't have any experience or any equipment?"

"I've never done anything. But I want to learn."

He looked me up and down.

"Okay. It's twenty bucks a month. Do you have twenty bucks?"

"Yeah, I can do that."

I found out later that if you didn't have the money but were serious about fighting, it was free.

There was no hazing, no ball-busting, no bullying. There was also no chitchat. We were all there to work, period, end of story. Tony didn't mess around. He'd work the mitts with you, have you throw combination after combination. When you started to get tired and your hands didn't snap right back to your chin after a combo, wham, he'd smash you in the side of the head with one of the crusty old mitts.

"Keep your hands up, kid."

Tony was no softie, but he was protective of his fighters. One time a guy came in, a kid I vaguely knew, a southpaw.

"Kenny, what's up, bro? I didn't know you were training these days."

"Yeah, I've only been doing it for a minute."

"You want to spar?"

I'd maybe sparred once if at all. But I was here to get over my fear of fighting—I wasn't about to say no.

"Yeah, sure."

I told my trainer and I got in the ring with this kid and we went a few rounds. He worked me over, and by the end, I had a huge black eye.

Afterward, Tony yelled over to the other trainer.

"Barry, what the fuck. You want me to lose guys over here? You can't put a new guy sparring with another new guy. The fuck are you thinking?"

When he was cleaning me up, Tony grabbed me by the back of my neck and looked in my eyes.

"Kenny, you never do that again. Don't ever say you'll spar somebody without talking to me first. You understand, son?"

It was funny because once I'd agreed to do it, Tony didn't step in and say, "No, no, no. He's just a kid, he's not ready to spar." He cared enough to let me make the mistake, stuck around to make sure I didn't get killed, then made it clear I wasn't to make the same mistake again.

After a couple of months of showing up five days a week and putting in work, I'd get acknowledgment from some of the other guys.

"Good to see you, buddy."

"How you doing, champ?"

"Straight cross starting to look decent."

If Tony wasn't around, they'd tell me to keep my elbows down or get my elbow up on my left hook or show me footwork drills. As other new guys came in, I became one of the guys who was already there, and my status ticked up a little bit. I even held my head a little higher when walking down the halls of my high school. I had no delusions of grandeur when it came to boxing. I knew my capabilities and my limitations. But the veterans at the Somerville Boxing Club treated me like I was part of the club, like I was a real fighter. It felt incredibly good to belong.

—

My senior year got off to a rocky start. Our football team was struggling, and I was the starting quarterback so I took the brunt of it. I could tell people thought it was my fault. I already felt completely out of my element. I really wasn't that good, there just wasn't anyone better. I tried incredibly hard, but I had no natural talent. I felt like a fraud. I wanted so desperately to be good, and I was hyperaware that I wasn't. I could tell people were thinking, *This kid sucks. If we had a decent quarterback, we'd be a better team.* But they hadn't liked me from the moment I set foot on the field.

My father had grown up in Medford, so when it came to youth hockey, he insisted I go play in Medford. Medford was a little more upscale, so maybe their programs were slightly better. He didn't even live in Medford anymore. Maybe my dad thought it'd help me? But the Somerville High hockey coach seemed to hate me because my dad had steered me to Medford. And when I entered ninth grade and decided to try out for football, I had to go try out at Somerville High. A lot of the kids hated me, thinking or even saying, "Why the fuck were you playing over at Medford?" The Medford kids hated me for going to the other side. Of course, all that lingering animosity only ratcheted up when I was tapped to be the starting quarterback.

One of our early games was against our rivals the Medford Mustangs. We were 1–1–1 going into it and I knew that if we lost, they weren't going to let me play anymore. We battled back and forth the whole game. Finally, we were tied with only a few seconds left on the clock, and Somerville had possession. The instant I got the snap, I faded back and threw a wild, last-ditch Hail Mary.

Somerville High had this wide receiver, a Black kid named Norman Kennedy. Great player. Norman was on another level. He was smart, he could run, he could jump . . . you got the ball close to him, I swear he could fly.

When that ball left my hands, I was a pariah, the fucking janitor's kid, an outsider hated as a traitor by both teams on the field. When that ball landed in the outstretched hands of our hot-shit wide receiver

Norman Kennedy for a touchdown, securing us the win over Medford, everything changed. In the blink of an eye, I went from an outcast to Somerville's favorite son. The same assholes who'd been backbiting and undermining me for two years were ready to carry me off the field like a conquering hero. It was undeniable—victory transformed you. I couldn't wait for my sports career to take off so I could leave these shitbirds behind forever.

I didn't live for football like I did for hockey, but that didn't stop football from opening doors for me. One day, I got a recruiting letter from the football coach at Framingham State College. No one in my family had gone to college, my friends weren't going, and I doubted Keith would even make it through ninth grade. For those very reasons, I knew from a very young age that I'd go to college. But to be able to play football in college? Yeah, sure, I'd go to Framingham State.

The last game of the season fell on Thanksgiving weekend. It would be my final game of high school football. It was against another rival team, the Arlington Spy Ponders. Corny name for a team but somehow, they managed to destroy us every time. Still, there were murmurs that this was our year, that we could finally get revenge.

The whole town came out and the stands were packed—parents, faculty, and students from both Somerville and Arlington. I felt like I was playing for the Patriots in a sold-out Foxboro stadium. Our team was good and we were playing well, but this team blew us out every single year. We were deadlocked in a tie, and I was getting sacked hard on every other play.

The crowd was rowdy, yelling and cheering every second the ball was in play, chanting in support of their team, heckling the ref. Then I heard something start up in the stands—our stands. It was just a couple of voices at first, probably a couple of wise-guy kids. But then it caught fire and the whole field started chanting it, everyone on both sides: *"Rideout sucks! Rideout sucks! Rideout sucks!"*

I felt completely out of control. This was the exact opposite of everything I'd ever dreamed of. Here it was, my greatest fear, dragged out into the light and magnified a thousand times. I believed with all my heart that I was better than this, that I deserved more than getting my ass kicked by my stepfather, getting clowned at school, and landing some dead-end job driving a forklift as a prelude to slowly drinking myself to death. I mean, I *wanted* to believe that with all my heart; I *tried* to believe that with all my heart. But there was a part of me, which I never showed to anyone, that believed the opposite. When that part looked in the mirror it saw a fraud and a loser, a guy who didn't deserve to be quarterback, who didn't even deserve to be alive. There, on the football field with everyone chanting about how fucking awful I was, I just wanted to crawl into a hole and die.

But I dug in. I fought harder. I pushed my team to fight harder. Soon, the stands were chanting "the line sucks" because someone realized that I was one guy on an eleven-man team and that maybe, just maybe I kept getting sacked because my linemen were leaving holes big enough for a truck to drive through.

We fought the Ponders to a tie. That left us at 5–3–2 for the season. It was disappointing but at least we didn't lose. The "Rideout sucks" chant died. Well, it died for everyone but me. Who knows, maybe it was only ten people chanting, but for me it felt like it was every single person in a packed gladiators' arena. That memory of being humiliated in front of everyone I was trying to impress, of being condescended to and ridiculed in public, of having a crowd chant gleefully that I wasn't good enough, that I was failing, that I sucked—it felt like a sharp chip of gravel lodged in my heart. It was the most painful sensation I'd ever endured. I wanted to forget it immediately and forever. And I knew that it would shadow me till the day I died. Before I even changed out of my muddy, sweat-drenched uniform, I swore that no one would ever be able to ridicule me like that again. Every single thing I did, people would see me sweating blood, putting every ounce of exertion into it. Even if it killed me.

Our coach was an older guy named Emerson Dickey, a math teacher in one of the towns nearby. He was a Bill Parcells type—an old-school New England ballbuster. He'd ride me all the time. And he could be a real monster, screaming at me and berating me if I made a bad pass. I wondered sometimes whether he was trying to make me better or just break me down. But he was a good coach, and he made me a better player. In one tackling drill, I kept getting taken down.

"Jesus Christ, Rideout, can you ever take a hit. Come over here, numb nuts, take a knee."

"Yeah, Coach?"

"You're literally out there just getting creamed. Instead of just taking the hit, did it ever occur to you to *give* the hit, even when you're carrying the ball? Run it hard, show these motherfuckers what you're all about."

From that day forward, I ran like I was trying to kill someone. It worked.

Maybe a week after my "Rideout sucks" nightmare, the phone rang in our house one evening. We had one phone, a big brown rotary dial hanging on the wall in the kitchen.

"Hello?"

"Rideout. It's Coach Dickey."

His voice sounded weird to me, and I realized that it may have been the first time I'd talked to him that he didn't sound angry.

"Oh, hey, Coach, how are you?"

"I just wanted you to know that you've been named to the Greater Boston League All-Star team as the starting quarterback."

"Oh my God, are you serious?"

"You did a good job, Kenny. You worked incredibly hard, for yourself and for your team. You weren't afraid to put your body on the line. You weren't afraid to lead, but you were ready to listen and learn, too. I'm proud of you. And you should be proud of yourself."

"Wow, Coach. Thanks so much. Man, I can't believe it."

"Have a good night, son."

As soon as I got off the phone, I beat it to my room so the rest of my family wouldn't catch me crying. It was impossible for me to communicate to Coach Dickey how much this meant to me. We were Division I, the highest league in the state. A couple of the other teams had good quarterbacks who also played defensive back, so they got on the team in those positions. But I'd be starting at quarterback. It was my greatest athletic accomplishment ever.

About a week after I graduated from high school, I got my first real job: prison guard at the Billerica House of Correction, where my stepfather had done time. I'd just turned eighteen. No one told me what to expect. I didn't even know I was going to be a guard. I thought I was going to be cutting grass at the prison when they first sent me the acceptance letter. In my work uniform, I looked like a little kid dressing up for Halloween. I can't believe I didn't get eaten alive.

Prison guard is a union job, and all the regular guards want to take their time off in the summer. So Billerica hired additional summer help—college kids. It was bananas to put college kids in this position. We got maybe four hours of classroom training before they put us to work.

"All right, look for contraband, look for weapons, look for drugs. These guys might hide weapons in their cells, or they might hide weapons on their person. They may hide weapons *in* their person. Remember: they've got twenty-four hours a day, seven days a week, three hundred and sixty-five days a year to think of ways to beat you. You're only thinking about them when you're in there. So whatever you think, think again, because they're always trying to get one over on you."

And then they sent us into the prison for our assignment for the day. I can't believe we didn't all get killed.

The Billerica House of Correction was a county lockup, so they had different tiers of security. There was a work-release area for low-risk inmates who required little supervision, then a section of modular buildings where medium-security inmates bunked together in rooms that maybe held twenty guys, kind of like an army barracks. Then there was the maximum-security section, a building that they called the Wall.

One day this kid showed up: white, maybe twenty-five, never been locked up before, knew nobody at the prison. The prison was super segregated. If you went to Billerica and you weren't from the streets, you were going to have issues. Didn't matter what color you were. If you weren't affiliated with a gang or connected to any of the street people, you were going to have a fucking problem.

Immediately, the Puerto Rican inmates started fucking with this white kid. They were talking shit and calling him names. Then they threw some cocoa butter on him, intimating that they were going to rape him.

They *weren't* going to rape him. That shit almost never happened in the modular section. There were fights and stuff but rarely sexual assaults—there were more than enough willing participants. The modular section was like a high school full of fresh pricks. They were wise guys and dickheads, all jerky fucking kids. They were just teasing this kid, but he didn't know it was just teasing, so it scared him. Once the kid was scared, he was dangerous. He could do anything. The guards must've seen this and sent him down to the warden of the modular unit.

I got sent down there with Brendan Daly, another one of the summer hires, typical kid from the city. We were very similar, by far the two youngest people working there, and we'd become close friends for life.

When we got down there, this kid was talking to the warden, Paul Norton, whom they called "Flash." Flash was a tough man from the Malden projects who looked like the Irish Tony Soprano. Every inmate was scared of Flash. The kid was trying to save face. He clearly wanted to get the fuck out of the modular buildings but didn't want to check in to protective custody. That was like a death sentence. That's where they kept the rapists, child molesters, and snitches. If a riot breaks out, the first thing the inmates do is go kill all the people in protective custody.

Flash had an old shackle on his desk—a big piece of metal

with two cuffs on it. In a desperate attempt to get in trouble, the kid picked up the antique restraint on the warden's desk, almost in slow motion.

"What if I bash your head in with this thing?" the kid said to Flash.

Brendan and I just looked at each other like, "This poor fucking kid."

And we bundled him. We tackled him to the floor, roughed him up a bit but not too much. We put his hands behind his back, handcuffed him, then shackled his legs together so he was hog-tied on his belly. Everyone knew what was going on, so we were sort of just going through the motions.

A common way guys avoid General Population is by getting in trouble. Then they'd have to go to the Hole—a special solitary housing unit in the basement. It sucked because you'd be in a tiny cell with bars, but you'd be isolated from the rest of the prisoners. You could stay in your cell all day and not have to interact with people if you didn't want to. Clearly, this kid preferred the isolation of the Hole to maybe getting raped.

"All right, guys," Flash said, "get him up. Call a van over here to take him back to the main building."

In the van, we tried to calm the guy down.

"Dude, can you chill out enough that we can sit you down?"

"Fuck you, motherfucker! Fuck you all."

During the drive to the main building, Brendan and I had to keep him on his belly on the floor in the back of the van. We didn't kneel on him as he was no threat to us, but he was acting crazy enough that we had to hold him down, even if just to protect him from himself.

I looked at Brendan.

"What the fuck, man."

"This job sucks," he said under his breath.

We carried this guy into the prison face down, each of us with an arm through his handcuffs and shackles. Flash met us as we carried him through the front door of the facility.

"Bring the kid in," he said, "get him to isolation."

We dragged him down there with a couple of other guys and got him in a cell. It was just a bed and a shitter in a concrete box with a steel door. We took his leg irons off, stood him up, then backed out so he could turn around. Now we had to do a strip search because you have to do a strip search every time you move someone.

"All right," Flash said, "we're going to take the cuffs off you and you're going to strip it down. Can we take the cuffs off you?"

"Fuck you. Take these handcuffs off and find out."

If he wanted to do this the hard way, fine. We'd go in there as a crew and none of us were going to get hurt. We'd hold him fast while we took the cuffs off, strip him down, do the search, leave him in his cell, game over.

Then Flash looked over at me.

"Kenny," he said, "get in there and take his fucking handcuffs off. If he doesn't want to take his clothes off, you rip them off."

It was me, Brendan, a couple of other grown men, this stupid kid in the cell, and Flash. Every single one was looking at me. I was eighteen years old. I grew up around violence. Even trained a little at the Somerville Boxing Club. But Flash didn't know that the reason I went to the Somerville Boxing Club was because, like everyone else, I was scared to fight. At the same time, they had me on the spot.

My buddy Brendan put his hand up a little and looked at me. "You want me to do it?"

We were the same exact size, same age. He must have been able to see how scared I was. I'll never forget that he was willing to get in there for me. That's the kind of person you wanted on your team. As much as I didn't want to do it, I knew I had to. I pushed his hand away.

"I got this."

When I stepped into the cell, they closed the door behind me.

For the first time since we started dealing with this idiot, the kid was actually dangerous. None of us knew who he really was, we had no idea what he was really capable of. It's not so hard to gouge out an eye or rip off an ear. He might punch me in the throat or just catch me with a hook or uppercut. The other guys would be on him in a heartbeat, but the right punch can knock anyone out, maybe turn you into a vegetable.

With my heart kicking like a rabbit in my throat, I walked over and took the kid's handcuffs off. He just stood there, mean-mugging me. Without looking away, I took one step closer.

"What are we gonna do?" I said, and stared through him.

After a long moment, the kid slowly started taking his clothes off. We did the search and that was the end of it.

In the fall of 1989, I started at Framingham State, playing hockey and football when most of the guys only made one team. I think I only made the football team because I'd been named to the All-Star team, but I was on it. My father was ecstatic that I was going to play college sports, but he didn't necessarily care about the college part. My mother would've been just as happy if I took any shit job. With no guidance from them, I took my lead from the other athletes around me and chose sociology as my major, since it had the lightest course load and was the easiest to pass. Still, it felt like a huge victory getting out of my mother's house, getting out of Somerville, and playing two sports at the collegiate level.

As a freshman, I lived in the dorms. I kept my head down, just going to practice, doing my homework, and occasionally going out carousing with the boys. As the Columbus Day long weekend approached, I didn't even realize that the following Monday was a holiday until that Thursday when the dorms started emptying out. No one was traveling from California to go to Framingham State—they were all local kids, and they were all going home. Somerville was twenty-five miles away, a forty-minute drive at most. A pain in the ass to come get me, maybe, but not an insurmountable obstacle. I called my mom.

"Ma, yeah, hi. Ma, I didn't realize it was Columbus Day weekend. Everyone here is leaving. Can you come pick me up?"

"What?"

"Can you come get me?"

"Kenny... no. I'm not driving all the way there and all the way back just to do it again on Monday."

"Ma, please! There's nobody else here. I'm like trapped here."

"Take a bus. Isn't there a bus to Boston from there? Then from Tremont Street, there's a bus to Somerville. I'll pick you up on Highland Ave."

"Ma, it'll take me like two days to get there on a bus—you can't just come and pick me up? It's like a ghost town here, you want me to stay here the whole damn weekend?"

"Uh-uh, Kenny, I ain't driving. You can take the bus or you can stay there."

"I swear to fucking God, Ma, you're gonna regret this. You're gonna regret treating me like a speck of shit. I'm gonna repay you ten times over for this."

"Okay, hon, that's fine. Bye-bye now."

I was consumed with bitterness toward my mother. Maybe it was a minor situation on the surface, but it felt like the culmination of years of selfishness. Initially, my parents had agreed to each pay half of my college tuition. But earlier that year, my mother had declared she couldn't afford to cover her half. My father carried on paying half of my tuition (and, on occasion, even covered my mother's portion), but I quickly had to turn to student loans to cover the many shortfalls.

It was a stressful time, and this painful humiliation really set me off. My mother had never encouraged me to excel and wasn't doing a thing to help me now that I'd made it to college. When I got the job at the prison, my folks were like, "That's great, you're going to be good to go as soon as you get out of college. You can start there full-time."

I couldn't believe it. *That's your dream job, working in a prison? Are you out of your fucking mind?* Of course, they thought I was crazy not to lunge at the opportunity.

"Kenny, a civil service job with a pension? That's a great job. You could probably make seventy-five grand there."

It felt impossible to communicate with them—it was as if we were from different planets.

When football season wrapped, I knew I wouldn't be playing the next year. It was too much. Between football, hockey, and filling in at Billerica when I could, my grades were garbage. Football had been a bonus. Now it was a distraction, and it had to go. Hockey was what was going to change my life.

In the spring, I got a call from my father. My brother Keith had been admitted to Mount Auburn Hospital for a kidney infection. While he was there, the doctor's examination revealed that he'd been shooting heroin.

I knew right then that Keith was gone forever. I'd seen heroin make Barney its slave over the years, and I knew my brother wasn't strong enough to turn it around. Jesus, he'd probably gotten the poison from Barney. Not that my uncle had given it to him, but his habit was impossible to hide in our shitty little house with paper-thin walls. Keith had probably sniffed out what Barney was doing and then forced him to show him how it all worked.

Underneath the fucked-up tough-guy front he always tried to put on, Keith was a nice kid. My mom still had this old picture of us as little kids in our ugly matching Christmas sweaters and matching bowl cuts, clutching hastily wrapped Christmas presents with big orange bows on them. The way I'm beaming at the camera makes me feel like it was probably Granny who'd taken the picture. Keith wasn't smiling though. He had this weird look on his face, like he'd seen the truth and knew what was coming. He was holding his gift up in front of him, almost in a defensive posture. His eyes said "This means nothing." Or maybe "I know you can't keep me safe."

I felt disgusted that my parents hadn't done more to help him. From a very early age, it was obvious that he was deeply troubled, that he needed help. But they did nothing to get him what he needed. As with everything else in life, they'd taken the path of least resistance. When Keith threw a fit, they'd do anything to make it go away, then pretend like it never happened. They never tried to figure out what was going on under his screaming and thrashing around.

Ah, what the fuck did I know, contemplating all this from my college dorm. My parents were the same age I was now when they had us, and I had no clue what I was doing in this world. If I had a baby now, it'd be impossible for me to prevent my frustration with everything else in the world from spilling over onto him or her. And to be like my mother and have *two* kids with no partner—I wasn't about to forgive her, but no fucking wonder everything had gone sideways. Still, I hated my parents for letting Keith come to this.

And I hated *myself* for letting Keith come to this. I tried to tell myself it was on them, that I hadn't been old enough or mature enough or tough enough to help him. The truth was, I'd turned my back on him. From the moment I could string a thought together, I knew I had to get out of my mother's house and get out of Somerville. From that moment and at every turn, I'd given up on Keith. He was too loud, too crazy, an embarrassment. The truth was, he wasn't crazy at all, we were both just reacting to the same bullshit and abuse in different ways. Had it just been a coin toss that I was born to excel, and he was born to explode? What if it'd gone the other way? The only thing that mattered was that he was my fucking brother. Jesus, if there was one person I should have dragged out of that hellhole with me, it was Keith. Instead, I'd abandoned him. I'd failed him.

I spent the summer of my freshman year back at Billerica, watching the inmates, talking with the inmates, and fighting the inmates. Violence was always one step away.

The prison was very segregated. There were the Hispanics, the Blacks, and the whites. Any time someone tried to cross that line, there was a problem. Sometimes it felt like the only thing these three warring factions had in common was their contempt for the guards.

There might be a quick scuffle in the hallway or something minor in the chow hall, but the most dangerous place by far was the yard. If there was a premeditated gang fight, that's where it would go down. We kept our heads on a swivel at all times, but these fights were an unavoidable occurrence, and dealing with them was just part of the job.

For the most part, I managed to get along with the inmates. My first day on the job, a big Irish gangster I knew from the neighborhood came running up when we were out in the yard. He grabbed me around the waist, threw me around his shoulder, and carried me around like a fireman before putting me down. It had freaked me out in the moment, but I realized after a while that he had been sending a message to the other inmates. He was saying "Maybe he's on the other team right now, but this guy is one of us."

Most of them got the message, but not all. There was a Puerto Rican guy a few years older than me who decided he hated my guts. He mean-mugged me constantly. I didn't want to go down that road with him, mostly because I didn't want to have to write a discipline report if he popped off. I wasn't about to back down, but I kept hoping he'd just stay away from me.

One day, about two hundred of the inmates were walking to the chow hall. I was standing there with another guard. As he walked past, this guy who hated me mumbled under his breath, "Fuck you, screw."

"Dude, what the fuck is your problem?"

"If you didn't have that badge on, I'd punch you right in your face."

"Oh, really?"

I put my hands on the badge to take it off, because if it was going to be like this, I was just going to fight him. The instant my hands touched my badge, boom, he fired off a straight right that broke my nose. My nose started gushing blood, but I didn't go down. I started swinging and we scrapped for a minute. But the guards got there quickly, tackled him, and threw him down in the hole without further incident.

When I got to a bathroom to clean up, I was covered in blood. I washed my face and hands and did my best to wipe the worst smears off my uniform. And then I got back out on the floor. I was only halfway through my shift and still had four hours to go.

My sophomore year, I moved off campus to a windowless basement bunker I shared with some random kid I'd met in the dorms, one flimsy sheet of drywall separating our "rooms." I had no idea who I was or what I was supposed to be doing. I housed bowl after bowl of New England clam chowder at the dining hall and packed on the pounds. I cruised around Framingham in my father's old '79 Buick LeSabre he'd given me in high school. Every single night I went out with my buddies, and most of the time we got fucked up and into fights. Night after night the script was the same: pound some brews and bust some skulls.

I'd been overhearing people talking about coke for a while and it got me curious. Finally, I sought some out. There were a couple of kids at the school who were druggies and I talked them into giving me a taste. I remember walking home late at night in the freezing cold in the best fucking mood, just thinking, *Oh my God, this is the best. No wonder everybody likes this shit.* When I went home to Somerville, I told all my friends about it.

"Dude, you've got to try this. It's so fucking good."

I called it donkey dust: "Bro, let's go honk some stripes of donkey dust." And then we were off to the races, staying up for days at a stretch, hammering copious amounts of cheap beer, unloading on anyone who got in our way. My nickname for coke made sense to me because I knew I was being a jackass by doing drugs.

This entire time, I was working a couple of days a week at the Billerica House of Correction, surrounded by thousands of men who'd wound up there for the bad decisions they'd made when they were under the influence. It never occurred to me that I was one phone call away from winding up as a resident of Billerica instead of an employee. They were criminals and drug addicts, they were losers. For me, it was just one night. Or one weekend. Or one summer.

Hockey started to come apart. The past couple of years, I'd noticed my teammates making these great leaps forward as athletes. No one worked harder than I did, on and off the ice. I ground forward and made incremental progress, but the magic I was hoping for just never materialized. I kept working and waiting and hoping, but the breakthroughs never happened. It was easy to be decent, not much harder to be good. It was a shitload of work to get from good to great. To play in the NHL, you had to be elite. We were Division III. No one in Division III was elite. Week after week, game after game, the truth finally became impossible to deny. I was good, but I wasn't good enough. And if I didn't make the grade at hockey, I had no fallback plan. I began to worry that my dream was slipping away from me, and I had nothing waiting to take its place.

We had a new coach my sophomore year, Guy Angers. We got along really well, even though our team sucked. Toward the season's end, I wasn't playing really well, and they benched me for a game. Instead of being a good sport and coming to watch the game and support my team, I told myself "fuck it" and went and got dusted with my friends. The coaches didn't dress me for the next game—and, again, I didn't go. After a third missed game, my coach finally called me and said that if I wasn't going to come watch the games, I wasn't on the team anymore. Fine, fine, I came and watched the next one and they had me play the one after that.

But from that episode on, I took a very passive-aggressive approach to the sport. I wasn't trying to get kicked off the team, but Coach Guy's move had pissed me off. I didn't feel like I'd been treated fairly. That frustrated me, and I became defiant. I went through a bad stretch where I just wasn't playing well, which made things worse. From my first days playing hockey, I'd always valued sportsmanship. I played to win but I played fair, and I was gracious whether we won or lost. Every single game, every single shift, I gave it everything I had, 110 percent effort, to the degree that my coaches lectured the other players to be more like me. All that went out the window.

As I became less invested in hockey, I became more invested in coke. If I did a bump, I'd immediately have to do all the coke we had, then all the coke we could get. We stopped paying our drug dealers. We'd just invite them over, get the shit off them, then say,

"Ah, yeah, we're tight this week, we'll get you next week." What was one guy going to do against a room full of hockey players, ready to fight at the drop of a hat? Eventually, we'd have to find another guy, then another guy.

I knew I had to quit coke—or rather, *stay* quit. Coke was easy to quit—you just didn't start again after the last bender. I told all my friends I was quitting, commanded them to not get the stuff for me. But as soon as I had one drink—Bud or Bud Light only, purchased in thirty-packs—I'd immediately say, "Fuck it, call the guy. This will be my last night."

Ten or twelve hours later, we'd be sitting around someone's living room, Run-DMC or Guns N' Roses blasting from the stereo. I'd notice it getting light outside and I'd snap, furious at myself for giving in, for wasting the night, and for the day I was about to waste. My sports career was dead, maybe I should just follow suit?

"Look at you fucking losers!" I'd yell at my friends, then storm out.

After six months of "my last night doing coke," the vow was cemented as a punch line.

—

My junior year, we went through the whole tryout rigmarole. Of course I was on the team, I always made the team, why wouldn't I make the team? At the end of the training camp, they posted the roster, and I wasn't on it. I called the coach.

"Yeah, Coach, I'm just calling because I saw you posted the roster."

"Hey, Rideout. Yeah, I thought I might hear from you."

"Was there like a mistake or something? There's gotta be a mistake."

"No, the roster's correct."

"Coach, I'm just trying to understand here . . . I outplay half of the guys who made the cut."

"That ain't it. Your attitude at the end of the season there . . . it wasn't good, Kenny. We had a rough year and we're trying to turn this team around. There's lots of guys dying for a spot. We aren't going to turn this team around with resentment, with guys who feel like they're entitled to time on the ice. Everyone's gotta work for it, all of the time."

"Coach, I can make the change, I just had a rough season last year, just . . ."

"The time to make the change was last season, Kenny. Everyone goes through rough patches. This ain't about that. Your attitude sucked. You had plenty of opportunities to fix it and you didn't. If anything, it got worse. So here we are."

"I mean . . . damn. Okay, I guess it's your team, Coach. It's up to you."

"Good luck, Rideout."

Good luck, he says, like I'm going fishing, like he's not running a stake through the heart of my lifelong dream. He couldn't have sat me down after that first night I was benched and explained to me that he was giving me an opportunity to look inward and make adjustments, an opportunity I was blowing? He couldn't have told me that I was making enemies when there were none? No, that wasn't his job because I wasn't a fucking baby. I was a grown-ass man and it wasn't his job to spoon-feed me that shit. He'd given me multiple chances to figure it out and I'd blown every one.

Nothing he said was aggressive or nasty. Maybe it'd have felt less catastrophic if he'd been a prick and railed on me. But he'd laid it out for me, plain and clear. I was good enough to be on the team, but I'd been so arrogant and so entitled that it didn't matter. My whole life, that dumb cut-down "You think you're better than us" had shadowed me everywhere I'd gone. My response had always been, "Fuck you, I don't *think* I'm better than you, I *know* I'm better than you." And it'd worked. I'd been better at hockey, better at football, better at school, just plain better in every way than my ambitionless family. I wanted to show them *this is what trying looks like, and this is what it gets you.* Until finally now, I'd taken it too far. I'd believed so much that I was better that, well, I was back to being not good enough. And that was going to cost me everything.

I scrambled to find another league to play in. There were plenty of back doors to the NHL. I started playing for a couple of junior teams. Junior hockey was a league for fifteen- to twenty-year-olds but they played by pro rules. You drop the gloves playing college hockey, you're out of the game. In junior hockey, fighting was a five-minute major, same as the pros. You had to fight in the juniors—people weren't there to see you play. I played and I fought and I busted my ass, but I still had this nagging feeling that I was losing the thread.

—

I took a hard look at my academic performance and was appalled. Even with the easiest major in the school, my grades were dogshit. It was bad enough that I was turning teachers against me. The final class that I needed to pass for my sociology degree was Research Methods. The meat of the class was a yearlong group research project. I was still working at the prison and had access to the prisoners, so I knew we could come up with a killer social research project based on inmate behavior. I partnered up with a smart woman in the class and I knew we could knock it out of the park. I'd do the stuff I could do as a prison guard, she'd do the brainy stuff, and together we'd have a kick-ass project. The teacher—who happened to be my advisor—reached out to the woman and told her that I was such a poor student that she should work with someone else so I wouldn't tank her grade. There was an odd number of students in the class, so I ended up being the only student forced to do the project alone.

I was pissed at the girl, but I was enraged at my advisor. Wasn't part of her job to help me succeed? It made me furious to have someone count me out like that. I hated school and I didn't want to do the project at all, but I swore that I would show them both. I switched gears and labored for months doing a research project from the ground up on the academic success of children of divorced parents.

If I graduated, my degree would qualify me to be a prison guard at Billerica for the rest of my dumb life. No fucking way. I liked fitness so I decided I'd be a physical therapist. Another brilliant move from a twenty-year-old kid, completely lost in space.

I started looking at grad school requirements to become a physical therapist. I needed to take Anatomy and Physiology I and II, Physics I and II, Biology I and II, and Chemistry I and II. Two years in, I hadn't taken a single one of those courses. There wasn't even enough time to sign up for all those classes, let alone pass them. So the second semester of my junior year, I started taking night classes at Bunker Hill Community College. The place was a joke. At Somerville High, we'd called it Benny Hill, after the raunchy slapstick British comedian who ran around patting girls' butts on late-night TV. The school was an absolute clown show.

I could only get so many shifts at the prison, so I started working at the Hood milk factory. I worked six to two so I could go to night classes at Bunker Hill from three to ten. A friend's father got me the job. The maintenance manager had no idea what to do with the dumb college kids, just there for the summer. We got busywork and no supervision, so each day I went up on the factory's roof and napped for a couple of hours on a drop cloth.

For eight fucking weeks I double-timed it like that—eight-hour shifts at the job, seven-hour shifts at school. Of course, after grinding so hard, I'd have to blow off steam on the weekends. I'd go out and get blackout drunk and whacked out on coke with my buddies and wake up banged up and hating myself.

It was an insane schedule. I was always exhausted and on the edge of a meltdown, but I'd backed myself into a corner. The only person who could get me out of the mess I'd made was me. Though it was my own fault, my bitterness only grew.

When I finally turned in the group project I'd completed solo, I got an A minus, the highest grade in the entire class for the whole year. I smoked everyone and made dean's list. Once I'd gotten over my seething resentment and got going, it wasn't even that bad. Though I'd played sports from the minute I could walk, my advisor's counting me out unlocked in me for the first time a deep-in-the-bone feeling of competition. *I'll beat you at a running race, a strength contest, a fistfight, a spelling bee. I don't give a fuck what it is, I'm dominating you.* For the first time in my life, I felt like I could do anything. I'd slacked off during all of college and then, finally, in my last year, I figured out that all I needed to do to excel was *try*.

That revelation made me proud, but it also made me feel like a real jackass. I could have been doing this the entire time.

―

In the fall of my senior year, I took one last swing at hockey. My buddy Al Santilli was a year older, and he was playing his first season in the East Coast Hockey League, a tier-three junior league sanctioned by USA Hockey. The East Coast Hockey League was one of the lowest levels of professional hockey you could play. Al played for a team down in Florida called the Jacksonville Bullets.

"Yo, I'm telling you, Kenny, you should come down and check this out. It's a fucking free-for-all, bro."

"Yeah?"

"All you have to do is be willing to fight. If you can fight and you can skate, forget about it. Who doesn't want to fight and get paid for it?"

Al invited me to come down to check it out, suggesting that maybe he could get me on the team. I worried that I couldn't really play at that level, but I had to find out.

I got down there on a Thursday night and went out for drinks with him and the team, some rowdy bar in Jacksonville. I don't even know how the fight started but the whole bar got going. It was kind of chaotic but not like it was in Boston, where everyone's whacked out on coke. Boston was dangerous, you were always waiting for someone to get shot or stabbed. This was just a regular fight, no big deal. Somebody called the cops and they came rushing in. They kicked the shit out of us, handcuffed us, then kicked the shit out of us again. I was handcuffed face down on the ground, cuts on my face, some cop standing on my neck. I saw Al face down and bleeding pretty good from a cut over his eye. Then another cop came over, casually leaned down and maced us both in the face, then threw us in the back of a cop car.

You ever been maced? It was like getting hit with a flamethrower. My eyes and lungs were on fire. Snot and tears were running down my face, more snot than I'd ever produced in my life. I still had my hands cuffed behind my back so I couldn't even rub my eyes. It was so hard to breathe, I thought I might have a heart attack, and I started panicking.

"Guys," I said to the cops in front, "seriously, I can't breathe. Can I at least get some water on my face?"

Without looking back, the cop said, "No. It's not really burning. It's just a burning *sensation*." Guy could not give a fuck.

Al was a fucking lunatic, a six-foot-four goon who lived to watch blood drip on the ice. He put his feet up and started trying to boot out the side window from the back of the cop car. Now I really started to panic. They were going to fucking kill him.

At the Jacksonville County Jail, we got stripped and searched and assigned numbered jumpsuits. They gave us little toiletry kits with soap, a toothbrush, and toothpaste, then released us into different cell blocks in General Population. The minute I hit the cell block, this gangster dude with neck tattoos came up to me.

"Yo, man, let me get that toothpaste."

Jesus Christ, here we go again. Was toothpaste a hot commodity in here or was it just a test to see whether I was a pushover? It didn't matter, my response was the same.

"Not a chance, my guy. Ain't fucking happening."

You give up your toothpaste, they'd be taking your ass next. He moved on, looking for an easier target.

You'd think that because I'd worked at Billerica for two years, I'd be at ease being locked up. It's true that I knew the rules. *Mind your business. Keep your mouth shut. Stay with your race. Don't start shit but don't let yourself be pushed around.* But I knew something my hockey buddies didn't: jail is way, way more dangerous than prison.

We were in there for dumb shit, kid stuff. Most of the other people were, too—disorderly conduct, disturbing the peace, DUI. But because we were in Gen Pop, we were alongside the hardened inmates awaiting trial, too: career criminals, gangbangers, rapists, murderers. Without knowing it, you could be standing in line for chow next to some guy up on triple homicide charges for butchering his whole family. And if he decided he didn't like you or you had something he wanted . . .

After walking on eggshells for two long days, Al and I finally got to see a judge. He pled us out to disorderly conduct. We had to pay a hundred-dollar fine, but that's it, we were free to leave. At discharge, we had to strip down again and they gave us back our clothes. When I pulled my shirt over my head, I forgot it'd gotten drenched in pepper spray, and immediately my face, eyes, and hands started burning like hot lava all over again.

It was a long, miserable journey back to Massachusetts. My lifelong dream of playing hockey—a dream that'd lifted me up through all the bullshit—was deader than a stone.

CHAPTER THREE

PERCS OF THE JOB

WITH HOCKEY GONE, I FELT LIKE I WAS IN FREE FALL. MY WHOLE LIFE, I'D condescended to my family. I felt that they were ambitionless fuckups. Maybe they didn't deserve all the hardship in their lives, but they certainly didn't do anything to show that they deserved anything better. Now that I'd washed out at hockey and was about to graduate with a useless degree, I had new empathy for them. You didn't have to be a worthless piece of shit to wind up wasting your life in a dead-end job in Somerville. All you had to do was make a couple of mistakes.

I'd been unfair to my family. I'd spent the first twenty years of my life hating them and now that I was about to be ejected into the world on my own, I realized that they hadn't been all bad. Sure, they'd bitched and moaned about it, but my mother and father had shelled out a bunch of money to make sure that I'd been able to attend college, something not all of my friends could say. My father had given me his old Buick LeSabre so I could go back and forth to and from work. A couple of times when I ran out of money, Granny had paid the vehicle insurance so I could keep it on the road. Our family was messed up, but that didn't mean that my childhood had been completely devoid of peace or normalcy. I remembered Granny singing all day long in the kitchen while she worked. Not a great singer but it was comforting nonetheless, one of the little ways she expressed her love for us. Always the same songs over and over, "When Irish Eyes Are Smiling" and "Que Sera Sera." At the time, it drove me nuts.

"Jesus, Granny, you ever going to add any new songs to your repertoire?"

"I like what I like, Kenny, I like what I like. Make yourself useful—run down to the packy and get me a double six-pack."

"Granny, it's not even noon."

"Mind your damn business, you little shit. Now bring me my purse."

—

That final year at Framingham, something had hardened inside of me. Sports, specifically hockey, had been the one thing my dad and I had connected on—the one way I got any kind of validation from him. It wasn't like I was losing some loving, supportive relationship, but it was what we had. Either way, it was gone now. The semester after I'd gotten cut from the hockey team, he'd refused to even pay for the books I needed for class, claiming he didn't have the money. So be it.

Gone, too, was my one dream of doing something great. I'd never thought I was going to be some hero, but I thought I could do better than the people who'd come before me. Now the challenge was simply surviving. I had to hunker down, retreat into myself, do anything and everything to get ahead. It was down to me, and me alone. I'd die before I went back to Somerville. There had to be something else.

Having busted my ass in my final year at Framingham to prepare for a graduate program in physical therapy, I finally realized I had no desire to be a physical therapist. I wanted to be an athlete, I wanted to compete, and I wanted to win. I didn't want to rehabilitate the winner's tight hamstrings behind the scenes.

Some buddies a year ahead of me had started working different sales jobs. One was in pharmaceuticals, making decent money. At a loss for what else to do, as graduation approached I started applying for every pharmaceutical sales job I saw in the *Boston Globe*'s "Help Wanted" section. I interviewed with Pfizer for a job in Maine. That went nowhere. I landed another interview at Roberts Pharmaceutical. A bunch of guys from nearby towns including Saugus and Melrose worked there. It turned out that the interviewer and I knew a couple of people in common, so I worked that angle hard. The job was in New York City.

I'd been to New York City once before in my life. My mother and Kenneth dragged me and Keith and our kid brother, Matt, to the city for a family vacation when I was sixteen. Of course, my mother and Kenneth crammed all of us into the cheapest, shittiest hotel room in Hell's Kitchen. Keith acted like a maniac, running off into traffic. Kenneth bought a gold rope chain off a guy on the street in the Financial District that was already flaking before we even got home. I'd been transfixed by the guys on the corner who'd set up a game of three-card monte on a couple of cardboard boxes.

Each time we encountered them, I knew exactly where the ace was. I was furious that Kenneth wouldn't let me play.

A few years later when I was working at Billerica, a Black inmate named Spider fell into step with me during my rounds in the yard and broke it all down for me. The game of three-card monte was rigged at every level. Walking by, you'd see a bus driver win, then maybe a taxi driver, then a businesswoman. Every round, it was obvious where the ace was, impossible to resist throwing down a five and trying your luck. The dealer would let you win a couple of hands at double or nothing, till the pot got big. Suddenly, the ace would disappear. The three cards were folded exactly the same so that when the dealer picked them up, he could stack them. When he put them back down, you couldn't tell whether he was dropping the top card or the bottom card. Boom—in one hand, all your winnings and a pile of twenties gone. Then someone would yell, "Cops!" The dealer would kick over the boxes and everyone would scatter . . . because the bus driver, the taxi driver, and the businesswoman—they were all in on the scam, too. And if you were a card sharp, fast enough to decipher the sleight of hand, and you took the dealer for a stack of bills? Didn't matter because as soon as you walked around the corner, one of his cronies had a gun to your head. They'd take their money, *your* money, and maybe your watch and sneakers for the trouble. Listening to Spider tell me how it all worked, I'd decided that New York City was a den of thieves, degenerates, and con men. I'd have nothing to do with the place.

A couple of days after my interview with Roberts Pharmaceutical, I got a call back. They wanted to offer me a position in New York City. I took the job. I'd have taken it if it was in Afghanistan.

I packed up all my belongings, barely enough to fill a single suitcase. People from the neighborhood gave me some old furniture. My mother gave me her old sofa, a couple of wobbly chairs, and an old card table. I loaded it all into a rented U-Haul van.

That was the thing with my mother—she wasn't always horrible. She was capable of kindness. It made me realize that it was her kindness that made her impossible to live with. Had she been a vicious, unrelenting hag, well, violence and cruelty were in the water in Somerville. But she could be kind, even sweet at times. That was the most destabilizing experience of all because you'd let your guard down and next thing you knew, you were getting whipped with a belt.

I moved into a fifth-floor walk-up studio on Seventy-Eighth Street and First Avenue. It looked out onto Seventy-Eighth instead of the alley so I guess that was nice. If I opened my window, I could hypothetically go out and sit on the fire escape, watch the other city dwellers scurrying around below me. But no one would ever do that. The ancient fire escape would probably peel right off the side of the building.

The apartment was small. A tiny little kitchenette and a closet of a bathroom with the type of black-and-white toilet you might find in a prison, with the flush handle on the exposed metal pipe. It had to be the bottom-of-the-line cheapest industrial toilet you could buy, but it flushed with the sound of a jet engine. Careful if you had any loose garments close by when you flushed, because it'd suck everything down the toilet.

Everything in the apartment had been painted probably a hundred times. You know how it goes—after one person moves out and before the next person moves in, the super comes in and paints everything: the walls, the cabinets, the cabinet handles, the radiator, the outlet covers, even the damn light switch. Thick, high-gloss latex paint, layer upon layer upon layer so it never looked dry and it never stopped stinking. The interior was coated in so much paint, I was surprised they hadn't painted the lightbulbs. It was your run-of-the-mill New York City shithole. But it was mine.

I felt what could only be described as irrational exuberance—fury that my parents hadn't done a fucking thing to prepare me for real life, but glee that I'd made it anyway. Here, finally, was my fresh start. I'd discovered in my final months in Somerville that, to quit coke, I had to quit drinking, so I was finally off everything and feeling great. I was an actual adult with an actual job at an actual pharmaceutical company in New York fucking City. My final pay package ended up being $36,000 a year, a sum so large in 1996, I could hardly comprehend it. Of course, after I paid my rent, student loans, utilities, and other obligations, I was operating on the thinnest of margins . . . but my excitement at being out in the real world was so massive, it overwhelmed anything in its path.

Before I left Somerville, Granny had taken me on a shopping trip to make sure her golden boy had everything he needed. If I was going to be a salesman, I'd need a nice suit, so she took me to the best place she could afford—Filene's Basement. Grab any guy off the street and stick him in a department store to pick out professional work clothes and he's going to pick out one navy suit and one gray suit. I couldn't get more than one suit, and my grandmother had to buy me that one, so I knew I had to make it count.

I had no sense of fashion. I didn't know how to tie a tie. I didn't know anything about anything. I was like an alien who'd been dropped in the middle of Manhattan knowing only two things: how to fight and how to skate. I walked out of Filene's Basement with a lime-green suit with a pattern on the front, a striped shirt, a floral-print tie, a brown belt, and black leather Rockport wing tip shoes with rubber soles. I thought I looked like a gangster. I probably looked like I'd lost a bet.

This pharmaceutical sales gig wasn't a dream job, but it'd gotten me out of Somerville, and I knew other opportunities were swirling around me in New York. The position came with a lot of freedom—maybe too much. Roberts Pharmaceutical didn't even have an office in the city. My only responsibility was to go visit doctors in my territory of downtown Manhattan, make sure they knew about our drugs, and facilitate their prescribing our drugs. Roberts bought drugs that were coming off patent but weren't yet being manufactured as generics. So we were selling drugs that'd been around forever. We sold something for urinary tract infections, a nitroglycerin patch, and an antiemetic injection that cured nausea. I had samples of this antiemetic, and when I started drinking again, I probably used it once a month. If I woke up hungover and nauseous, I'd inject this stuff into my ass muscle. Boom, my nausea would instantly be cured. It was a lifesaver.

I'd never had a white-collar job before and I was terrible at it. I had zero polish and almost no life skills. Since I was a teenager, I'd worked every kind of crummy low-level job: supermarket bagger, landscaper, roofer, maintenance worker. There was always some abusive alcoholic lifer screaming at you if you slacked off. Or, in the case of the prison, hundreds of lowlifes and criminals and gang members ready to get one over on you if you weren't paying constant attention and nailing every detail. Now I had all this freedom, no office to go to, and no one checking in on me. If a salesman like me had a decent territory, there'd be doctors writing prescriptions for the drugs they were representing, so the salesman would be getting paid for doing nothing. That was me, essentially. If I didn't want to work one day, I just didn't work. I *never* wanted to work. I put in maybe four hours a week, tops.

I was given a calling card so I could check in with my boss from a pay phone because, presumably, I was on the street all day. I was supposed to call the guy at ten one morning. Of course, I slept till nine and then just kept hitting the snooze button. Finally, I dragged myself out of bed and got on the call with him. Ten minutes into the call, my fucking alarm went off.

"Ken . . . is that your alarm clock?"

"No, it's, uh . . . Hang on. It, uh, I think it was a car alarm. The guy just shut it off."

He had to have known right away. *This dirtbag kid from Somerville we took a chance on is lying in bed till ten a.m. on his mattress on the floor, surrounded by floor-to-ceiling boxes of drug samples for old people.*

But man, I had the greatest time. When I wasn't schmoozing with doctors in my lime-green pimp suit, I was working out. I played hockey at Chelsea Piers, and on a lark, I ran the New York City Marathon in three hours, twenty minutes with no dedicated training. I found it long and boring, totally not my thing.

I became a regular at the Vertical Club, New York's hippest gym. During the time I was training there it was the Studio 54 of New York City fitness: models and celebrities working out alongside financial bigwigs and social climbers. It had the visual aesthetic of a nightclub, with floor-to-ceiling mirrors, a booming sound system, and flashing neon lights. Everyone close to my age whom I met there seemed to be flush. While I had my fifth-floor one-room walk-up full of worn-out furniture and a quarter closet of clothes, they were living in these sick pads with elevators, doormen, Jacuzzis, and views of the East River or Central Park. On weekends, a bunch of them would rent a house in the Hamptons and throw decadent parties that lasted for three days. Every single one of these people worked in finance.

At one meeting at a doctor's office, I found myself standing next to a perfectly polished pharmaceutical sales rep. Not a hair out of place on this woman—tight navy pencil skirt, suit jacket, pristine black pumps, perfect makeup, perfect bun. She worked for Pfizer, I worked for second-tier Roberts out of New Jersey. She looked like a Mercedes S-Class luxury sedan; I looked like a lowered Hyundai with neon under-glow. My very next paycheck, I was down at Brooks Brothers, picking out one gray suit and one navy suit. I was ignorant, but I wasn't stupid. I was starting to figure it out.

When I'd moved to the city months earlier, I was so unprepared for life in New York that I didn't even know what I didn't know. But I was a fast learner. Moving from a home life that could spin into violence at any second to overachieving in high school to fist-fighting inmates in prison to navigating college, I'd learned to adapt quickly to anything. The only constant was that anywhere I went, I didn't belong. But I learned how to fake it long enough to figure things out. I learned how to talk, how to dress, and how to carry myself to convince people I did belong. It was all about survival. *More* than survival actually. I wanted to show everyone not just that I deserved to be there, but that I was going to blow them out of the water.

In the men's hockey league at Chelsea Piers, I played with a kid named Mike Peltier. A good guy and great hockey player, this unflappable French Canadian. He was an interdealer commodities broker, meaning he didn't have to deal with retail clients, just brokered deals between institutions. He mentioned one day that they were looking for a trading assistant on their desk—was I interested? I ran down there the next day. They hired me on the spot.

The place was called Euro Brokers. The office was out in Greenwich, Connecticut. They sent a limousine every morning to drive us out there, then we took the train back into the city after work. The ritual was a perfect metaphor for what I experienced on a daily basis—because I woke up feeling like a rock star, ready to kick ass at my first job in the financial sector, then, after getting berated and bullied all day by my coworkers in this isolated office park in the middle of nowhere, I'd creep back into the city on public transit, just another downtrodden working stiff on the train.

Euro Brokers bought and sold electricity. We'd get contracts for a specific number of megawatts on a specific transmission line in a specific territory for a period of time—a month, three months, maybe a whole calendar year. There was a big whiteboard labeled "Bids" on one side and "Offers" on the other. The traders would yell out a territory, a length of time, and a number, like "February Ercot Fifty-Two bid," and I'd have to write it on the board. Pretty straightforward, right? For the life of me, I couldn't fucking get it right. The traders were merciless, screaming at me, belittling me. They were arrogant dickheads, a little gang of bullies making tons of money. Torturing me was just a game to them. One woman whom I'll call Valerie James made it her life's mission to make me suffer.

I don't know what it was about me that rankled her so much.

Maybe because I was young and athletic and clueless, bumbling around in the only area of her life that held any meaning for her? I never figured it out, but she never missed an opportunity for petty cruelty, whether it was mocking my clothes or making insinuations about any personal call I received at the office.

Peltier had a very even keel and never let it get to him.

"That's just how they are, Ken," he told me one day, "let it roll off your back."

I just took it and took it and took it. But it fucking drove me crazy.

One day, maybe a month into the job, I snapped. We were all working in this open office together, people yelling orders across the room and screaming into their phones. Someone called out a trade and, yeah, I was trying to move too fast and I wrote it down on the wrong side again.

"Yo, that's the offer, not the fucking bid, Rideout."

I felt the eraser for the whiteboard hit me in the back. Because why wouldn't someone toss an eraser at me? I was Valerie James's little bitch, so I should be the bitch for the whole office, right?

Not today, motherfucker, I thought to myself, *this shit ends right now.*

I'd been working out every day. I was in good shape, throwing a lot of punches at the New York Athletic Club. The last thing I was worried about was getting into a fight. I put my marker down, turned around, wound up down to my heels, and just about slapped this idiot trader out of his socks. He didn't know whether to shit or go blind.

"Now you're coming outside," I said quietly. "I'm going to fucking kill you."

What's crazy is the office was so busy and loud that the only people who clocked it were Mike Peltier and the guy I slapped, who looked like he was about to cry.

"Dude," Peltier said, "what the fuck are you doing?"

"What do you mean what am I doing, you saw what this fucking guy did."

"Bro, calm down. Go take a walk, get some air, cool off."

Mike was unfazed. He'd watched guys pound each other's teeth out for lesser offenses on the ice, so he wasn't going to get his feathers ruffled by a little slap. Still, as cruel as their hazing had been, I knew I'd crossed a line. Sure enough, later that day I got called to the office of one of Valerie's cronies.

"Yeah, Ken . . . things aren't working out for you here at Euro Brokers. We're going to have to let you go."

My head started spinning and I felt the walls closing in. I'd hated it there—every single person who worked there was a mercenary dickhead, but it was the first time I'd been fired from a job. I hadn't even been in New York for six months and I'd already blown it at two jobs. I refused to go back home with my tail tucked between my legs, but how was I going to pay my bills?

"Your termination will be effective immediately. We're giving you two weeks' severance."

Severance? They were going to pay me not to go into work? Jackpot! I could find another job in two weeks. Within twenty-four hours, I had a job offer with a competitor.

The same day I got fired, I cold-called Peter McNally, a competitor of Euro Brokers who ended up being a real class act. He said he'd poke around on my behalf, make some calls. The next day, I got a call from Darren Lobdell, the head trainer at Enron. He was like the Gordon Gekko of commodities—a big deal. I gave him the full rundown on my termination with Euro Brokers and he laughed. He said Intercapital was looking for someone. Later that day, I got a call from a guy named Lee Taylor, the head of the desk. He was from Boston. I gave him the full-court press.

"Can you start on Monday?"

It was Thursday.

"Yeah, yeah, that sounds great."

"I'll see you then."

"Um, so . . . what's compensation?"

"The position pays eighty grand."

"Right on, I'll see you Monday, bro."

Eighty thousand fucking dollars. It may as well have been a million. The office was in the iconic World Trade Center. I felt like I'd hit the lottery. I'd been barely scraping by on forty grand but was now making double that after getting canned for slapping a guy? Thank God I'd stood up for myself. The icing on the cake was that Darren Lobdell had been one of Valerie's customers. With every trade I made with Darren, I was taking money out of my torturer's pocket. For the rest of my life I'll remain grateful to Lee Taylor for the opportunity he gave me.

When I got my first check, I went out and bought myself an Omega Seamaster, the same watch James Bond had. It was the most expensive thing I'd ever owned in my life. A month later, I gave it away to my little brother Matt when ICAP gave me a $50,000 bonus and bumped my yearly salary up to $125,000. When that bonus landed, I went out and bought a Rolex Sea-Dweller. It was like a Rolex Submariner, but whereas the Submariner was only good to a thousand feet underwater, the Sea-Dweller was good to four thousand feet. I'd never been diving in my life and had no intention of going, but that watch looked amazing. I was on my way.

—

Nothing in my early life had prepared me for working as a trader. If you'd told me as a kid that I'd be an astronaut, that would've seemed more likely. But oddly enough, lots of things from my early life served me well as a trader. I'd learned as a kid that you never complain—someone always had it harder than you. You keep your eyes open, but you don't rat someone out. There were all kinds of criminal enterprises unfolding around me on the street in Somerville and it was good to know what was up, but it was none of my business, and certainly none of the cops' business. Reputation matters: you do what you say you're going to do. Hockey taught me loyalty over everything. It doesn't matter if I hate my goalie, you so much as bump into him, I'm going to take out your entire top row. On or off the ice, my teammates were my blood, and I'd do anything to protect them. Working in the prison, that'd been my PhD program. Don't make a problem where there isn't one. Know your role and stick to it. If someone messes with you, you don't go tit for tat. You either ignore it completely or you hammer them with overwhelming force. It doesn't matter who you are, it doesn't matter what the situation is, even if you got to draw blood or burn the house down, you never let anyone bully you. I'd made that mistake at Euro Brokers, but no one would ever step on my toes again.

Within six months of getting canned for slapping that guy, I was one of the top brokers in New York. I was living the life, but the gulf between my past and present made me insane. When I first moved to the city, I'd felt insecure just stepping out of my rented U-Haul van, like I didn't deserve to be there. But my sales gig at Roberts Pharmaceutical had barely been a real job. Working as a trading assistant at Euro Brokers was still small potatoes. ICAP was a genuine breakthrough, my first serious job where I felt like an adult in control of my destiny. I was working shoulder to shoulder with guys from Harvard and Yale, with MBAs in finance and ten years' experience. Every single day, I had this voice in my head telling me I wasn't good enough, I wasn't smart enough, that one day they'd figure out I didn't belong here, and I'd be finished. They'd discover I'd graduated from a state university one step up from a vocational school with a major in sociology and minors in fighting and cocaine and run me out of town. I worked some of that nervous energy off on the ice or in the ring at the New York Athletic Club, one of the best private athletic clubs in the world. In my early days in New York, I never could have afforded a membership there, but I'd secured a free membership in exchange for competing on the boxing team. I was still scared to fight, but I convinced myself that the fear would eventually end. It never did, but I got good at both boxing and doing things while scared.

Mostly, I harnessed my insecurity and anxiety to work harder than anyone at my office. It paid off handsomely. But the only thing worse than having no money is having money and worrying you're going to lose it. I was convinced that all my success could fly away at any moment.

Friends? Who had time for that? I was so busy working, training, and entertaining clients that I had nothing left for making friends. I got along with the majority of folks I worked with, and some would end up becoming lifelong friends, but there was no shortage of bullshit artists working in finance. I checked in with my old crew from Somerville only occasionally. My old friend Sully hadn't made it to college, so he became a security guard. He had a kid super young with a local Somerville girl we'd gone to school with who treated him like trash. He was such a sweet guy and he'd fallen into the same life I'd run from.

I was friendly with the people I worked with, but they were all aggressive cutthroat personalities. They did things for me and I did things for them but I knew that the minute that went away, everything went away. New York was such a bizarre world. I was constantly surrounded by people—playing hockey at Chelsea Piers, boxing at the New York Athletic Club, shouting out trades while surrounded by other shouting traders, late nights at Peter Luger or the W or the Four Seasons—so how was it that I felt lonely? Whatever, it didn't matter.

In 1998, I went to a podiatrist with an ankle issue. After our first consultation, the doctor wrote me a script for seven Percocet. I went directly to the pharmacy and filled the script. I took one pill as I walked out of the store and felt it kick in even before I got home. Alcohol had never worked for me and coke hadn't worked for me in the long term, but this, this was something different. I'd felt happy and confident, even optimistic and excited for the future. Yeah, it killed the pain in my foot, but who gave a fuck about the pain when the side effects were this good.

I spent every single day at my job racked with anxiety that, eventually, they were going to realize that I was just some dumb meathead from a dirtbag town who had no business playing with rich, educated people's money. Percocet made that anxiety and inadequacy disappear as if by a magic spell. That little white pill made me feel like I was going to be okay. I felt like I was going to make it. I even got a little warm glow in my chest. This Percocet shit, it felt like love.

I got another seven on my visit the next week. And then another seven at the visit the week after. Then I started altering the script, changing the numeral 7 into a 2 and adding a zero. Suddenly, I had a script for twenty Percs a week. I brought my scripts to all these different little mom-and-pop pharmacies around Manhattan where I knew they wouldn't call to verify it. I had this new career where I was making shitloads of money and I had my secret, this little white pill that made everything better. I was on top of the fucking world.

In the beginning, I got the shit directly from the professionals. New York City was full of shady doctors willing to scratch your back if you scratched theirs. But I couldn't just stroll in and pay them to write me a prescription. I'd go in and bullshit them, go through a whole thing of like, "Oh, my back hurts, yes, right there, ow ow ow." Like they didn't know exactly what I was after. Like they didn't have a line of other jerk-offs like me doing the same ham acting job for the same reason. They didn't care. They knew they were providing a service, and we were paying for that service, and that was enough.

Once in a blue moon, I'd speak to my grandmother and get an incidental update on the rest of the family.

"So, what's up, Granny? How you been doing?"

"Oh, I'm just sitting here with your brother Keith."

"He's there with you on a weekday, huh? Does he have the day off today?"

"Don't be fucking funny, Kenny. You know he doesn't have a job."

"Keep letting him live there with you, that'll definitely motivate him to change."

I loved Granny, but God, it was so hard to deal with any of them.

—

In 2000, I got invited to interview with Cantor Fitzgerald in London to run their European commodities trading desk. The higher-up negotiating the contract was Lee Amaitis, a Brooklyn-born guy whose dad had been a coal miner in Pennsylvania. Lee's first job had been training horses when he was a teenager. He was a hard man—the British press called him the "Brooklyn Bruiser"—and he definitely didn't mix with the rank-and-file brokers.

Unlike in the United States, spread betting was legal in London and they had a betting platform in the UK called Cantor Gaming. That was Lee's baby. Lee loved horse racing and gambling in all forms. He was like an old-school mafia guy—he would have done great in 1950s Vegas. Lee had a rep for being notoriously ruthless. He had this aura where you didn't know whether he was going to punch you in the face, stab you, or shoot you. I never felt intimidated by that routine. Go play in the NHL for ten years as an enforcer, yeah, then you're tough. Lee was a businessman, and I was a businessman. We got along fine.

We were sitting in Lee's office in London, hammering out the contract. Bernie Cantor, one of Cantor Fitzgerald's namesakes, had been the largest private collector of Rodin sculptures in the world. Lee had a limited-edition bronze copy of *The Thinker* sitting on his desk. Must have weighed sixty pounds. We were going back and forth, back and forth.

"Listen," I said finally, "I'll tell you what. I'll agree to the contract as written if you give me that sculpture."

"You like that, huh?"

I shrugged.

"Be nice to have it kicking around the apartment. Good paperweight, you know?"

Lee gave me a hard look.

"If you sign this contract right fucking now, when you come over here and do your first trade, I'll give you this statue."

I signed the contract. When I did my first trade in London for Cantor Fitzgerald, Lee gave me the statue. I still have it. It could be some incredibly valuable Rodin limited-edition artwork or some worthless piece-of-shit replica, I don't know. But whether it's worth a hundred dollars or a hundred million, it's mine, it's priceless, and it's one of my most prized possessions.

The money was bonkers. Cantor gave me a $250,000 cash signing bonus, an unfathomable amount for a twenty-nine-year-old kid. Best part was that it was treated as a forgivable loan, so no taxes until the loan was forgiven. And at this stage of my life, I wasn't worried about next week, never mind two years. I was also made a partner at Cantor, which meant I got a small share of the firm's overall profits every quarter I worked there. I was hired as an expat, which meant that when I got to London, Cantor paid for everything. They paid my rent. They paid my tax expenses. Any living expenses, anything associated with me living in London . . . it was all on Cantor's tab.

They put me up in a Mews House in Kensington, the nicest

house I'd ever lived in. The rent was £5,000 a week—all paid for. It was a three-story stand-alone building on the street. It opened into a little cobblestone alley called a mews off the main road. It'd been an old stable that'd been converted into this super-modern three-bedroom house. There was a massive flat-screen plasma TV, and in the third-story loft half the floor was glass, so you could look down into the kitchen and living room below. The house had a great finished roof deck on top of it. On the ground floor, there was a garage with a door that made it look like the whole front of the house was lifting up.

That first night in Kensington, late December 2000, I stayed up late with jet lag, restless with energy from my few remaining Percocet, wandering around my new digs, marveling at the opulence. I'd be making over a million dollars a year. My mother's tongue-lashing, Kenneth's belt dangling from his hand, that soft spot in our living room floor—they felt as distant and unreal as a bad dream. Nothing could stop me now.

CHAPTER FOUR

FULLY LOADED

Less than a week after I made it to London, I got sick. It felt like the worst flu of my life. My nose was running, I was racked with fever and chills, a pounding headache that wouldn't go away, zero energy. I figured I'd picked up a bug on the flight over and tried to sleep my way out of it. But as bad as I felt the first day it hit, I kept getting worse. By the third day, I was delirious from loss of sleep, curled up in the fetal position in my bed, sweating through my sheets, afraid I was going to die. By the fourth day, I was ready to die. Worse than all the physical elements of my mysterious illness combined was the soul-crushing depression. I felt hopeless, useless, trapped a million miles away from home, and unworthy of drawing another breath.

I felt like I'd witnessed this type of sickness before but I couldn't recall where. Finally, it hit me: *Barney.* A couple of times a year when I was a kid, I'd seen my uncle laid up like this when he'd run out of heroin. I was in withdrawal.

By this point, I'd been popping Percocets around the clock for maybe a year. It'd never occurred to me that I was becoming addicted, or that one could even get addicted to pills. When I landed the position in London, I figured it was going to be so good, I wouldn't need the pills. Moving to New York had cured my coke problem, so I figured moving to London would cure my pill habit. But no, apparently there were horrific consequences for taking drugs all day, every day. Dear God, what had I done?

I got my little brother Matt on the phone. As things had started popping in New York, I'd brought him in and gotten him a job working in the financial sector. I hadn't introduced him to drugs and certainly never spoke to him about using drugs, but you didn't make it out of Somerville without finding out a thing or two. This new pill marketed by Purdue had gotten popular in the last few years, a painkiller named OxyContin. Percocet only had five milligrams of oxycodone per pill. They made OxyContin with ten, twenty, forty, even 160 milligrams of oxycodone.

I forced myself to be very low-key on the phone with Matt. I had to ask a favor for a friend, no big deal. I told him to reach out to a couple of different guys we knew from Somerville and find me a big bottle of OxyContin, the strongest he could find. He was to overnight it to me in London. Whatever it cost, I'd pay.

Within a couple of hours after FedEx pounded on my door with the delivery, I'd eaten, worked out, and showered for the first time in days and was back at my desk, catching up. I didn't just feel cured of the plague that'd descended on me, I felt amazing, the best I had in years, like I was seeing the sun shine for the first time. But there was a nagging voice deep down inside of me. I knew now that I was hooked. No way around it, I was an addict.

It never occurred to me that, as far as I'd gone into withdrawal, I could have just powered through and been free of this shit once and for all. But getting sober didn't even feel like an option. The only way to cure myself was to get more drugs. The only way to not get sick again was to not run out. I had money. I just had to find a way to never run out again.

Within days I started shopping for doctors. The UK had public health services, so anyone could go see a doctor at any time. But if you had private health insurance or were willing to pay for a private doctor, it was like concierge service. The private doctors were very, very accommodating. So I called up a twenty-four-hour doctor call service in London.

When the doctor showed up at my office, I could tell he'd been drinking. He was this Walter Mitty type—bad suit, kind of disheveled, probably forty but he looked fifty or sixty. I ushered him into an empty conference room and gave him my standard song and dance about a herniated disc. I'd thought I'd only be able to get Percs from him, but the only thing he had was OxyContin. Yeah, that'd get the job done.

Every time I used that doctor, he showed up reeking of booze. I didn't feel one flicker of compassion toward him when I recognized he was drowning like me, I just remember thinking *now I got your number*. After a while, I suggested we just meet in the bar downstairs. In London back then, it wasn't unusual to have a beer anytime, like "Hey, let's go downstairs, talk about these commodity prices at the pub." They'd have a beer at breakfast. I wouldn't drink a thing when I was working—had to stay sharp. Sure, I'd swallow a handful of pills the moment I woke up, with more for lunch and dinner, but that was just part of the job.

I always paid cash. Cash opens a lot of doors. Of course, my doctor loved it, he was a drunk. I wondered sometimes how much of the money I paid him even made it out of that pub. He'd come and collect my cash and drink the beer I bought him and write a script for as many as I wanted. One day, he wrote me a prescription for a hundred pills. I couldn't believe my good fortune. But a hidden part of my soul started quaking. If I hadn't been out of control before, this was going to tip me over the line.

I was probably single-handedly responsible for the first big wave of Oxy prescriptions in London. It was almost funny: I'd started out as a pharmaceutical sales rep, trying to get doctors to prescribe my drugs. Now, in what felt like an entirely different universe, I was still pressing doctors to prescribe my drugs, but some other pharmaceutical sales rep was cashing in.

—

I'd always been resourceful, and I quickly learned how to get drugs anywhere. When I learned to get drugs anywhere, I got them everywhere. I'd go to the Four Seasons in Maui, ask the front desk to connect me with a local doctor who made house calls. I didn't give a shit about spending two hundred bucks to get the doctor to come to the hotel so I could roll the dice to try to convince him to write me a prescription. I'd always lay out cash, so the doctor understood I was willing to pay him off the record. Take ten twenty-dollar bills and put it on the table. Guy would walk in, see the cash, and human psychology immediately kicked in. Some of these doctors were addicts like me, only difference was they were hooked on my money while I was hooked on their pills. The guy wasn't going to make the trip and leave two hundred dollars cash on the table. As soon as I asked for the pills, he'd know what was up. *You don't give me the prescription, you're not getting the cash.* Nine times out of ten, I got my pills.

—

When I was coming up on the trading desk, it was still the rules of the jungle. It was very aggressive, very cutthroat. If you weren't standing on the gas all day long, you'd get run over. Not the way I wanted to work or live, but I adapted and learned to thrive. The position of greatest power on the trading desk was the manager. But it was like a lion ruling over a pack of hyenas—they were always trying to charm and seduce the lion for favorable treatment while conspiring with the other hyenas to undermine or even overthrow the lion.

When I got the job at Cantor in London, I was hired to be the manager of the energy commodities trading desk. I was a good broker, but I had zero managerial skills. It was like someone said "This is a great hyena, he's good at all the things hyenas do—let's make him a lion." They were asking me to be an entirely different animal. And I'd signed up for it. I was worried from the minute that I landed there that all the other hyenas were going to be like, "This guy ain't no lion, he's a hyena. If they're trying to stick him in on top, that means any one of us can do it. Let's band together and get him out."

I knew that traders weren't literally hyenas and managers weren't lions. We weren't in the jungle, we were on the trading desk. Successful managers weren't always just tyrants, they often had unique characteristics or personality traits they used to keep the traders in line to keep everything moving smoothly. Though I later discovered

I had some of these latent managerial qualities, they were so buried under insecurity, anxiety, and low self-opinion at the time as to be nonexistent. Brute strength concealed all those faults. If I couldn't be the wisest, most charming, most experienced lion in the jungle, I'd be the biggest, baddest, most brutal lion anyone ever saw.

I wasn't comfortable being super aggressive all the time. While it didn't come naturally to me, intimidation was so central to my survival in London that I quickly got better at it. It was never something I reveled in. I'd never been a bully, but to succeed at managing a trading desk in a new job in a foreign country where I knew few people, that's what I had to become. I hated it. I hated going into work every morning, ready for war. I hated berating my traders in front of their peers, I hated the way everyone on the floor tightened up around me, I hated the way they hated me, because I hated me, too. The pills made it easier to play my role. They were like a mask I put on to play the bully. They gave me something to hide my real self behind—helped me forget I was an insecure blue-collar kid way out of his league, crippled with anxiety and self-loathing, living in terror of being exposed, shamed, and exiled.

I killed it at work. The money was insane. By this point, I'd been making big money for a couple of years, so with a huge new job, it was time to spend some of that cheddar. I was a Wall Street bigwig now, and so I was buying all the best. I'd go to the Armani store once a week and buy suits, overcoats, raincoats, anything they had, everything they had. I had custom Armani Black Label cashmere suits, top of the line. Everything I wore was Armani, down to my ties. Long gone was my lime-green embarrassment of a suit—now I was dressing to the nines.

Some people bought the act. They looked at me and thought, *Wow, this guy is really dialed in.* I'm sure other people thought I cared way too much about how I was dressed, that I was trying too hard. They were right. It was like my two-tone Jordache jeans in tenth grade all over again. I wanted so badly to belong that I was wildly overcompensating in trying to conceal my hardscrabble childhood, my questionable academic credentials, and my lack of social pedigree.

I took the Concorde back and forth from New York to London. I flew first class all over the world. I stayed in every Four Seasons in Europe. I'd go online and find out where the best hotels in the world were, then I'd zip over for a weekend of decadence. I had the best of everything: Tom Ford tuxedos, Rolex watches, linens and towels from Frette. It wasn't enough to have all the best stuff, I needed the world to *know* I had the best stuff.

The money made me feel like I was bulletproof. I once brought an ounce of coke on an international flight to France from the UK, then on to Monaco in a chopper. Every year, Cantor Fitzgerald threw a big bash in Monaco for the Grand Prix. They chartered a private jet for us from London to Nice, a plane full of people drinking and smoking cigarettes and getting lit up. I had the coke folded up neatly in the inside pocket of my tuxedo in my luggage, because why would they suspect a clean-cut guy like me? It wasn't just careless, it was reckless. I was daring the universe to take me down.

Cantor Fitzgerald threw a crazy black-tie formal dinner the Saturday night before the race. Halfway through the night, the roof of the venue retracted so we could watch fireworks that were going off over the Mediterranean. The entertainment was James Brown.

There were maybe two hundred people there. It was insane watching "The Hardest Working Man in Showbiz" put on such a powerful show for such an intimate crowd. They had a charity auction. On a whim, I bid $3,500 for the Formula One star Jos Verstappen's signed racing suit. I had no desire to win it. If you put a gun to my head, I couldn't have told you why I bid, but I won it. I got lit up the next day at the race, then put it on before we left and flew home in this Formula One driving suit.

My friends thought I was a crazy bastard, but I was just an idiot, drunk on money and power. I should have felt on top of the world, but the more money I made, the more my anxiety mounted. Any day now, one of the jealous traders I managed would expose me as a fraud. When my new social sphere figured out I was just dumb, worthless white trash, they'd run me out of town like the fucking bum I was. With the amount of money I'd been making, they wouldn't just run me out of town. They'd want blood. I had to make as much as I could, spend as much as I could, and live as much as I could before the whole thing blew up in my face.

Having a car in London wasn't as ridiculous as having one in New York, but I could've easily gone without a car my entire time there. Nonetheless, one day, I convinced myself I needed a car. I went on the Porsche website, then dialed the company's office in Germany. I told them I wanted a new black 2002 Porsche Carrera Cabriolet, the top of the line, the best of the best. Yes, it had to be convertible with the optional hard top (which would end up being a royal pain to store). GPS navigation in cars was brand-new at the time—did I need GPS? Damn right I did. I needed every single option available, this car must be fully loaded. Did they have any other options, anything else I didn't know about, anything not on the website that I should get on the car? I needed that salesman to tell me that the car would be so special that everyone would know I was special. It must have been the easiest sale of his life.

The last car I'd owned had been an ancient Toyota Tercel with tires thinner and slicker than bologna skin. The transmission was falling apart, and when I was on the highway, it kept slipping out of fifth gear. I'd attached a bungee cord to the dashboard and looped the other end around the gearshift when I was in fifth to hold it in place. One night before I'd moved to New York, I'd had a date, so I took down the bungee cord. Of course, it'd slipped out of fifth on the highway, causing the transmission to grind like mad and scaring the shit out of the poor girl.

I booked a first-class one-way ticket to Stuttgart and flew over to pick the car up directly from the factory. It looked immaculate, smelled immaculate, 320 horsepower with a six-speed manual transmission. I didn't know anything about cars, had never owned a nice car in my life, but I loved that Porsche. I'd go ripping around town in my hundred-thousand-dollar sports car like I was driving the Batmobile.

There were women but never anything serious. I'd become a master at "nothing serious." I'd meet someone through the job—a banker, a flight attendant, an heiress. We'd sail to France or go skiing in Switzerland or stay at the nicest hotel in Hong Kong for a weekend. And then that was it. I was busy, I told myself, too busy to sustain a real relationship. When the right one came along, I'd go all in. But I had a nagging suspicion that I wasn't just failing to make a deep investment, I was investing deeply in the shallowest things: mountains of pills, the finest of everything money could buy, crushing the competition. Whatever, it was fine.

My old life found me, even in my fortress of OxyContin and opulence. When I moved out of Boston, I'd dropped almost all communication with any of my family. Somewhere in the back of my head, I knew Matt was on pills and messing up. Keith had gotten pinched and was serving time in the very same prison where I'd been employed as a guard. I worked hard not to know any more than that.

But when I moved to London, word got around in Boston that I'd started making serious money. One day, I got a call from my dear old mother.

"Kenny! There he is, there's our world traveler."

"Oh hey, Ma, how you doing?"

"Oh, I'm fine, sweetie, we're all fine. Same old, same old. You know Keith is trying to get on his feet still . . . same old, same old. But how are you? You must be so successful to be working over in England. You know everyone in the neighborhood is so proud of you, we're all so proud of you."

"That's nice, Ma. Doing good."

"That's good, honey, that's great."

I didn't say anything for a minute. She was being so syrupy sweet, it made my antennae go up immediately. Something was up. She and my stepfather had divorced after I'd left home—was she looking for a new meal ticket? She paused, then went for it.

"Say, Kenny, I think it's finally time I get out of Somerville. They're building a bunch of new condos in Stoneham. I wanted to ask if you could lend me the money for the down payment."

"How much is it?"

"I think it's around eighty thousand dollars."

"Ma. For me to give you eighty thousand dollars . . ."

"It'd be a loan, Kenny."

"No, I loan you that eighty grand, I'm never getting it back. Let's just call it what it is, I'd be giving you eighty grand. You know how much effort it takes to make eighty grand? That means I got to make one-fifty, get taxed for seventy, then put the other eighty aside and not spend one dollar of it for a whole fucking year. And then I just hand it to you? What the fuck are you talking about? I'd never do that."

"I knew you'd get angry at me just for asking."

"Let me ask you something, Ma. Do you remember my first semester at Framingham State? When I didn't realize it was a three-day weekend and then I called you and begged you to pick me up? What did I tell you then?"

"Kenny, you don't have to be nasty about it."

"Ma, I fucking begged you for a ride home when I was stuck at Framingham over a holiday weekend. And you wouldn't do it. You acted like I was crazy for asking. And I told you then that, one day, you'd be sorry for the way you treated me. Do you remember that? Today is that day. You're not getting a fucking dime. I'll set my money on fire before you see any of it."

It should have felt good. Here it was—the revenge I'd dreamed of. It just made me feel twisted up inside, like I'd been poisoned. She was my mother. I should have given her everything she asked for and more. I should have made her every dream come true. The only thing standing in the way was the mountain of cruelty she'd inflicted on me as a child, all the times she'd cut me down and mocked me and belittled me and slapped me around. And if I'd said yes and given her the eighty grand? It'd never be enough. She'd bleed me dry. She'd been looking for a free ride since the day I was born, I'd be goddamned if I was going to be her next mark.

—

That September, I'd treated myself to first-class airfare and ringside seats for a boxing championship fight at Madison Square Garden. The afternoon before my flight was to leave, I was on the trading desk at Cantor. It was a large, open trading floor with the stock tickers going and flat-screen TVs mounted on all the columns. I had my head down when I heard someone say something I'll never forget.

"Someone just flew a plane into the World Trade Center."

I looked up and there it was on the TV, a big smoking hole in the side of the North Tower.

We were alarmed, of course. But traders were people who spent all day every day calculating risk. It was our job to not freak out. We hadn't yet seen the footage of the Boeing 767 carrying ninety-two passengers (including the five hijackers) and crew disappearing into the building.

I think most people assumed it was some idiot amateur pilot who'd crashed his Cessna. It was unnerving that some nitwit had flown his hobby plane into the most prominent symbol of US global financial leadership, but it was our job to take disturbing events like this in stride and keep rolling.

There were some mutterings that it'd actually been a commercial airliner, but that was just some crackpot conspiracy theory. It was unheard of. I'd sooner believe that we'd been hit with a nuclear bomb. And if it'd been a commercial flight, where was the debris? It made no sense.

We had open lines of communication between New York and London. You'd just pick up the phone, push the button, and it'd broadcast your voice on a speaker we called a squawk box. There were multiple desks with open lines for interest rate swaps, treasuries, and government bonds. For the first few minutes after the plane hit, there were people talking back and forth.

"Okay, yeah, they're telling us we got to get out of here. We're going to head to the stairwell now."

"All right, guys, be safe. Just get out of there, get out of the building."

From the TV, we could see a crazy amount of smoke, but it wasn't like the building was on fire. Sure, there was a hole in the side of the building with smoke billowing out, so obviously something was on fire, but it wasn't like the building was engulfed in flames.

"We're watching you guys on TV right now. Wow, this is fucking crazy. Yeah, don't panic but definitely get out of there as soon as you can."

"Yeah, I think we're going up to the roof. There's so much smoke, and it's so far down to the street, it's safer to not use the stairs. We're going to go up to the roof. They'll get the fire out and get choppers up there to get us down."

Cantor Fitzgerald occupied the 101st to the 105th floors of the North Tower, so it was much easier for people to go up to the roof to await rescue rather than try to brave the stairwells.

Seventeen minutes after the first plane strike, we watched with eyes glued to the TV as United Airlines Flight 175 hurtled out of the clear blue sky, then disappeared into the South Tower in a splash of fire and debris. The whole floor gasped. Some people cried out in terror. I felt a chill of horror and panic blossom at the base of my neck, then run all the way down my spine. The reality of what was going down finally slammed into us all. Oh my fucking God, it was terrorists. We were under attack.

The floor was calm chaos. It was terrifying, it was horrifying, it was appalling—every bad thing you could think of to say about it was true. But we dealt with bedlam every day. We were there because we had a job to do. Goldman Sachs had gone offline only seconds after the first plane strike, and as bad as the scene in New York was, we were already catastrophizing about the impact this would have on the global financial markets. Through our dread and horror, we did everything we could to stop the bleeding. But the blood kept coming.

Thirty-four minutes later, American Airlines Flight 77 crashed into the Pentagon. Five minutes after that, the FAA grounded all air traffic in US airspace for the first time in history. Another flight was reported off course and zooming toward lower Manhattan. We were hearing rumors of people finding bombs on the ambulances sent to the World Trade Center to rescue the wounded. No way this could get worse.

A little over an hour after the first plane strike, we watched the South Tower implode upon itself and, almost in slow motion, shred itself to the ground. The entire trading floor was just stunned shock and silence. There were some people crying, but it wasn't yet madness. People didn't want to be too dramatic. None of us really understood what we were watching or what it meant.

Half an hour later, the North Tower came down. The North Tower held the entirety of Cantor Fitzgerald's New York operations.

One guy on the floor, both his brother and father were in the North Tower. My buddy Mike Peltier, the laid-back French Canadian who'd given me my start in finance, was there, too.

Everyone had been frantically calling their people in New York, but there was no cell service. When the towers came down, it wasn't like, "Oh my God, they're all dead." Everyone was holding out hope that our people made it out because so much time had passed from the first plane strike till the towers came down. We had no point of reference. No one was like, "Oh, I remember when that hundred-and-ten-story building in Chicago collapsed a couple of years ago." It was totally unprecedented.

I felt numb. It didn't register with me. It looked so unreal, like we were watching a disaster movie. In 1993, they'd set off a giant truck bomb in the basement and couldn't knock the World Trade Center down. One month later, it was business as usual. And now some madmen had flown planes into the sides of the towers and taken the entire fucking thing down? I could not wrap my brain around it.

We worked to exhaustion that night. The whole mood was subdued. We were trying not to jump to conclusions, trying to stay calm, trying not to panic, just holding the line and waiting for information.

Over the next day or two, the madness struck. Anyone who hadn't been in the North Tower was now in London working on the trading desk there. Overnight, we had to try to get all the desks from New York up and running from London. We were operating this business around the clock. The London market opened at eight o'clock local time, then New York came online at one thirty. That meant that shit would be jumping till around eleven or midnight in London, then light up again around seven the next morning. We had a conference room set up with cots because so many people were sleeping in the office.

It felt like we were at war. The level of camaraderie and patriotism took your breath away. The Brits had loved to take the piss out of the American expats, but all of that was instantly gone. The English had seen London bombed to the ground twice in the last hundred years, and they were furious on our behalf. There was an unspoken consensus on the trading floor: *Fuck those guys straight to hell. No one's going to take us out. Let's go, all of us together.*

On September 14, Howard Lutnick, the chairman and CEO of Cantor Fitzgerald at the time, established the Cantor Fitzgerald Relief Fund for the victims' families with a million dollars of his own money. Lutnick also pledged 25 percent of the company's profits over five years, in addition to providing ten years of health insurance for the surviving family members. The fund's goal was to help families until every child of a 9/11 Cantor Fitzgerald victim had finished college. They'd go on to raise $180 million for the victims' families.

For once, in the most shark-eat-shark industry in the world, we all became selfless. On September 10, we were traders, protecting our clients and covering our own asses, grinding to get that cheddar. On September 12, we were soldiers serving a greater cause, doing everything in our power to steer this ship into safe harbor. We donated to charities and organized benefits and gave blood. We held our breath, waiting for news about the survivors.

That news never came. In the end, the blood we gave was useless.

The missing stayed missing. Not one person from the floors above the plane strikes survived. Every single Cantor employee who was in the office on 104 and 105 that day died. Of the 978 Cantor employees in New York, 658 of them perished. We lost almost 70 percent of our New York workforce. Most of them, no trace was ever found. The implosion of the towers had disappeared them completely. The only proof we had that they'd ever existed were the smoldering scars on our hearts and minds.

The markets went crazy. These days, every trading company has redundancy. Every transaction is tracked multiple times in multiple places. But at the time, the idea of maintaining disaster relief center backups to servers seemed like a paranoid hassle. When 9/11 happened, mountains of records were destroyed. Nothing was left. And it wasn't just Cantor Fitzgerald—the World Trade Center had housed Bank of America, Morgan Stanley, the futures trader Salomon Smith Barney, the US Securities and Exchange Commission, and the New York Stock Exchange.

The uncertainty was through the roof. We worked till we were cross-eyed, trying to stabilize the global markets. Looking back now, I can't believe we made it through that. The shot-callers figured it out and the rank-and-file guys fell in line and picked up the slack. That the global economic systems didn't completely melt down felt like a miracle. Financial markets eventually leveled out.

It was all so instantaneous and so heavy and then so all-consuming. In the months following 9/11, I never had the opportunity to process the massive trauma I'd witnessed. But then, I'd never been big on processing trauma. I was already blocking out so many emotions and numbing so much pain, the destruction of the World Trade Center was just one more thing to throw on the pile. I worked like a fiend, worked out like a fiend, and sought refuge in my painkillers.

It was late October before the adrenaline finally wore off. The markets were calming down and as much as we knew it'd never be business as usual again, we were finding our feet in this new world we'd been thrust into. I knew I had to get sober. The coke and the drinking, that was part of the job. Honking some stripes and getting banged up with clients and coworkers was just good business, a way to strengthen those bonds. The pills, well, those were my secret shame. I wasn't tossing a couple back on a Friday night to wipe away the stress of a busy week. I was chowing down a handful before breakfast so I had the courage to put my fucking socks on.

There's nothing like a global catastrophe to make one reflect on the stupid bullshit we use to fill up our days: all the ways in which, minute by minute, we throw our lives away. Even in the worst throes of my addiction, I knew my consumption was unsustainable. And after 9/11, it hit me like a freight train—I had to quit this shit immediately. Thousands of my peers, my fellow New Yorkers, were dead. And I was honoring their memory, their unlived lives by gobbling pills like Pac-Man? I could have easily been in the North Tower that day. If I hadn't gotten the contract to come to London, that's exactly where I would have been. I'd gotten a second chance at life, a second chance that'd been denied to thousands of others. I couldn't blow it.

The first time I'd gone through withdrawals, it'd caught me by surprise. Now I knew exactly what was coming: sweats and chills, cramps like a shiv in your guts, hammering headaches, sleeplessness and exhaustion, horrifying nightmares, and worst of all, the depression that felt like your soul was slowly being torn apart, fiber by fiber.

I made the decision to white-knuckle at home, by myself. Other people had gotten through it, I'd get through it, too. It felt like standing on the precipice of hell and gazing down into the immeasurable suffering, torture, and ruin below, and then throwing yourself in.

CHAPTER FIVE

JOYKILLERS

AFTER WHAT FELT LIKE A SUICIDAL ETERNITY, I FINALLY EMERGED FROM that long, lightless tunnel of withdrawal. No, it wasn't like after an earth-shaking thunderstorm where the clouds recede and the sun comes out and there's a rainbow. It was more like dragging yourself from the basement of a building that's been shelled with heavy artillery for a week. You're weak, you're terrified, the sun hurts your eyes, and you just stand there in shock and horror, staring at the ruins around you.

I crawled back to the office to catch up on the work I'd missed after calling out for a week. I tried to get back into a day-to-day routine. Though I was through the acute withdrawals where it felt like a demon had its icy claws around my throat, I still craved Percocet every minute of every day, even dreaming about those pills at night. I knew I wouldn't make it without help, so, with a heart full of shame and disgust, I dragged myself to a Narcotics Anonymous meeting at a dingy community center in London.

As I approached the grimy building where the meeting was held, I immediately noticed the tattooed hipsters and run-down addict types lingering around the building, sucking down one last smoke before the meeting. I'd just gotten out of work, not a hair out of place, even though I felt like death. I must have stuck out like a sore thumb. I felt a wave of disgust at having to share space with these people for the next hour. *Fuck these people. Fuck this place. I have nothing to learn from them.* And then I felt a bigger wave of shame: *Look at what I've become. I'm here with them because this is where I belong.*

This kid from Northern Ireland who looked like a character from *Trainspotting* walked over to me.

"What's up, mate? I'm Gareth. This your first day?"

He must have been a regular there and could recognize the specific mixture of anxiety, humiliation, and resignation on the face of a newcomer.

"Is it that obvious?"

"We've all been there, man. Just keep coming back."

"Yeah?"

"Only two things you need to do. Make it through today. And keep coming back. You'll get through it."

"We'll see."

"There's that can-do attitude I knew you had in you! I'll walk you in. The coffee's shit but there's loads of it."

In that meeting, the same people I'd judged mercilessly my entire life welcomed me with open arms. I became a regular at meetings all over London. I got into a good groove there. I enjoyed the people and I enjoyed the atmosphere. As different as we were, in one crucial way, we were all the same, and that was enough for incredible camaraderie. I even stood up and shared a few times. I was shocked at the level of support all these people in need provided for each other.

Though we only had one thing in common, I ended up hanging out with Gareth all the time. He never officially became my sponsor, but he looked out for me, and I really learned a lot from him. He was a savage dude and an incredible photographer. His work was hardcore. He showed me some brutal, beautiful pictures he'd taken in Northern Ireland during the Troubles—the aftermath of terrorist attacks, young junkies shooting up, people with hatchet wounds still gushing from IRA fighting.

As soon as I got sober, I started getting in crazy-good shape. I'd always been athletic as a kid, and as I got older, taking care of my body became an important way in which I set myself apart from all the people I'd left behind in Somerville. Now that I was staying out of bars and avoiding social gatherings, I had nothing else to do but train. I hit it hard. I'd never found a boxing gym in London I really liked so I was lifting weights five days a week at the gym below our office. Weekends, I'd go running. Three, four, maybe five miles at a time just to mix it up, blow off some steam. I had no passion for it, but then I had no passion for anything. It was a means to an end.

Gareth gave me shit about working out so much. It didn't matter how long he'd been clean, he still looked as skinny and disheveled as the worst Skid Row junkie.

"Mate, every time I see you, you got bigger muscles."

"Yeah, I'm too vain to go through life being skinny-fat. And when I'm training, I'm not thinking about getting high. You should try it sometime. Have you been to the gym one time in your entire life?"

"Aye, you know what they say about the gym: it's so good, you should never even try it once."

I liked myself so much better sober, but the job wore on me. It was the same life I'd lived for years, but it felt radically different when I wasn't popping pills all the time. I was counting on myself to have the same level of performance and interact with people on the same level. But without my secret superpower, everything was harder.

And in the spring of 2002, shit started falling apart at work. Trading electricity was the main moneymaker for the desk I was running. When Enron filed for bankruptcy in December 2001 after concealing billions of dollars in debt, the stock plummeted to less than $1 per share after a high of $90.75 eighteen months prior. At the time, the $63.4 billion Chapter 11 filing was the largest ever. Investors lost their shirts, Enron's founder and CEO, Kenneth Lay, was indicted and convicted, and energy traders were saddled with a bunch of new restrictions. As a result, all our business was drying up.

At that same time, the most lucrative business that Cantor Fitzgerald had in the New York office was credit derivatives. I was a good broker with an underwhelming product in London. My contract in London was up. When Cantor reached out and asked me to come back to New York and take over the credit derivative business, I jumped at the opportunity. I'd been making more than five hundred thousand dollars a year at Cantor before Enron went bust. When they sent me back to New York, my new contract paid ten grand a month draw, meaning I'd have to make the money up in sales. Far from an ideal situation, but I was eager to get back to New York.

Thing was, when I landed and got to work, no one wanted to work with Cantor. Emotions were raw, tensions were high, and there was a lot of misinformation swirling around. Some of the clients I was calling on had long-standing, deep-rooted relationships with Cantor brokers who had died in the attacks. Though the 9/11 attacks were no fault of Cantor Fitzgerald, Howard Lutnick (the chairman and CEO at the time) pledged 25 percent of the company's profits for five years and ten years of health-care coverage for the victims' families. To date, $300 million has been donated through the Cantor Fitzgerald Relief Fund. Still, some clients felt that Cantor didn't do enough to take care of the families of the employees who died when the towers fell. It's true that Cantor Fitzgerald made a lot of money, but no company was prepared from one day to the next to have all business cease at the drop of a dime. Could they have done more? Yes, absolutely, we can always give more. It's also true that for the men and women who lost their partners and the kids who lost their moms or dads, no amount of money in the world could fill that hole.

Time and again, I'd make calls to customers to try to get this credit derivative desk booming. It did not go well.

"Nothing to do with you, Ken, but until Cantor fixes this, nothing is happening."

"Don't call me anymore. Until they make this right, lose my number."

"Get fucked, Rideout. I'm never doing business with Cantor again."

Not only was I trying to establish myself, I was working in this new field of credit derivatives that I knew nothing about. While I was scrambling to get up to speed on the product, eight out of ten customers wouldn't give me the time of day. The jig was up.

During that first month I was on the credit derivative desk in New York, I got a call from Fimat, a bank owned by the French financial services company Societe Generale, known in America as SocGen. They weren't in credit derivatives at the time, they were doing other financial products such as interest rate swaps, corporate bond trading, currency exchange, and foreign currency trading. They didn't know whether I was good, bad, or indifferent—they just knew that credit derivatives were a lucrative product to broker and that I ran the desk at Cantor Fitzgerald, one of the top firms. They wanted to know whether I'd consider coming to work for them. The position paid a $250,000 signing bonus, a $250,000 salary, and a guaranteed minimum bonus of $250,000 after the first year. If I had to start over and learn everything new from scratch, I might as well go over to Fimat and get paid $750,000 to do it.

I had a few weeks off before the new job started, so I booked a suite at the Maui Four Seasons, my own personal boondoggle. I told myself it'd be good for me. I'd had a hard time staying clean since I'd gotten back to New York and watched my new job turn to dust in my hands. The only thing standing between you and your old life is one bad day, and a few bad days had turned into last-minute trips to one of my previous doctors. I'd tried half-heartedly to find a new NA group that I vibed with like the ones I'd had in London, then given up.

In Hawaii, though I worked out like a fiend, I just couldn't find a way to calm my brain down. Finally, I called the concierge and asked them to connect me with a doctor for a house call. When the doctor came to my room, I convinced him to write me a script for thirty Percocet. I'd quit again when I got back to New York, I told myself. Two days later, I called the concierge for another house call. And another.

When I returned to New York and started working at Fimat, I quickly reestablished my underground network of pill suppliers. I had shady doctor connections all over the city, all those poisonous relationships just waiting to spring back to life.

I had a Chinese doctor off Canal Street where I could just show up in the middle of the day with no appointment. The receptionist was in on it, too. I'd hand her forty bucks, and she'd grab my folder and walk me directly into his office ahead of twenty-five other legit patients waiting for him. Big smile and handshake, then he'd write me a prescription for anything I wanted and hustle me out the door. That guy would have written me a prescription for cyanide if I asked.

One day, I read in the paper about these Florida pill mills—sketchy pharmacies eager to prescribe mass quantities of potent painkillers for the slightest complaint to anyone who could pay. So many people were traveling to Florida from out of state for these drugs that the pharmacies had started taking the pill racket online. The paper described it as a real problem. My junkie brain saw it as the solution.

I immediately got online to figure out what the deal was. You had to fill out a questionnaire about your pain—what caused it, how long you'd had it, what the severity was, blah-blah-blah. It was all bullshit. You fill out this form required by the state, some crooked doctor approves every single application, they send you pills. They'd found a loophole in the prescribing practices and were exploiting the shit out of it.

Within days, I'd set up ten different profiles with ten different pharmacies and started ordering thirty or forty Lortabs through each of them. Every few days, a new batch of pills would show up at my office in a FedEx envelope. Scoring pills was now so effortless, I felt like I'd cracked the code. For two years, I went off the rails.

—

Very gradually and then all at once, the magic disappeared. I needed increasing amounts of pills just to not get sick. You get deep enough into painkillers, you realize that killing pain is only part of what they do. They kill joy, too. Not just joy and happiness but any sense of pleasure, any sense of completion or fulfillment or basic human connection. All my natural highs and lows had been destroyed. I had one high: taking pills, and one low: needing pills. Everything else was gone.

—

One day, Seth Flowerman, a kid whom I'd mentored in London, invited me to come and speak in front of a hundred high schoolers at Juilliard. Ordinarily I'd have blown off the invitation, but I liked Seth, so I said I'd do it. The speech was fine, I got through it. Afterward, one of the other speakers, a talent agent who repped models and actors, invited me out for drinks. He said he'd be getting together with a bunch of the models he repped, if I wanted to meet some pretty girls. This was before dating apps, when you actually had to meet people in person. Sure, why not?

We connected at the Soho Grand in lower Manhattan. It was a Friday night so the place was starting to fill up, but I was thinking about moving on because no one there had caught my eye. Then this beautiful woman walked in. An absolute showstopper. She was tall and blonde and looked like Daryl Hannah as Darien Taylor in Oliver Stone's *Wall Street*. But everything about her made it clear she was nothing like the money- and status-obsessed interior decorator from the movie. Her face was warm and open. Her eyes were kind. And whereas every other woman who'd walked through the door was dressed to the nines, this one was dressed incredibly low-key. She wore a black sleeveless, form-fitting top with a long, flowing floral skirt. But her shoes were these drab inexpensive flats. Old-lady shoes, like she'd picked them up from some granny's yard sale.

Some people remember every face they see. Other people can quote extended passages from every movie they've watched. For me, it's clothes. I could tell you exactly what someone was wearing, instantly, in one glance. It was a blessing and a curse. I wasn't a label whore. I didn't have anything from Gucci, I didn't have anything from Louis Vuitton, I never subscribed to high-end magazines. But even at work, someone would have on a cashmere sweater, and I'd know instantly it was Brunello Cucinelli just from the leather tab on the quarter zip. So I watched this woman walk in and I remember thinking, *Geez, that girl is so pretty and so fit and so put together . . . how is she wearing the cheapest, most basic flats from Payless Shoe-Source?*

She wasn't rocking Manolos or Jimmy Choos because she didn't *need* Manolos or Jimmy Choos. She owned the room the minute she walked in, and she would've if she was wearing a barrel and suspenders. What her shoes put on display was her sensibility. She was practical, she was secure, she was grounded. She was the exact kind of woman I could see myself settling down with.

The talent agent greeted her and introduced her to me: Shelby.

Years earlier, she and the talent agent had attended the same tony New Jersey private high school, Pingry. Shelby and I chatted for a minute and hit it off right away. She was a fast talker, like me. She wasn't a model; she was an actress who'd fallen into modeling. But her real passion was kids. She'd gone to Vanderbilt and double majored in elementary education and special education. I was sold. At some point, she got up to go to the bathroom and I leaned over to the talent agent.

"Dude, I really like her. Do you mind if I ask her to go out sometime?"

"She's great, right? I kind of invited her for myself. We go way back, you know?"

I barely knew the guy, but I've never been shy.

"Bro, then why did you invite me? Where are the other people? She is it, man."

He was a nice guy, so I let it go for the time being. A few minutes later, he got up to use the restroom. I immediately ratted him out to Shelby.

"Let me tell you a funny story."

"Okay."

"When you got up to go to the ladies' room, I asked your friend if I could ask you out."

She grinned at me, this beautiful, wide, easy smile. Not going to lie, it got my heart going a little.

"Oh, really? And what did he say?"

"He said no because he's interested in you."

"Well, I have no interest in him."

I'm no dummy—this was a huge green light. Game on. How could I get her out of here, away from this other joker?

Eventually the talent agent came back and we decided to bail on the bar at Soho Grand for another nightclub downtown called Spa. It was a cool, hip spot with lines around the block. I knew one of the club promoters, this Haitian dude from Boston called Unik. I gave him a call and got us on the list. The three of us bypassed the whole line and walked right in.

The place was packed with young, rich, and beautiful people. The club promoters gave tables to groups of models from all the different agencies so dudes would walk in and decide this was where they needed to set up camp. It was Club Promotion 101. The talent agent immediately started working the room, going table to table, buying drinks and chatting up all these different models. After we'd been there maybe thirty minutes, I leaned over to Shelby.

"Hey, you want to get out of here?"

"Do you?"

"Yeah, let's split."

She glanced over at the talent agent.

"Okay, you go that way. I'll go the other way, past the coat check, and I'll meet you at the front door."

I loved it. Our first time meeting and we were already conspiring together. We ditched him and left. We went back to her place, a plain little apartment on Fifty-Eighth Street between Sixth and Seventh Avenues that she shared with a roommate. We stayed up all night, just talking.

Shelby was fantastic. She was smart and funny, a good listener and a sharp conversationalist, not afraid to bust my balls at times. She felt like the perfect foil for me. I was self-obsessed, insecure, far too concerned with what people thought of me: my job, my clothes, my car, my money. I was constantly seeking validation from the world, validation that never seemed to land. Shelby was the opposite—a model who cared little about clothes and fashion. She was fit, but not for vanity's sake. She'd played soccer in high school and had considered playing at the college level. She was so secure, she seemed unable to worry what people thought of her. While I was grimly focused on getting to the next level—better job, bigger paycheck, better apartment—her passion was helping others. Her ultimate goal was to get a job working with developmentally disabled children. While I'd seesawed back and forth on coke and pills, Shelby had never done any drugs in her life. She'd never even *seen* marijuana.

Her family was perfect. Her father had gone to Tabor Academy, Princeton undergrad, and was a Columbia MBA. He was the CFO of a plastics company. Her parents were still married and had paid for all their kids to go to college: Georgetown, Richmond, Michigan, Vanderbilt. Her parents sounded like good and successful people: serious, down-to-earth, not frivolous with money.

We talked about wanting large families, about adopting kids from less fortunate situations. I shared with her everything from my past—my rough upbringing, my failed athletic dreams, my insecurity, everything. Shelby represented everything that was missing in my life: the security, the stability, the selflessness, the traditional family values. I knew instantly that I wanted her to be the mother of my children. Maybe part of me wanted her to be the mother I wished I'd had.

AC Milan was playing Manchester United in an exhibition game at Giants Stadium the next day. Fimat had a bunch of tickets through the brokerage desk to give to customers who were into it, and I happened to have a couple of extra. I knew Shelby was a soccer fan and it seemed like an easy way to impress her—free tickets to a match between two global powerhouses at a classic stadium. Before we crashed in the wee hours of the morning, I asked her whether she wanted to go. She accepted.

When I woke up the next morning, I was so hungover, I felt like death. Had I known her better, I'd have been like, "Fuck this, let's not even go to the soccer game. Let's just hang out and watch sports all day." But I was determined to impress.

It was maybe a hundred degrees outside by the time the car service finally dropped us off at Giants Stadium. Our seats were great, but they were in the direct sun. It was miserable. I was crazy about this girl, but I felt like I was going to pass out. Finally, I caved.

"Shelby, I'm sorry, I don't know how much more of this I can take. This heat is killing me."

"Oh, thank God, let's get out of here."

"You're not bummed about missing the end of the match?"

"Oh God no, I don't care about either of these teams."

Jesus Christ, neither of us had wanted to go, but both of us went along with it just to spend more time together. We couldn't get out of there fast enough. We grabbed another car service back to my place. I was making a lot of money at that point, so I was living on Seventy-Second Street and Third Avenue in an apartment on the thirty-second floor. It was nice. I grabbed the remote and threw on some nondescript golf tournament just to justify sitting around in the apartment, hanging out together. That night, we went to dinner at Atlantic Grill on the Upper East Side. We couldn't get enough of each other.

The following week, I asked her what she had planned for the weekend.

"I don't really have anything going on."

"You want to go to Nantucket?"

"Nantucket? Like . . . in Massachusetts?"

"Is there another one?"

"Ken, I . . . it's awfully kind of you to offer. I can't say yes right away, I mean . . . we've only just met, you know? I mean, how would we even get there? Would you rent a car? Isn't it kind of a long drive?"

"Nah, we'll fly. You know, one of those little planes, like Cape Air."

At the time, it wasn't well-known that you could fly into these little out-of-the-way places. It was considered a huge luxury to be able to fly over to Nantucket.

"I had no idea they even had airports there. I mean, I'd need to think about it. Where would we even stay?"

It was a big deal to her to go away for a weekend with a man she'd just met, but eventually she accepted. I put us up in the Wauwinet, the finest hotel on Nantucket or Martha's Vineyard. After that, we went everywhere together: London, Capri, Positano on the Amalfi Coast in Italy. We went skiing in Aspen and Beaver Creek. We went skiing in Whistler—flew into Vancouver, then took a private chopper up to the mountain, stayed in a huge penthouse suite at the Ritz-Carlton. We stayed at the Fairmont Chateau on Lake Louise. We did everything.

Shelby was kind of shocked by it all.

"Ken, these trips, they've been amazing."

"I'm glad you like it."

"It's just . . . it's all so much, so fast."

"Is it too much? We can lay off for a while, just hang in the city."

"No, that's not what I'm trying to say. Ken, these are the best trips I've ever been on in my life. It's just all happening so quickly. It's really good, it's just overwhelming."

I should have been over the moon to have found the woman I wanted to build a life with, the woman I'd always dreamed of. But I was a nervous wreck. Every trip we took, I had to make sure I had enough pills to get me through the time we were away. Every day, I was terrified that she'd find out and the whole charade would come crashing down.

It was mental torture. From the moment I met her, all I was doing was trying to quit. I'd be irritable and depressed when I was going through withdrawals, then happy and euphoric when I gave in and started taking pills again. I was miserable. And it was hard for Shelby, too, because I didn't tell her, I couldn't bear to. I wanted so bad to get clean. I knew firsthand the hardships of living with an addict—I'd grown up with them and I was determined not to subject her to that. But kicking pills brought out the worst in me, so time and again, I canceled plans or flew off the handle at her, only to break down and get high again just to try to repair the damage I'd done. Poor girl, she must have thought I was mentally ill. I certainly felt like I was going insane.

I signed up to do the Boston Marathon through a charity, hoping that the process of training for and then running it would get me sober. In the ramp-up to it, my focus was only training, not sobriety. I did a bunch of shorter runs and one eighteen-mile run before it and convinced myself I was ready. I took off like a bullet at the start, but the last third was a death march. I limped over the line at 3:31—more than ten minutes slower than I'd run in New York years before when I was unfocused but not strung out on pills. Had

I thought sobriety was something that would just magically happen the minute I crossed the finish line? It didn't. Still, that race planted a tiny seed: if a degenerate drug addict could run a 3:31 marathon undertrained and strung out on Percs, how fast could that same person run properly trained up and sober?

—

The first time I read about Subutex online, it sounded like a miracle cure. Methadone had been around for a while but that was hardcore junkie shit, and I knew you could get addicted to it. I knew people who'd been on methadone for a decade, and you wouldn't know they weren't still using heroin. Subutex was supposed to ease your withdrawal symptoms without getting you high. There was a medically assisted withdrawal program in New York with a doctor who specialized in opiate addiction, so I called for an appointment immediately.

They told me that you had to be off drugs for twenty-four hours, otherwise the Subutex would make you sick. A day without pills would put me into full-blown withdrawal. *Fuck it, this is it*, I told myself, *let's fucking go*.

When I woke up the day before my appointment, I swallowed my last pills with my morning coffee, already feeling a chill of terror for what lay ahead of me. I worked the whole day, only starting to get dopesick when I got home. I was up all night, drenching my sheets in sweat like I was about to die from heatstroke, or shivering and shuddering like I was freezing to death. I was in hardcore withdrawal by the time I woke up: exhausted and dizzy, my head pounding, sweating bullets. I crawled down to this shitty little office in Murray Hill in Manhattan for my eight o'clock appointment. All my senses were incredibly heightened. I was just one open nerve, and the city felt like it was too hot, too crowded, and just screaming. The doctor's staff put me through all the typical bullshit of check-in, and I felt like my head was going to implode.

Finally, they got me in an examination room. I wasn't just sweating through my shirt, I was sweating through my pants. This doctor came in with a little pill in a little paper cup, the same way they'd handed out prescription meds in prison, yet another reminder of how far I'd fallen.

"All right," he said, "put this under your tongue and let it dissolve. Do not swallow."

I looked in the cup. It was one-half of one pill. Half a pill, are you kidding me? No fucking way this was going to do anything for me. What an idiotic waste of time. The minute I got out of there, I was going to call my Chinatown doctor and head down there to re-up.

With a shaking hand, I reached out and took the paper cup and put the pill under my tongue to let it dissolve. Not even twenty seconds later, I was like, *Dude, I'm back.*

Almost instantly, I felt back to 100 percent, more myself than I had in years. I wasn't high and I wasn't in withdrawal. Most important, I wasn't even craving drugs. I remember thinking, *Holy shit, I'm good, I'm so fucking good.*

"Better?"

"Holy shit, Doc, that was profound. I feel so much better."

"All right now, remember the dosage instructions. Take half a pill for three days, then a quarter pill for three days, then an eighth of a pill for three days, then stop. The first couple of days completely off the Subutex might be a little difficult, but you'll be good."

I did everything on the schedule. I followed his instructions to a T. But somehow, I just never got to the point where I could stop taking a little shred of a pill, just a half milligram. Whenever I stopped completely, I'd feel a little bit sick, and the cravings would come roaring back. In my mind, I was like, *Ah, fuck it. I'll do that tomorrow. Tomorrow I'll be sick.*

But who wants to be sick? Tomorrow never came. And then something would happen—Shelby and I would have a fight, or a deal would blow up, or I'd just have a rough day and my brain would turn on me. *I haven't been on drugs in two or three weeks. Fuck it. What's one time going to hurt anybody?* I'd get idiotically high for a week. Then I'd call the Subutex clinic and tell them I'd messed up, and I'd have to get another prescription to try again.

I did this so many times, I finally found myself back at my Chinatown doctor's office, asking him for a script for Subutex instead of Percocet. He'd never even heard of it. He took out his pill-prescribing manual, looked up how to prescribe Subutex, then wrote it down for me. Before long, I had him writing me scripts for Subutex and Percocet on the same trip.

On the one hand, Subutex was a godsend. My life no longer revolved around buying, eating, and chasing pills, because the Subutex would allow me to stay off opiates for months at a time. But on the other hand, the active ingredients in that drug were ten times more physically addictive than the pills. White-knuckling it off Subutex was way harder than getting off opioids.

When I took the Subutex, I wasn't high, but I certainly wasn't me. It made me irritable, moody, and incredibly temperamental. Once every two months, it'd give me a stifling migraine that was so intense that I couldn't get out of bed for two days. And the migraines always seemed to come at the worst possible time. Shelby and I booked a week's vacation in Miami, and I spent nearly the entire vacation in the darkened hotel room with the worst migraine you can imagine. It felt like someone was drilling a hole in my temple.

It felt like a curse. By seeking a cure, all I'd found was a new, tougher addiction. I knew I loved Shelby with my entire being, and I knew I had to get clean for her, so I kept trying. All I did was whiplash back and forth from Percocet to Subutex, dragging myself and the love of my life across the razor's edge of withdrawal each time.

It drove me mad. I had to quit Percs. I had to quit Subutex. I had to try again. I found myself quitting pills or Subutex—and sometimes both—for the next six fucking years.

CHAPTER SIX
RUNNING THROUGH HELL

SHELBY AND I MARRIED IN 2007 AND IMMEDIATELY SET TO WORK TRYING TO build our dream family. She was thirty-three and I was thirty-six and we knew we wanted a lot of kids, so no time to waste. We started trying to get pregnant on our honeymoon and began the adoption process as soon as we got home.

We quickly discovered that trying to adopt was radically less fun than trying to conceive. Put it this way—there was no risk of *accidentally* adopting a baby. The adoption process was so convoluted, the only way you were going to get a baby was if you were absolutely determined. We had to get six letters of recommendation, which had to be notarized once by a regular notary, then notarized again by their county supervisor. We had to get fingerprinted by local authorities *and* federal authorities. Adopting was important to both of us, but my wife was in the driver's seat. Starting a family quickly became her greatest concern. I was normally so tense, anxious, and obsessed with minutiae, but for some reason, I had blind faith that it was all going to work out.

When the financial crisis hit in 2008, I was working at Natixis, a French bank. It was a job I'd felt lucky to have as I didn't have the academic or professional pedigree to justify getting hired. I'd been selling structured credit products—the exact industry that blew the economy up. Ninety percent of the people in that field lost their jobs, including me.

Jobs were scarce and the economy was in the toilet bowl. I was living in a brand-new $2.5 million penthouse apartment with a $12,000 a month mortgage and I was running out of runway. I interviewed at a bunch of different places, most of them hopeless wastes of time at garbage banks because, on paper, I looked horrible. My résumé probably closed more doors for me than it opened.

Eventually, a buddy went to bat for me and I got an interview at Crédit Agricole, another French bank. I had a couple of interviews, and I hit it off with the interviewers, but every single person told me they'd never have guessed I'd led such an interesting life based on my terrible résumé.

Finally, I got an interview with the head of sales and trading—a decision-maker. He owned a Ferrari and a bunch of expensive watches . . . the guy had money. The day of my interview, he wore a Patek Philippe—a hundred-thousand-dollar watch. He was reading my résumé and then he looked up at me.

"This résumé is dogshit."

"Yeah, I know. Who gives a fuck? You know how I got this interview? A friend at Western Asset called you and told you to have a conversation with me. These are real clients that you need because your desk is weak. You need me."

He leaned back and looked me over, really scrutinizing every detail of my appearance. Then he pointed at the watch on my wrist.

"What says more about you—the Rolex Daytona or the shamrock cuff links?"

The cuff links were these nondescript, hand-painted, antique ones that I'd bought at some vintage shop in the West Village years earlier. They were green shamrocks with gold accents on them. Nothing flashy, they were just cool. And the Daytona . . . it was a stainless-steel Rolex. Of course I had to have it.

"The shamrock cuff links remind me where I'm from. I grew up in an Irish Catholic area of Boston. They were blue-collar, hardworking people. I didn't love growing up there and I busted my ass to make it to Manhattan, but I identify with that kind of background. Those experiences made me who I am.

"The Rolex watch is one of my favorite physical possessions. I wanted a Rolex since I was a little kid and saw one of the made men in my neighborhood wearing one. But the Rolex kind of says, 'I'm so insecure that I have to show you I made enough money to buy a thirty-thousand-dollar watch.' I'm proud of it, but it doesn't really tell you anything about me other than I have the means to spend a stupid amount of money on a watch I don't need.

"I gotta go with the shamrock cuff links. I'm much prouder of who I am and where I came from and what I've overcome to get to this point in my life."

He stared at me for a moment from across his desk, then he spoke.

"You're hired," he said.

Within six months, I was getting paid more than anyone else on the trading desk. I cold-called these huge customers and got them to do business with us. There were some people there with Ivy League MBAs who were pissed. They hated that some working-class guy with an unrelated degree from a shit university just swept in and outhustled them. But I deserved it. I built some incredible relationships with huge customers for Crédit Agricole. And I was glad I was able to deliver for them. They never knew it, but my entire life hinged on that one interview. I was on the brink of financial collapse and if I hadn't gotten that job, I don't know what would've happened to me.

Though I'd let most of my old relationships die, I'd kept in touch with my childhood friend Sully. One day it occurred to me I hadn't gotten a call back in a long time. I rang up one of my other buddies at home.

"Yo, where the fuck is Ray Sullivan? I haven't heard from that kid in years."

"Dude, you are never going to believe this. Google 'Ray Sullivan bank robber.'"

"Get the fuck out."

"Seriously, bro, look it up."

I could not believe what I found. There was an image from a bank surveillance video of Sully in huge aviator sunglasses, handing a note to the teller. He'd gotten strung out on heroin, tried to rob a bank, and gotten popped on his first heist. They'd given him seven years.

—

After two years of our trying to have a kid with no success, my blind faith that everything was going to work out was starting to falter. We just could not get pregnant. There were no identifiable medical issues or concerns. We were both incredibly healthy. One doctor theorized that if anything, maybe Shelby was so healthy that her immune system treated an embryo like a foreign body and destroyed it before it could implant. I was determined to stay positive, but after seven rounds of in vitro fertilization and three miscarriages, I was starting to worry that it just wasn't going to happen. At the same time, I genuinely felt in my heart that if we couldn't have biological kids, it wasn't the end of the world. We'd just have to go another route.

It hit differently for Shelby. Ever since she was a little girl, she knew that being a mother would fulfill her ultimate purpose. The way she saw it, two years of failing to conceive was twenty-four cycles, twenty-four times at bat, and twenty-four strikeouts. There were many times in the process when Shelby would just fall apart because she felt like a failure—as a mother, wife, and woman. I was always trying to talk her off the ledge, but after a year or two she started to convince herself it was never going to happen. She was starting to break down emotionally. It was an incredibly difficult time for us. It was hard for me, but I knew it was much, much harder for Shelby and that it was a burden I was powerless to shoulder on her behalf.

The adoption process wasn't going much better. As motivated as we were, it still took us forever to get through the mountain of paperwork, court-mandated verifications, and background checks. And there were so many adoption agencies. One in Sacramento scammed us out of $17,000. It was a decent chunk of money, but okay, fine, you got me, not the end of the world. What made me want to really firebomb the whole place was thinking about the other good-hearted people they'd scammed—the farmers in Iowa who'd taken out a second mortgage on their house in hopes of getting a baby, just to have their application go right in the trash.

It didn't help that I was still lost in the quagmire of Subutex. Never forget that the lesser of two evils is still evil. I'd get down to the most minute dose, just this shitty little crumb of a pill. That tiny dose was still so incredibly powerful that when I stopped taking it, I'd immediately plunge into full-blown withdrawals. No way around it, I was addicted to Subutex.

I'd gotten myself hooked on a drug that had no high. The only benefit of Subutex was that it kept me from getting sick, but it dulled my senses and kept me irritable, moody, and constantly on edge. Poor Shelby. At least I was sunny when I was high on Percs, but on Subutex, I was a sour old crank 24/7, always either in mild withdrawals or just agonizing because I'd relapsed and I knew I could never get off this shit. I was like Sisyphus, rolling that boulder up the hill only to lose it at the last second and watch it roll all the way to the bottom. There were days I wanted that boulder to just roll over on top of me.

—

While I was hammering lap after manic lap around Central Park one day, I noticed the guys out on their bikes. Running had started to bother my knee so one day after my run, I fell into a conversation with a few of the cyclists. Maybe there was something to it. I went to a bike shop and cautiously picked up an entry-level bike to try it out. A week later, I returned the beginner bike they'd sold me and told them to set me up with the best they had. I was hooked. For years, I'd been curious about the world of triathlon. Maybe this was my time.

I signed up for a local sprint triathlon, the Mighty North Fork out on Long Island, in 2008. I'd gotten off pills and was taking Subutex, which, while it kept me moody, made training with consistency so much easier. I'd been working my ass off on the bike, I was in sick shape, and now I'd go out and school the locals in this little race with my superior conditioning.

I fucking sucked. In hindsight, I knew nothing. I didn't know one single thing it takes to win a triathlon. I was riding a road bike instead of a time trial bike. I made every possible mistake. My transitions were garbage . . . it's crazy how bad I was. With my gear I had a little Tupperware bowl into which I put fresh water so I could rinse off my feet after swimming before I put my bike shoes on. I was changing my top and washing my feet off like I was Mariah Carey changing outfits between songs.

I got beat. I got my ass handed to me. I think I came in nineteenth overall. I went home with this stink of shame on me, like I was outclassed, like I didn't deserve to be there. I didn't know what I didn't know. But I knew there was a way to learn.

I knew my swimming sucked and that I needed help. I went down to the New York Athletic Club and I jumped in the pool. There were former Olympic swimmers in the lanes next to me. When one stopped to rest for a second, I said, "Hey, buddy, do me a favor and watch me swim to the end and back and tell me what I'm doing wrong?" At first, the guy seemed a little taken aback. The elite swimmers were there to work; they weren't there to waste time teaching some amateur. But the guy did give me a few tips, and it helped. Before long, I was there twice a day. As soon as the other swimmers saw that I was willing to do the work, that I was there grinding every day, everyone rallied behind me. I became the NYAC swimming community's pet project.

I signed up for another tri. And another. I did something stupid in every single race. But as much as I was getting humbled, I kept coming back for more. My times started to tick down. My place among the finishers started to tick up.

Never content with the status quo, I set my sights on joining the elite of the elite. I considered competing in an Ironman, the legendary triathlon that includes a 2.4-mile swim, 112-mile bike ride, and full-length marathon. But any schlub can complete an Ironman, right? I'd worked with plenty of weekend warriors who'd managed to get over the line. I had to make it to the Ironman World Championships in Kona, Hawaii. That meant finishing in the top 1 or 2 percent in my age group. Fuck it, if I could get off Percs, I could do anything.

Well, *almost*. In 2009, I ran my first Ironman in Louisville, Kentucky. I came in seventy-eighth out of 369 in my age group, a far cry from qualifying for the World Championships. My time was 11:07:35. At that point, I'd gotten down to just the smallest crumb of Subutex. But my body was still so physically dependent on the drug that, partway through the race, I felt the heavy weakness that comes with early-stage withdrawal.

Getting off Percs had been a revelation. Yes, you can be a pill head and run a marathon, but you're never going to hit your goals. It felt like I'd been trying to swim in overalls and been finally allowed to take them off. But as I spent months and then years on a drug doctors intended patients to take for a week at most, it became clear that I'd made it out of hell only to be trapped in purgatory. Subutex had gotten me closer to my performance goals, but it'd never let me reach them. I caved and went back to Percs.

Finally, Shelby and I saw our luck turn. In August 2010, we got a call from WACAP, the adoption agency we'd been working with. They had a four-week-old baby girl available in Ethiopia. She'd been born on July 14—Bastille Day. It was very rare for a child that young to become available. They said she was ours if we wanted her. Yes, *of course*, we wanted her. In our hearts, she was already ours.

The agency said they'd send over a physical by a local doctor. We had an adoption specialist in Manhattan they'd recommended to us who'd evaluate the medical report. The unspoken part was that, if our specialist found any serious health concerns, we'd be able to decline the adoption without penalty.

Are you fucking kidding me? Here she was—the child we'd hoped and prayed for, separately and together, for so long. If it'd been our pregnancy, we wouldn't have been saying, "Oh, she's not perfect? Send her back." It didn't matter to me whether she was malnourished, or physically or mentally disabled. This was my daughter, my child, my baby. She couldn't have been more mine than if I'd given birth to her myself. Whatever came with her, good or bad, was exactly what we wanted.

The approval went through without a hitch. On paper, we were the perfect couple. We'd go to pick up our daughter from the orphanage in November. Shelby and I had never been so in love as we were in the days we were celebrating the impending arrival of our new daughter.

I woke up one day in October and realized that we were picking up our baby in Ethiopia in less than thirty days. By this point, I'd traveled all over the world with pills, so I wasn't clutching my pearls and inwardly wailing, "Oh my God, what am I going to do if I need to go away for seven days?" I knew I needed a minimum of seventy pills to avoid going into withdrawals. Whatever I needed, I'd get. But in my heart, I knew it was over.

We were picking up a baby, a real live human being, a child of our own. This had been a lifelong dream. I was going to love this baby like I'd never loved another human. I hadn't even seen her and already, I knew she was going to rule my heart. I couldn't be around my wife, my baby, my new family, and be whacked out of my mind on these cursed joy killers. I couldn't subject this innocent child to the horrors of life with an addict for a parent. I *had* to get off these fucking drugs for good.

I found an outpatient detox facility in New York called Parallax, located in this shitty nondescript brick building in Murray Hill. The lobby smelled like old skin, with an oily three-ring binder for a sign-in book and a bored security guard who looked like he couldn't knock a sick old lady off a toilet. I stepped into this creaky closet of an elevator to go up to the seventh floor. When the elevator chimed, the door opened onto a cramped, depressing waiting room filled with strung-out dope fiends. The scene felt insane to me, unreal, like this couldn't be my life. I'd grown up around heroin addicts and alcoholics, I'd seen firsthand the carnage that drugs wrought on a human being, the evil that addiction brought into a person's life. I couldn't believe it'd gotten me, too.

The goal was just to get you through the week. Each morning, they'd check my vitals, then give me my meds for the day: Ritalin to stay awake at work, Xanax to go to sleep at night, blood pressure medication, some kind of fast-acting antidepressant . . . it was a lot of drugs. And I had to go there each morning for my dose. They weren't going to give me a bag of Ritalin and a bag of Xanax. They knew I'd take it all the first day because I was a fucking junkie.

If you made it through the seven days sober and passed a drug test, you could then get a shot of Vivitrol, an opioid blocker that lasted for thirty days. Once they injected that shit deep into the muscle in your ass, you couldn't get high. It blocked all the opioid receptors in your brain and was even supposed to repair some of the damage to your pleasure centers from years of addiction. It didn't just sound like a miracle drug; it sounded like an outright miracle.

I knew I could gut it out for seven days. I'd stand on my fucking head for seven days for this baby if I had to. Once I got through seven days of misery, they'd shoot me full of Vivitrol and I'd be home free. Shelby would never even have to know.

The first day, not too bad. The second day, not too bad. I'd get up in the morning, go to the detox and get my pills, go to work, go running, then come home at night and have dinner. Just a normal guy living a normal life. I hadn't told my wife what I was doing because why would I? When you're a fucking junkie and a liar, why not just keep lying? My self-respect had fled years before.

The third day leveled me. I was so depressed I could barely put on my socks. I'd known it was coming. But the intense, shuddering waves of self-loathing—I wanted to crawl out of my body and disappear into the gutter. This was exactly why I'd been high for ten years, self-medicating at the most extreme levels, just to avoid this plunge. We've all heard that "light at the end of the tunnel" shit, and it's true, there *is* light at the end of the tunnel. But I was in the *middle* of the tunnel . . . and it was pitch fucking black—as if light had never existed.

I crawled to Parallax for my morning dose of meds, the only guy in a pressed shirt and business suit in purgatory's waiting room full of zombies. Instead of my clothes making me feel like I was better than them, they made me feel worse. Here, finally, was proof that I was a fraud. Sure, I had the Thom Browne suit, but underneath it I was covered in flop sweat, my skin trying to turn itself inside out just like theirs.

Through all of this, I was still running every day after work. I'd gotten a bike maybe a year earlier with the intention of training for a triathlon, but running was the only part that'd become part of my daily practice: my mental health exercise, my antidepressant, the only way I kept my shit together. During this detox period, running became my punishment and absolution, a cleansing fire.

The first day, running wasn't so bad. The second day, I felt something approaching confidence, like maybe I could get through this. That third day, I was dripping with sweat and shivering from my very core even as I was lacing up my Reeboks.

Fuck you, I told myself. *You don't get a day off just because you sabotaged your entire fucking life. We're going.*

I felt like I was going to have a heart attack. But the worse I felt, the harder I ran. *I'd* done this to me, no one else.

That third night, I woke up a few hours after my head hit the pillow, needing to piss. I stumbled to the bathroom and flipped on the light. In front of me our pristine, contemporary white marble bathroom shined with straight edges, a floating vanity, and absolutely nothing out of place. Months before, Shelby and I had purchased this luxury two-bedroom apartment, which was located in a new, all-glass high-rise on West End Avenue between Fifty-Ninth and Sixtieth Streets. We'd talked ourselves into the place after admiring the breathtaking views of the Hudson River and the New York City skyline. The bathroom was perfect, the building was perfect, my wife was perfect, the life I'd built was perfect. And in that moment, it all felt like a sham—a meaningless, glittering bauble forged from secrets and lies. Then the darkness came roaring up from the shadows in the bathroom's corners and crashed over my head, and I sank into oblivion.

I came to lying in a puddle of my own piss in my boxer briefs. My head was screaming with pain from where I'd hit my head when I fell, a big throbbing egg of a contusion already coming up. Shelby was crying and cradling my head, pleading for an explanation, begging God for me to be okay.

"Ken! Ken? Oh my God, honey, what is going on? Are you okay? Ken, what the hell is going on?"

It took me a minute to piece it all together. *Oh my God, what am I doing down here? What the fuck, did I piss myself?* My head was killing me, I probably had a concussion, not like I gave a shit. *How am I going to tell Shelby I blacked out while withdrawing from fucking pain pills?* God damn it. And I wasn't even high. I was just dopesick.

Shelby was crying and kneeling on the floor, still cradling my head.

"Damn it, Ken, what the *hell* is going on?"

Jesus, I'd put so much fucking pressure on her, piling my whole fantasy life on her narrow shoulders. She'd carried that burden with grace, and I'd rewarded her by lying to her over and over, again and again—a new lie forming with every pill I swallowed. I wanted to throw myself off a balcony and just end it all forever.

But I didn't. Instead, I came clean. I told Shelby everything. She knew I'd been on and off drugs. I told her that my problem had been more serious than I'd let on—first Percs and then Oxys and then that disastrous Subutex, then Subutex *and* Percs—but that I was finally taking steps to deal with it once and for all.

"Shelby, I'm so sorry for the number of times I've made you watch me try to get sober and fail. Now I'm in a fucking outpatient detox with professionals watching over me. I can't do it by myself."

I'd spent my entire relationship with my wife in terror of this very moment. It's every addict's nightmare: getting caught.

And then, much to my surprise, Shelby couldn't have been more supportive. She helped me get cleaned up and I got back in bed.

The morning held a new reckoning. What now? The cat was out of the bag. Would we survive? There was a hundred times more pressure on me now that my wife knew. As low as I felt, I knew there was only one option: hold fast and stay the fucking course.

Walking out for my run that afternoon was like walking out to a fistfight that I knew I was going to lose. I felt like utter dogshit and my mind was just screaming. How was I going to do this? I knew I wasn't running to get sober. I was getting sober to get sober. But if I got sober . . . what could I do as a runner?

Every single step hurt. I'd been jacked to the gills on painkillers for ten years, and now, finally, there was no pain medicine in my system. That opened the floodgates for the very thing all that crap had been holding back: pain.

With each step, I could feel every inch of every bone in my body. Every bone in each of my feet clanking . . . the ankle bones grinding . . . and from there the pain shooting up my shin all the way to my hips, ribs, spine, and idiot skull. It felt like someone was standing on my kidneys and grinding them into the pavement. Every chilly breath I took somehow transformed into a lungful of smoldering fire. Snot poured out of my nose, tears streamed from my eyes, sweat dripped off my forehead into my eyes even though I was shaking with cold. My teeth hurt, my veins hurt, my fucking *blood* hurt. Every single cell of my body had been replaced—by Percocets, by secrets, by lies—and with each step, I waited for the whole shit show to collapse.

But it didn't. I kept running.

CHAPTER SEVEN

A NEW LIFE

I FINISHED MY RUN THAT DAY. AND THE NEXT DAY...AND THE DAY AFTER THAT. Running became my personal penance. I finished my week clean and got my shot of Vivitrol that would prevent me from getting high for thirty days—a huge needle full of thick, white syrup deep in my ass cheek that hurt like a motherfucker. And I needed it.

Maybe twenty-six days into my thirty days, something went sideways with one of my clients. In hindsight, it was a minor altercation, some trifle that affected me emotionally for some reason. I just remember saying *fuck that* in my head, reached out to my drug dealer, and bought thirty Percocets. I dry-swallowed three and waited for that blissful feeling of escape to overtake me. Nothing. I might as well have eaten chalk. What a fucking waste of money. I'd let myself down, I'd let my wife down, and I'd let our baby daughter down—for nothing. Thank God for that Vivitrol, which was silently hanging out in my body doing its job.

That part of my life was over. Walking home from work that night, I chucked the Percs in the trash in a fit of rage—then felt a shudder of straight fear. What if the Vivitrol hadn't worked? What if the opiates had gotten through? I'd be right back on the same fun house merry-go-round I'd been killing myself to get off for years.

As soon as I arrived home, I changed into my running clothes. Since getting clean, I'd started running in the mornings but sometimes, I'd have time to bang out another workout in the afternoon. Carving one more lap around Central Park in the waning fall light, I felt—through my exhaustion and fear—a thin sliver of hope.

In November, we traveled with several other adoptive families to Addis Ababa, the capital of Ethiopia, to pick up our new daughter, now four months old. I'd been all over the world, but Addis Ababa still blew my mind. With brutal poverty set against a backdrop of modern high-rises and a light-rail, it was a thoroughly modern city—an explosion of all the hope and desperation of humanity.

The adoption agency didn't put us up in some fancy chain hotel, because they were sensitive to the perceived optics of rich white Westerners spiriting Ethiopian babies away to America. WACAP had booked us rooms in a discreet, low-profile guesthouse considered to be a decent place. It looked like a military barracks, just a low concrete bunker full of ants with a huge stone security wall around it. Inside, crown molding peeled off the walls and mildew coated the shower stall. The beds had no mattresses, just box springs. Every single night, the power would go off all over the city and the gigantic diesel truck engine that powered the guesthouse's emergency generator would fire up. It was like trying to sleep while nearby an overloaded dump truck growled up a hill. I refused to be bothered by it, though—we were here, it was happening. Some of the other families were wringing their hands and griping about the conditions, saying things like, "Oh, these poor people, the poverty and the deprivation." I kept my mouth shut. I'd seen nothing in Addis Ababa worse than the conditions in Somerville or Alabama or the Mystic River projects. Poverty knows no borders.

On our sixth day in Addis Ababa, WACAP finally loaded Shelby and me and four other families into this dilapidated old van to bring us down to the orphanage in Hawassa where our babies were waiting. I like to be able to see where I'm going, so, already on edge from having observed how they drove here, I sat in the front with the driver. It was maybe a hundred-mile journey and WACAP said it'd take five hours. *Twenty miles an hour, are you crazy?*

Yeah, it was *that* slow because we were on a two-lane highway traveling through middle-of-nowhere Ethiopia, just rolling farmland and pastures and some truly incredible *Land Before Time* scenery. The driver wasn't about to make that trip any longer, so he took every opportunity to pass a slower vehicle, regardless of how tight or terrifying it was.

Once we made it to Hawassa, we went straight to the orphanage. The organizers put these black-and-white-striped scarves around our necks, then they brought us to a big empty room with chairs all around the exterior and some Ethiopian rugs on the floor.

Watching my wife take our new daughter in her arms, I felt overwhelmed in the best way. Shelby is a beautiful woman, a stunner on her worst day. But I'd never seen her shine the way she did cradling our daughter in her arms. There was this majestic sense of completion. The battle had been tough and we'd fought so hard for so long, but we kept the faith and we never gave up. Now, we'd done it.

So many feelings ran through me all at once when I held my

new daughter. I was nervous, anxious, overjoyed, and awed by the sense of responsibility I felt. It was like being born again, but in the healthiest way. I thought of my own parents and all the mistakes they'd made and felt determined to give this child the exact opposite childhood that I'd had.

We kept the Amharic name that our daughter's birth mother had given her, Tensae. It referred to Easter, a holiday more important than Christmas in Ethiopia because in Ethiopian Orthodox theology the Resurrection of Jesus is more important than his birth. In the Ge'ez language, Tensae literally means "to rise." It fit perfectly with how I felt in that moment.

Tensae had been born severely malnourished and, at four months, was still only seven pounds and change with a big, distended belly. We were concerned that she hadn't been getting adequate care. The adoption process is lengthy anywhere, especially for an international adoption, and the Ethiopian officials seemed like they were in no rush. We were very intent on making sure Tensae got whatever medical care she needed as soon as possible.

At the end of the day, one of the organizers gathered all the families together before we climbed into the van to head to our accommodations for the evening. "Tomorrow," he announced, "we have arranged for a sightseeing tour of Hawassa. We'll meet in the reception area at the hotel at nine. Around five, we'll return to the orphanage for another brief visit before dinner."

"Hang on, brother," I said, "it's a beautiful country but we're not here for the sightseeing. I'm here to be with my baby. What time can we come back in the morning?"

The organizer looked perplexed. "I don't know, I guess everyone gets here around seven or eight."

"Great. We'll get back here at eight. And we'll stay here all day with the baby."

The organizer sputtered a little.

"Sir, the tour is part of the package. It's been planned."

"I'm not interested in the tour. It's already paid for, right? Someone else can take my wife's seat and my seat. We want to sit here all day in this room with the baby."

There was some eye-rolling and sideways glances, but then the organizers said that was fine. Then all the other parents started chiming in. No one wanted to go on the tour, everyone just wanted to spend time with their babies.

We hung out at the orphanage with the babies the whole next day. All of the families were in heaven. By the end of the day, it was like we'd all been friends for years.

The day after that, we had to return to Addis Ababa to go in front of the judge to officially adopt Tensae in the Ethiopian court. Supposedly, it would take eight weeks for the paperwork to process before she'd be cleared to leave the country. Most adopting parents would be forced to go home during that time because they couldn't afford to take off so much work. But Shelby and I had made up our minds. No way were we leaving our four-month-old, malnourished daughter alone for that long. I'd run back to New York to deal with work and Shelby would stay with Tensae in the guesthouse.

An Ethiopian lawyer had been assigned to the parents by WACAP to shepherd us through the process. He was about seventy, no niceties, all business.

"We're going to go in front of the judge, a Muslim woman," he announced to Shelby and me. "Do *not* say anything. Let me do all the talking. After we go through this process, one week later, the babies will all be transported to Addis Ababa. Since you're staying here, you'll be granted temporary custody, and your new baby will be allowed to stay with you in Ethiopia until she's granted permission to leave the country."

"Hang on," I said. "After today, she's ours, right? So why are we going to let her sit in an orphanage for another week? My wife's here, she's going to stay here, our baby can come up tomorrow."

"The driver has already been arranged."

"I'll pay for another driver."

"No, no, no, all the babies are transported together."

"How about this—I'll pay for a private car for each family. Five different trips. Your driver is going to be stoked."

"Sir, we can't do that."

"Why not? I'm paying for it. What do you care?"

"Sir, that's not how we do things here. The matter is closed."

We went in front of the judge and started sorting through all the rigmarole. The judge was fine, this was just another day for her. She signed off on our adoption and the lawyer said that they'd have the babies brought up next week. I raised my hand.

"Excuse me, Judge?"

Immediately, I could see our lawyer panicking.

"Yes," the judge said, looking at me coolly.

"Your Honor, our baby is at the orphanage, and she's super iron-deficient. I talked to several doctors in the United States who specialize in infant nutrition. They have all agreed that she needs to be on fortified formula."

This was all lies. I knew Tensae was sick, and I was pretty confident that the formula would help her, but I hadn't talked to any doctor in Ethiopia or the States, let alone several. But I kept going.

 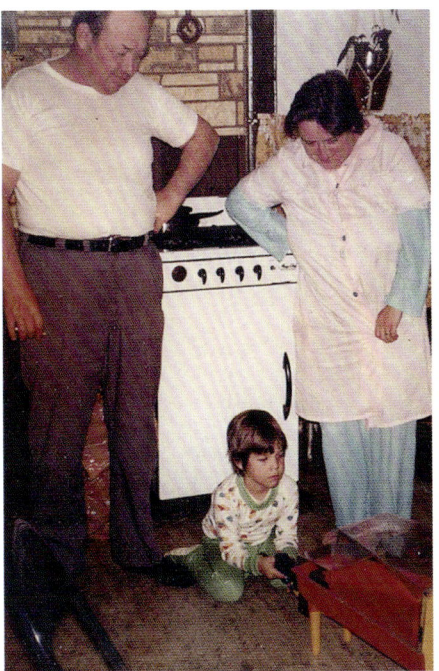

My mother had me when she was nineteen. I'm sure she started with good intentions, but she was divorced soon after, and the men who entered her life tended to bring out her worst while often inflicting the same on me.

We lived on the top floor of a run-down two-family home in inner-city Somerville, with my maternal grandparents on the bottom floor. I received little love from the adults in the house. Not Granny, though. She was tough as nails, but the one person who was unconditionally kind to me.

Once a flourishing industry town, Somerville hit rock bottom in the 1970s. It wasn't a place where people had big dreams. I knew from an early age that I had to get out. (Bill Curtis/*The Boston Globe* via Getty Images)

My father took me to hockey practice and games multiple times per week, which always felt like an escape. Sure, he could get worked up over how I performed on the ice or the playing fields, but he helped us when he needed to. My brother Keith (left) and I thought of him as something of a savior.

When I was a kid, all I wanted was to be a professional hockey player. It was my first dream—the one nobody told me was unrealistic. Here I am playing in the 1989 Massachusetts high school state tournament at the old Boston Garden, home of the Bruins.

I was the starting quarterback my senior year of high school and learned what it was like to have people's opinion of you soar or plummet, depending on what the scoreboard said. I won some big games and even made an all-star team, but that didn't stop the crowd from chanting "Rideout sucks" the last game of the season.

With my mother at high school graduation. She was a destabilizing person to live with: kind in some moments, vicious and cruel in others. But there were times when she really did try her best.

A week after high school ended, I got my first real job: prison guard at the Billerica House of Correction, where my stepfather had done time. At eighteen years old, I was an innocent kid being thrown to the lions.

Here I am at Framingham State, about to go in against Tufts. When we had an edge on them, their fans would chant, "That's all right, that's okay, you're gonna work for us someday." At college, I couldn't quite shake the weight of my childhood and often turned to cocaine to dull the pain.

Connections: If you have them, life tends to work out. Within two years of graduating from college I was a top broker on Wall Street, but my demons still hung around. I spent every single day at my job racked with the fear that, eventually, someone was going to realize I didn't belong.

On September 11, 2001, I was in London—running the European commodities trading desk for Cantor Fitzgerald. We were on the phone with our colleagues minutes before they lost their lives as the towers crumbled. Having such a close connection with that tragedy made me want to get clean and do something valuable with my life.
(AP Photo/Suzanne Plunkett)

ABOVE: In 2002, while still fighting an addiction to Percocet, I met Shelby and knew immediately that I wanted to build a life with her.

RIGHT: We adopted our daughter, Tensae, in 2010. I was nervous, anxious, overjoyed, and, yes, awed by the sense of responsibility.

When I got sober and stayed sober, I threw myself into triathlons. At the 2012 Ironman World Championships in Kona, Hawaii, I underestimated the blistering heat. Here I am giving my wife the "cut" sign. This is the moment I found out that quitting is always harder than persevering. The sting and shame of quitting that day in Kona still lingers.

In my boyhood, there was so much violence surrounding me that I took up boxing. The sport continued to be a refuge when times got tough. Here I am in 2019 sparring with Mike Lee, former super middleweight champ.

In early 2020, I won my first big race: the Pasadena Half. With nine thousand runners trailing behind, I crossed the finish line first in the Rose Bowl.

Winning the masters division at the 2021 New York Marathon opened up a lot of doors, allowing me to grab a position at the front of the 2022 Boston Marathon starting line. Overhead, out of sight, military jets flew by just as the gun was about to fire. I was the only runner staring down the course, completely locked in. (Craig F. Walker/*The Boston Globe* via Getty Images)

Even though I was finally sober, I just couldn't be at peace. The races I won, the work I did, the money I made—were never enough. Deeper healing was necessary. So, in early 2023, I checked into the Onsite trauma healing program, located an hour outside of Nashville, with former NFL player Eric Decker as my roommate. My experience at Onsite wound up being a ticket to freedom.

When I first heard about the Gobi March, all anyone would tell me was how difficult it was. So I flew 6,500 miles from Nashville to Mongolia to see if I had what it took. Here I am resting after the grueling second stage of the race.

anyone were betting on the Gobi ce, their pick would have been avid "Dudu" Danu from Israel ft) or Reinhold Hugo from vitzerland (not pictured)—not me, e guy with zero ultramarathon perience. But I slugged it out— d kept a promise I made to myself: cross the finish line first. On my ght is Filippo Rossi from Italy, who ssed me late in stage 1 to finish in ird place on the day.

Yeah, I have a trophy or two. That's the Gobi March trophy in front, with the New York Marathon trophy to the right. None are as important as the family and friends who helped me find my way to the other side of hard.

My wife and kids—that's my team, my family, my entire heart. From left to right: Shelby, Cameron, Jack, Tensae, Luke, and me. And, yes, Shelby got her Weimaraner as well as Vizsla.

The grind never stops. In 2025, at age fifty-four, I found myself training for Hyrox, a competition that combines eight kilometers of running with eight different workout stations. Here I am doing lunges with a seventy-pound sandbag. (Photograph by Rafael Voegtli)

"We have fortified formula here for her and we're ready to take over her care. And technically, if she's ours . . . Judge, I've offered to pay for a private car to get not just my daughter but all of the individual kids whenever they're ready. I don't want to be difficult. I just want to say there's no sense in her staying there another day if she doesn't have to. I'm happy to cover all the bills. For all the kids."

The judge didn't say one word, just turned that cool gaze on our attorney.

"Judge, we have made arrangements to transport all the babies together next week."

"You can transport all the babies together tomorrow," the judge said. "What's the sense in waiting? Put them all in the orphanage in Addis Ababa and the parents who are here can take custody immediately."

When we left the courtroom and the other parents found out what I'd done, they were practically carrying me on their shoulders. "Ken for mayor," one of the other dads said, and shook my hand hard for a long time, tears welling up in his eyes. Sometimes you got to fight for what you love.

———

Then things started going sideways. I had to fly home the next day, and by the time I landed, I was sick as a dog. I took a car service directly from JFK to the emergency room at Beth Israel, where I was diagnosed with walking pneumonia. And despite the sage advice from all my made-up American doctors, the formula didn't cure Tensae. She kept losing weight. Shelby took her to every emergency room in Addis Ababa. Was she lactose intolerant? Did she have giardia? Maybe it was the formula? No one could figure out what was wrong. Then *Shelby* started getting sick. I was back in New York, losing my mind, counting down the days till I could get my wife and new daughter home.

—

We never found out what had been ailing Tensae, but from the day she arrived in America she never had another GI issue. And Shelby? My wonderful wife had been feeling sick in Ethiopia because she was seven weeks pregnant. Our first biological child was due July 14— Tensae's birthday.

CHAPTER EIGHT
WIN OR DIE TRYING

OUR SON JACK ARRIVED EARLY IN JUNE 2011, NEARLY A MONTH PREMATURE. Shelby was in the hospital for three days and Jack was in the NICU for a week. He was undersized and jaundiced, so they had to keep him under specialized lights to break down the excess bilirubin in his body. He looked like a little oven-roasted chicken under warming lights at a fast-food restaurant. When he was finally well enough to take home, I got a great photo of him in his car seat with Tensae peering down at him, like, "Hey, what's going on over here?" They were best friends from the jump. Shelby and I got into a great rhythm looking after the babies together. It was an incredible time in my life—it felt like there was nothing we couldn't do.

—

When I finally made it clean in late 2010, my training immediately leveled up. Even in the depths of my cocaine and opiate abuse,

I'd always been fit. I boxed, I ran, I lifted weights. It was a way I showed respect for myself and quieted my anxious mind. But whereas in the past I flailed around, doing a little of this and a little of that just to not be a slob or a lunatic, now I had focus. I was working *toward* something, not just trying to undo the damage of the night before.

With nothing holding me back, I ran like a man possessed. It was such an insanely freeing sensation to not have to worry about running out of pills. Gazing out at the Greenport waterfront one evening from my in-laws' house on Shelter Island, I thought, *Wow, I did it. What a great feeling to not be a prisoner.* It was a level of happiness I'd never known.

I even made contact with my childhood friend Sully, fresh out of prison after serving three years. I'd heard through the grapevine that he'd gotten out and I'd called the number I had for him, but I didn't get him on the line. While I was driving to Shelter Island with Shelby one day, his number popped up on my cell phone. I hit the phone button on the car console and picked up the call.

"Is this John Dillinger, the famous bank robber?"

Shelby started laughing and I could hear Sully's awkward laughter on the line.

"Sully, what made you think you could get away with robbing a bank, bro?"

"Uh, I don't know . . . heroin, I guess?"

We chatted for a couple of minutes, then made plans to have a proper catch-up soon. After two weeks of calling him with no answer, I reached out to another friend in Somerville.

"Bro, what the fuck is up with Sully? I've been calling him for weeks with no answer. No response, no nothing."

"Oh man, I hate to be the one to tell you this. Sully overdosed the other night, Ken. He's dead."

Sully must have found a connection as soon as he got out of prison and tried to go back to the same stuff he'd been taking before he got put away. It killed him. *Ah, Sully, you were such a good friend, such a sweet kid.* It was a somber gut-check reminder of the world I'd left behind, a world that could still easily claim me if I couldn't stay clean.

Very quickly, I found those extra workouts I'd been doing weren't a bonus but a necessity, not just for my triathlon goals but for my mental health. For more than a decade, I'd used drugs to suppress or mute or kill the feelings I couldn't deal with. Now completely clean, I felt everything. It's true that I was happier than I'd ever been. But, having lost the secret weapon I'd used to modulate all the negative feelings, I found it difficult to deal with the world. More specifically, *my* world—the screaming pressure cooker of global finance. Day after day, I pounded it out on the pavement, doing my best to kill off the junkie madman I'd been and build a better man in his place.

Qualifying for the Ironman World Championships eluded me. I went down to the Texas Ironman in May 2012 full of confidence, ready to destroy. Unfortunately, it was I who got destroyed, finishing twenty-fifth in my age group of 338 participants, nowhere near qualifying. I was absolutely gutted. I'd been sure that this was the one, and now it felt like getting to those championships was never going to happen.

But that August, Ironman was launching a new race in New York, the Ironman US Championships. Since it was a new race, they were trying to boost attendance by offering a couple of extra Kona qualifying spots in each age group. I had a good day and shaved nearly eight minutes off my time in Texas; my finishing time was 10:14:37. That put me in twelfth in my age group, still not fast enough to qualify.

But the next day when they were handing out medals for the age group winners, the qualifying spots were assigned in person. If you weren't there to claim your spot, it went to the next finisher. I stood there with bated breath as they called finisher after finisher in my age group and those precious qualifying slots trickled down. Finally, the last qualifying slot for the 2012 Ironman World Championships in Kona rolled down to the twelfth-place finisher in my age group—me. I was in.

I felt like an up-and-coming boxer who'd just gotten his first shot at the title. At this stage in my life, I knew I wasn't going to go to the Olympics or turn pro in anything, so this was the pinnacle of athletic competition for me, and I was on cloud nine. I was sober, I'd achieved this goal I'd pursued for so long, and I was ready to fucking rock. The World Championships were less than two months out, but I'd just raced New York, I figured I'd be fine. I rented a house on Ali'i Drive in Hawaii, right on the water next to the marathon course, then set up shop there with my wife and our two little kids. It was gorgeous, the atmosphere was so festive, and we really had an amazing time. There were tons of activities, all the expos were set up . . . it was like the Olympic Village but populated by triathlon dorks like me, everyone walking around in compression shorts and Hokas. It sounds funny, but it was a dream come true to be rubbing elbows with all these world-class competitors and feeling like I belonged.

The start of the race was chaos—the crush of too many bodies in the water, people kicking you in the face—but it's always chaos. The swim felt okay, but I recalled that in New York, we'd been swimming downstream in the swift current of the Hudson and my swim time had been maybe thirty minutes faster than I'd expected.

It'd been hot in New York, but nothing could prepare you for the blast furnace of this Hawaii-set bike ride. We were biking on blacktop, surrounded for miles by black lava fields with no cover, nothing to protect you from the blistering trade winds that sapped all the moisture from your body as they tried to throw you off your bike. It was like the surface of some distant sun-baked planet, an unending no-man's-land, just the same shit for 112 miles.

Like a green fighter distractedly preparing for his first title bout, I'd gotten so carried away celebrating the win that I'd forgotten that all I'd won was a shot at the title—an opportunity to get my ass beaten publicly, on a national stage, by opponents whose toughness had been proven many times over. If you show up to a championship fight just happy to be there, you're going home in a fucking body bag.

I'd gotten so wrapped up in getting to the race that I'd underestimated the difficulty of the race I was there to compete in. We weren't in Hawaii for a vacation. We weren't here for a victory lap. They didn't hold the World Championships on Kona because it was beautiful. They held them here because Kona wanted to eat you alive.

Ninety miles into the bike ride, I felt utterly destroyed. I couldn't wait for it to be over. I wanted to take the bike, break it over my knee, throw it in the ocean, and never ride again.

By the time I made it to the run, I was falling apart, just

stumbling and bumbling. But I'd done enough racing to know that sometimes your legs can come back around. *All right*, I told myself, *just ease into this. Even if you walk for a little while, you can start running again. It's such a long day. You can make up a lot of time if you come around.*

It never happened. My wife was at mile four or five, videotaping. By the time I got there, I was hobbling, half-crippled.

"I'm done," I gasped to her, "I'm done."

The smile drained from her face.

"Oh my God, are you serious?"

"Yeah."

"Ken, are you sure? You've come such a long way to be here."

"Babe, I can't do it. I'm fucking ruined."

She never uttered a word of judgment or criticism, just silently turned off the camera and helped me off the course. I'd convinced myself that because I couldn't win, I should just tap out. Like I was some professional hotshot: *If I'm not going to make the podium, what's the point of even finishing?*

And just like that, the entire experience turned on its head. This wasn't a loss, this was a failure. It hurt like nothing before, and that pain would transform me like no win ever had.

A friend once told me, "It's harder to quit than to persevere." Those words had never rung so true. I'd never considered how I'd feel if I quit, how I'd feel knowing that I'd tapped out. I walked back to collect my bike, so angry and disappointed in myself that I had tears in my eyes. Jesus, everyone in my business and personal life knew I was down here racing. Again and again, I'd be answering that haunting four-word question—*how'd the race go?*—and I'd have to explain that I'd failed.

I hadn't even made it into the shower before I was interrogating the entire experience in my head. I felt like I was composed solely of shame and weakness. We'd had a wonderful time leading up to the race, and now I was second-guessing every moment of our pleasure. In the blink of an eye, my greatest victory had turned into my greatest defeat.

In a life full of bad decisions, I'm hard-pressed to think of a decision I regret more than giving up on myself at Kona. Almost fifteen years later, it still feels like a hooked bone stuck in my throat. Even if I'd walked every step of the remaining twenty-two miles, I still could have gotten in under fifteen hours. I could have finished, I could have logged a result, I could have prevented that searing loss. Instead, I just fucking quit.

The next night, Shelby and I got someone to look after the kids and went out for dinner. I was super depressed from quitting, and was hating myself for how depressed I was. Shelby listened to me rant and ramble without complaint. When I finally ran out of steam, she spoke:

"Ken, I want you to know that this doesn't matter to me. Not a drop. You're an amazing husband. You're an amazing father. You're sober. I know you love this stuff, but if you'd gone out there and won it today I couldn't be any prouder of you than I am right now. It doesn't matter to me but I know it matters to you. I know it's incredibly important to you. If quitting yesterday bothers you that much, just come back again next year and go all out and make it right."

I stared at her for a minute. She stared right back.

"Shelby . . . are you sure?"

"Yes. With conditions. We all came here for you to do your race with the understanding that we were having a family vacation afterward. Your race is over, now it's not *your* time, it's *our* time. From the minute you dropped out, you've been completely miserable, a total sourpuss. You've got to get over it. And you have to engage with your children, you have to engage with me. When we go back, yes, you can train. But when you come home from training, I don't care how exhausted you are, you still need to be a dad. You can't just go eat a pizza and lie in the bed because you're tired. That's not what good fathers do. When you're home, I don't want you to talk about bikes, or shoes, or training. When you come home, we talk about the family, we talk about stuff that we're all interested in."

"Okay. I get it. Is that all?"

Shelby's eyes sparkled.

"And a foot massage once a week."

"Best I can do is one every two weeks. Final offer."

"Seriously, Ken. Your pursuits here are pretty selfish. We're a team. At some point, I'm going to have a dream—something I need to do. I'm counting on you to support me in that like I have supported you. But I know this will eat away at you if you don't get it right. So yes, if you can hold up your end of the bargain, I'll support you in trying again next year."

All I heard was that she was willing to let me race again.

"Fuck it," I said, "I'm all in."

On the flight back to New York, I stared out the window at the black lava fields of Kona, where my determination had crumbled. I knew I needed to etch that feeling of shame into my soul so I'd never repeat it. In one of the promo videos for the World Championships I'd watched, they'd talked briefly about how the Hawaiian Islands had been formed by active volcanos, then showed a clip of red-hot lava coursing down a hillside into the ocean and, with a puff of steam, hardening into Kona's trademark dense lava rock. I closed my eyes. I imagined a drop of that red-hot Hawaiian lava made of my humiliation, disappointment, and self-loathing dropping directly into my brain, searing the flesh around it, and transforming into a small but unbreakable shiny black pebble that I'd carry with me everywhere I went.

I'll never quit again. That was my vow.

Not only that, never again would I undertake a race without putting every single thing I had into it. Blood, sweat, and tears were for amateurs. I'd run till I went blind, till my lungs caught on fire, till my organs were hanging out of my body, till my feet became bloody stumps . . . and then I'd keep on running.

—

The experience galvanized me. Shelby had been incredibly patient to let me train my ass off in 2012, and incredibly generous to let me sign up for the same meat grinder again in 2013. I intended to honor her support, her sacrifices, and the love she'd shown me. There'd be no fucking around this time.

When I'd been unable to qualify for the World Championships at the other Ironmans I'd run, I'd latched on to the New York race as a back door to Kona because of the extra qualifying spots. Even then, I'd only made it in because other people hadn't shown up. I'd only made it to Kona because I'd exploited a loophole *and* gotten lucky. None of that was happening in 2013. I wouldn't be taking any shortcuts. Luck would play no role. I'd make it there honestly, by never skipping a workout and by busting my ass every single day.

My demeanor at races changed, too. I'd always come ready to compete, but now it was a vendetta. I shouldered my way to the front of every race to avoid getting caught up in that clusterfuck at the beginning that costs you precious seconds. I wasn't there to run with these people. I wasn't even there to run around these people. I was there to run right through them.

I ran the New York City Half Marathon in March and carved three minutes and change off my finishing time, dropping from a 6:12 pace to 5:56. Promising, but not enough. In April, I ran a 5K and my time was 17:31, bringing my pace down to 5:38 from my previous best of 5:44. Decent progress, but the Ironman wasn't a sprint.

Shelby got pregnant again and our second son, Luke, was due in June. When Shelby went into labor, we simply walked outside in the middle of the night and tried to catch a cab. For whatever reason there weren't many cabs that evening and Shelby was starting to have serious contractions. St. Luke's Hospital was on Fifty-Eighth Street and Tenth Avenue, only a few blocks away, so we did what any New Yorker would do—started walking. Piece of cake, right? I have some great pictures of Shelby leaning on a brick wall in Manhattan trying to catch her breath and recover from a contraction during our middle-of-the-night urban hike to birth our third child.

We arrived at St. Luke's around three in the morning. Less than six hours later, our new son was chilling in a bassinet. Like Jack, Luke was born via C-section, which meant we'd be in the hospital for three nights. Though spending three nights sleeping on a cot next to Shelby sucked, it's one of my fondest memories because I got to spend tons of time connecting with my new baby boy, Luke. He'd been born healthy after a normal, uncomplicated pregnancy—a nice break after the drama of retrieving Tensae from the Ethiopian orphanage and the anxiety of Jack's stint in the NICU. Holding Luke in my arms, this little warm nugget, I felt that same perfect feeling I'd felt with Tensae and Jack. I was proud of Luke just for existing and couldn't wait to show him the world.

—

That August, I took on the Subaru Ironman Canada, a brutal high-elevation full Ironman-distance triathlon. I finished in fifth place in a very competitive age group with a time of 9:44:21, knocking half an hour off my best Ironman time, making it to the podium for the first time, and qualifying for Kona 2013 in the process. No roll-down spot for me this time. This year, I'd fucking earned it and no one was going to take that away from me. Six weeks out from Kona, I was ready to kill. This was it—time to get it done.

In 2012, I'd rolled into Kona with my wife and kids like we were showing up to a party. I'd felt blessed, like the universe had pulled some strings on my behalf to make it happen. In 2013, I went back solo, dead-eyed, like a samurai with a blood debt. I hadn't gotten there because of a loophole or good luck or because the universe had smiled on me. I'd gotten there because I'd done every single bit of the work. I stayed in the race hotel by myself, right by the Start/Finish line. Like a hit man, I had my assignment, and I'd done my homework and my preparations. I was going to complete my mission in solitude and get the fuck out of there.

I crossed the line at 9:39:33, my fastest Ironman finish at the time. I only came in fifty-first out of 282 in my age group, but finishing the race with a time I was proud of after such a disgusting spectacle the year prior felt like a massive victory. Never again would I give up on myself. Going forward, anything I did, I'd give it my all. I'd win or die trying. No excuses, no whining, no bullshit, just pedal to the metal. Nothing but *nothing* would hold me back.

CHAPTER NINE

ESCAPE FROM NEW YORK

IN EARLY 2014, I STARTED WINNING SOME LITTLE RACES OUTRIGHT: FIRST out of 285, first out of 239, first out of 429. I wasn't going to lie to myself—these were rinky-dink local races that, in the grand scheme of things, counted for nothing. One involved a couple hundred people gathering at a frigid little park in Westchester for a 5K when it was fifteen below. Another, heavy with turkey trot vibes, drew a couple hundred people from the neighborhood, and I just smoked them. But I couldn't deny that the number one still felt good. I knew I was building up to something bigger. I wasn't yet sure what it was, but I knew it was going to be big.

As it turned out, I needed every single one of those victories because everything else in my life started going sideways. In 2013, we'd moved up to an affluent little hamlet called Katonah, part of the town of Bedford in Westchester County. It was definitely the country as far as I was concerned, and I felt a little out of my element after seventeen years in Manhattan. But we were stoked to get out of the city, lead a quieter life, and have a bigger place with a backyard for the kids. It was idyllic, our own little slice of suburban heaven, nothing like the shithole in Somerville where I'd grown up. Only problem was that getting back and forth between my office in lower Manhattan and that slice of heaven meant two daily trips through hell.

In the morning, my commute was a headache, maybe only a hassle on a good day. I'd leave at five, get there at six, run for an hour or so, show up at the office by eight. But then I'd be looking at the clock all afternoon and obsessively checking the Waze app to see how bad traffic was going to be. Even on the best days, it seemed like it was redlining by three thirty. That hour-long commute could quickly turn into a shouting, heart-pounding, two-hour stop-and-go shit show. As a result, I often tried to leave early, which didn't sit well with the rest of the team. And that just boosted my anxiety and stress.

This was not how I wanted to live. It made me question my sobriety. If I was going to feel this angry and alienated all the time, maybe I'd be better off just getting high. At least when I was high, I'd have a few minutes of happiness. It was self-sabotaging thinking to be sure, but I couldn't see a way out.

I loved my kids dearly. Tensae was now four, Jack was three, and Luke was one. I'd wished for them so hard for so long, but I'd ignored the fact that I had no idea how to raise one child, let alone three. Shelby, however—she hadn't just been wanting and waiting to be a mom, she'd been preparing, putting in the work. And parenting came naturally to her. Was I just not born with paternal instincts? Did I put up mental obstacles due to my miserable childhood in Somerville? Probably a bit of both.

I loved Luke and I was always happy to hold him, but the best and worst thing about little babies is that they're like a sack of potatoes. When they're happy, you can just look at them and make funny sounds and they'll be delighted. Shelby could do it all day, but it wouldn't take long before I got bored or antsy. When the kids were babies, there were many times when they'd start to fuss and nothing I did could calm them down. The minute I handed them off to Shelby, they'd instantly chill. A lot of dads are bad with babies, and I think part of it is that women have an instinctual sense of how to nurture children, while nurturing is something men need to learn. In the moment, though, it made me feel frustrated, powerless, even hopeless.

I knew I could be hard on the older kids, and I tried with everything I had to be more patient. But while I was learning to parent, I was also learning to be a human being again. Sobriety and parenting had this in common: I'd fantasized about them for so long as the solution to all my problems that there was no way to avoid disappointment when I discovered how complex and demanding they were.

Beyond deciphering how to properly nurture three little kids, I was also trying to support Shelby's launch of a small business, Bright Signs Learning. She'd taught our kids to read and use sign language before they could even speak. It blew my mind. One of her tools had been these little videos she'd created for the kids, and she wanted to share them with the rest of the world.

We'd hired a live-in nanny shortly before we left New York for Katonah. Her name is Whitney Van Rhee. She'd just graduated from the University of West Georgia and had never been a nanny before. But she was phenomenal and took a load of work off our backs from day one. Great maternal instincts just like Shelby, and to this day she's still like a member of our family.

One of the things that was challenging for me about our arrangement, though, was that, all of a sudden, Shelby had a female friend in the house. Since Whitney was fresh off the bus from Georgia, she didn't have a ton of friends close by. She and Shelby would spend loads of time together, doing girl stuff. Whitney was always careful not to take sides when Shelby and I fought, but the fights seemed to last longer now that Shelby had someone to talk to when she wasn't talking to me.

Whitney was a tremendous help with the kids, and they adored her. But now that Shelby had someone to help her, it was often easier for her and Whitney to just deal with all the kid stuff and for me to get out of their way. Soon, I was in the city from dawn till dusk, leaving Shelby and Whitney home with the kids, all of them developing great routines together. It was like there were two separate stories unfolding under one roof—one that included the five of them, and one that was just me.

When I did try to be involved with the kids, it seemed like I always messed it up. One time we were visiting the in-laws out on Shelter Island, and there was a little shopping wagon. Jack was probably two at the time.

"Come on, Jackie, get on the wagon and I'll push you down the hill."

"Ken, are you sure?" Shelby said. "The hill's a bit steep."

"He's going to be fine."

So I put Jackie in this stupid little thing. Maybe it was a Fisher Price toy shopping cart? Definitely not something that's designed to ride in. I gave him a tiny push and sent him down the hill. Of course, he immediately got going too fast. The front wheel hit a little bump, and the cart dumped him out and he went ass over teakettle. Poor little Jackie face-planted and skidded across the grass on his face. There was this terrifying moment of silence, then he popped up, bawling and screaming, his little face all scratched up.

"Ken, you can't do that with the kids, they're too little!"

Shelby ran and scooped him up off the grass, his little face red from screaming.

"Oh my God, Shelby, I'm so sorry!"

I was mortified.

Shelby never scolded me about my mistakes regarding the kids because she knew I was a compassionate person who loved his children. Still, I always felt horrible about it, and then a black cloud hung over the rest of the day.

Shelby and I talked about child-rearing and our own upbringings many times. One night, the kids were clamoring for ice cream after dinner. I knew it affected their sleep, so I was being the bad cop, arguing for them to have popcorn or fruit or basically anything but ice cream.

"Ken, come on, they're kids. I bet you can remember eating ice cream or candy before bed when you were a little kid."

"I don't."

"Your parents never gave you sweets or candy before bed?"

"I'm not saying they didn't, I'm just saying I don't remember it."

"Well, what did they give you after dinner if they were giving you a treat?"

"I don't know. Shelby, you're not going to believe this, but I swear to God, when I say I can't remember, I mean I can't remember *anything*. I remember feeling unsafe and riddled with anxiety and that's about it. It was so painful as a kid, I think I just did everything I could to block it out. And then as I got older, I just kept piling layers and layers of shit on it so I'd never have to deal with it. And now, I don't know, after taking pills for all those years, maybe it's just gone forever."

She didn't look at me like she was angry or didn't believe me. Instead, I saw on her face sadness and concern, maybe dismay. How could a man who couldn't recall ever having been a child understand his own children?

—

As I was failing some major parenting tests, I also found myself failing to stay sober. I'd make it a few months clean, then something would happen that'd throw me off—a fight with Shelby, a deal gone bad at work, some unexpected repair on the house or one of the cars. In a storm of emotional chaos, I'd break down and call my dealer, who always had plenty of Percs.

Crazy as it sounds, I bought only a small amount, though, because every single time I relapsed, I was convinced that'd be the last time I got high. As if I hadn't been "getting high for the last time" for years now. I'd buy just enough to get through the day. Then the next day, I'd have to see my guy again.

Finally, Shelby caught on.

After a particularly rough day, I'd taken too many Percs before dinner and I was struggling to keep my eyes open.

"Ken," Shelby said, raising an eyebrow, "you with us?"

"Yeah, yeah, I'm here."

"Did you take something?"

"Nah, I'm just exhausted."

Then she set a trap and I walked right into it.

"Did you take a Benadryl?"

"Oh yeah. I took a Benadryl."

"I got you, mister. I threw you an excuse. I threw you a bone, and you took it. You changed your story. Maybe I'm naive about drugs, Ken, but I'm not stupid. Get your shit together."

Training became my man cave, my safe space, and, though it wasn't totally healthy for me or my family, my training paid off. In October 2014, I won the Westchester Medical Center Half Marathon with a time of 1:17:29. It was a field of only 429 and my time certainly wasn't dazzling, but it felt wild to win a half marathon, even a tiny one. The victory gave me enough confidence to think, *I'm not a bad runner—I could start doing this for real.* A month later, I came in twenty-third out of nearly six thousand in my age group in the New York City Marathon with a time of 2:45:29. It was a full thirteen minutes faster than my previous fastest marathon. The rest of my life may have been hanging by a thread, but the running was starting to come together.

In September 2015, I went to Madison for Ironman Wisconsin and had the best race of my life. My swim performance sucked, but it always sucked. I was not a great swimmer—the swim was what it was. I came out of the water at seventy-five minutes. I always finished somewhere between sixty-five and seventy-five minutes. I did one swim at Kona in sixty-two minutes, but that took a huge effort. Earlier that year, we'd had our third son, Cameron. I'd been training in Westchester and commuting to the city, so I'd intentionally only done the bare minimum of swimming. But Ironman races are rarely won in the swim. From the elites to the middle of the pack, the swim is only a difference of a few minutes. The bike or the run is where a guy can really peel away and establish a lead.

Once I got out of the swim, I absolutely destroyed the bike ride. I had one of the fastest bike splits of the race in under five hours. Then I had a killer run through the Wisconsin countryside. Halfway through the race, I tweaked something in my back. It was a little pinch at first but after a couple of miles, it started screaming. The pain kept ratcheting up and up and up. It was killing me, but I'd die before I quit again.

I hated it when people put on this dramatic show at the finish line, so as much as I'd busted my ass to get there, I always tried to sneak across the line with low-key dignity. Not in Wisconsin. I was able to hold it together until the second I crossed the finish line, and then my back seized completely. They had to drag my carcass from the finish line like I was a dead man. After they completed an IV and a doctor's evaluation in the med tent, I discovered I couldn't stand up.

My buddy Mike Buteau, who was a reporter for Bloomberg, helped me back to my hotel, where they put me in a wheelchair and carted me up to my room. Then he went to the pharmacy for me and brought some dinner to my room. I thought I was going to have to stay there for two or three days because I could not get out of bed. I was in crippling pain, chewing up anti-inflammatories, muscle relaxants, anything but opioids. This was the kind of pain where even pain medicine doesn't work. I was just miserable. I eventually had to go to a chiropractor to fix my back enough to get on a plane.

None of that, though, obliterated the joy I felt at having performed so well in the race. I finished with my fastest Ironman time of 9:36:15, won my age group, and came in seventh overall. Poring over the results, incapacitated in my hotel bed, I saw that I was less than ten minutes out from the second-place finisher. Had I buckled down and done all my swim training, had my back not freaked out, I could have been the second amateur overall. I could have made it to the podium. Even then, drowning in pain, I thought to myself, *No more bullshit. It's time to get serious.*

—

A good friend of mine, Amar Kuchinad, had set up a financial technology firm called Electronifie and he asked me whether I wanted to come and run the sales department. Amar was a great guy, one of my most trusted and closest friends. He'd majored in mathematics at Harvard, ran a sub-three-hour marathon, and had completed the legendary Leadville ultramarathon. Just the sweetest guy and a hardcore Wall Street player, ran all the structured credit trading at Goldman Sachs. Absolutely the kind of guy I wanted to work with. I told him that I'd do it, but I wanted to cover West Coast clients because I wanted to be living in California within the year. It was a difficult decision to give up our beautiful new house in Westchester for LA, but the commute was killing me and, as collateral damage, bringing the whole house down.

After twenty years of grinding and hustling in New York, in January 2016, I packed up the wife and kids and bailed for LA. It was scary and jarring—the screaming, red-faced New York financial world had been my entire identity for so long. But I'd been miserable in it for years. The job had turned me into a bully and a tyrant and a drug addict, and that's not who I was inside. That was part of the old life, and it had to go.

I raced Kona again in October 2016 and lived on my bike in 2017 and 2018, hammering the hills around the Pacific Palisades. When my triathlon training made me a ghost in my own house, Shelby let me know that she was over it.

"Ken, I'm fine with you going biking for ten hours—I'm going to have a grand old time with the kids. But when you get back, you need to be present. And you're not, you just lie there like a lump. You have this entire secret life with your little triathlon buddies, a life we're not a part of. These are your *children*, Ken. This is what you always wanted. You keep letting us down, and we're running out of runway, buddy."

I couldn't even fight her on it. That little contract we'd agreed on after I quit Kona? I hadn't done any of the things she'd asked for and we both knew it. Ironman training just used up too much of my time and energy. I knew I was being selfish and my relationships with my wife and children were suffering. Something had to change.

I loved biking and I was good at it, but I knew I'd never be great. Although I tried to pin the needle the entire ride, there were always times where I'd be cruising or coasting. Running, though? If I was short on time, nothing gave me more bang for the buck than running fast. I knew that's where my gifts were—the strategy, the suffering, the purity of it. No one could suffer like I did.

I dropped my tri workouts and switched to running ten miles a day, every single day, no exceptions, as hard and as fast as I could. One day a week, I ran twenty. This was my version of a scale-down. I hoped it would be enough for me to become the husband and father my family deserved.

—

In 2018, I signed up to do the Malibu Half Marathon. It wasn't a huge race, maybe two thousand people, but I was there to win. When I got there, I immediately started sizing up other runners, which is always a mistake. There are some guys who fancy themselves good runners and they're all done up in top-notch gear like they're killers. And then the gun goes off and you're like, "Where's Harry Highsocks? The dude in the compression socks and the racing singlet? He looked like the guy to beat." And then some guy who wasn't on your radar at all will own you by six minutes.

Right away, I noticed this African dude warming up and I didn't like how good he looked. I wasn't a real runner but this guy, he was a real runner. As it turned out, he was the cross-country coach at Cal Berkeley, and he ran the 5K in the 2012 Olympics for Eritrea. He was in insane shape, like next level—an Olympic distance runner.

Shelby and the kids had come along to root for me. When she walked over, she could immediately see it on my face.

"What's the matter, Ken?"

"Look at this fucking guy. I'm not going to beat this guy. He's way out of my league."

"Oh, cut the shit, Ken. You got this."

I clawed my way to the front of the pack like I always did. We were standing there with maybe ten minutes to go before the start. The African dude was probably mid- to late thirties and he was standing there with this tall, skinny white kid in a long, loose-fitting T-shirt who looked to be in his mid-twenties. The kid was built like an elite runner, but he wasn't dressed like one. He started talking to the African guy.

"Yo, you see the time that won this race last year?"

"Nah, what was it?"

"It was like one-seventeen. That's hella slow, dude, hella slow. Never heard of the guy, either."

He was right, it wasn't a great time for that course. And I knew that because the guy who won the race the year before with a time of 1:17 was me. It just hadn't been a competitive race that year. But a win's a win, and I wasn't going to let him shit all over it. We were packed in tight at the starting line and I was maybe eighteen inches from this kid. If I wasn't ready to throw down before, now I was ready to go to war.

"Yeah, motherfucker," I said, "that guy was me. You only have to run faster than the guy in second. Let's see how it goes today."

I didn't know this guy from a hole in the wall, but I was already thinking to myself, *I'm going to kill you both.*

They both recoiled a little bit, but the African guy recovered first, a total gentleman.

"Yeah, that's it, man. You only have to beat the rest of the field. No use killing yourself if you're way out in front."

The white kid immediately started backpedaling. It was awkward. He knew he was staring down a lunatic.

"Uh, yeah," he said, "I'm not in the best shape. I didn't train as hard as I should have. I didn't even dress right. I should have worn a singlet."

I didn't give a fuck.

When the gun went off, those guys took off like they were running out of a house on fire. If I was running a 5:20 pace, they must have been running 4:45. Absolutely scorching.

The course wound along the beach in Malibu, out and back on the Pacific Coast Highway. Shelby and the kids had posted up at the one-mile marker, cheering and waving. I just ran by them, shrugging and cursing in my head. I didn't want them to have come out just to see me finish in third. I was pissed.

I could have easily convinced myself that top three is fine. No sense killing yourself, right? All three of us had just agreed on that at the starting line. And this race meant nothing to anyone who wasn't running. No one would ever look at the results of this race and say, "Oh, he's only a mediocre runner because he came in fifth. But if he'd come in second, then he'd have been a *good* runner." I'd won it the year before, I had nothing to prove, I didn't give a shit about the results.

Well, 49 percent of me didn't give a shit. The other 51 percent knew I'd rather drop dead than not get the most out of myself. It wasn't for anyone else. When it was time to compete, especially when it came to running, some primitive part of my brain just screamed *attack*. I started legging it.

The course was basically six and a half miles out along the PCH, then six and a half miles back. After the turnaround, the African guy was long gone but I could see the white kid running. He looked okay, but he didn't look great. Around eleven miles, I ran up on him. Normally I'd blow right by him, which is what you're supposed to do. But there was a part of me that knew I had him, and I wanted to toy with him for talking shit about me.

I fell in right behind him, almost touching him. After breathing down his neck for five or ten seconds, he tried to say something to me.

"What's up, man?"

"Later," I said.

I put the hammer down and I dropped him.

As soon as I crossed the finish line, I stopped and waited for him. The African guy was there, and I shook his hand and congratulated him on his win. The white kid rolled in about two minutes later.

"Hey, nice job, man."

"Thanks," he said between breaths, "good race."

"Listen," I said, "next time, make sure you wear all the right gear because I don't want you to have any fucking excuses."

The African dude slapped his thigh and laughed.

"You talked shit about the wrong guy, bro," he said with a grin.

I would come back for the Malibu Half the next year and win it. No excuses, no bullshit, no prisoners.

—

When Shelby picked me up after the 2018 Malibu Half, she dropped a bomb on me.

"Ken, I've been thinking about it and . . . I think it's time for us to get a dog."

I was exhausted and did not want to hear it.

"Well, I want a unicorn but not all dreams come true."

"Uh-uh, Pops, not so fast. When we were dating, I told you I had to have a dog when we were done having kids. Remember when we first moved out to California and we were walking on the beach in Malibu? I told you we were going to get a dog, and you said yes."

"Shelby . . . now? Are you kidding me? No."

"Ken, I've always supported your hobbies. This is my hobby. We're getting a dog."

"Ah, Shel . . . shit, that's tough. That's the only argument you've made that makes sense."

"What I hear you saying is, 'Yes, Shelby, that's a wonderful idea.'"

"We're getting a bulldog, then."

"What? Ken, no. They're terrible dogs, they can't breathe, they can't do anything, they have all kinds of health issues. We're getting a Weimaraner."

"I don't even know what that is. We're getting a bulldog."

"Ken, I don't tell you what kind of bike to ride, what kind of shoes to buy . . . I don't tell you how to train."

"Here we go. Well, we're getting a male at least."

"Nope. My hobby, my dog, my choice."

"Shelby, Jesus, you're killing me. I'm picking the name, at least."

"Wrong again. Ken, this is my dog. Your role is only to support me in this. And that's it."

What could I say? Last thing I wanted was to add a dog to our already chaotic home, but she had me dead to rights.

To her credit, Shelby did it right. I did my best to contribute. She found a puppy through a breeder and decided to make it a Christmas present for the kids. When they were opening their presents on Christmas morning, we made sure each kid got a dog-related gift: a doggie bed, some dog toys, dog treats, a book on dog training. Shelby tried to convince Cam that the dog toys were actually for little kids; I told Luke that the dog bed was actually a mat for him to lie on to watch movies. When all the presents were open, Shelby "found" a letter from Santa hidden on the tree, explaining that he'd had one last item left on his sleigh, and it was waiting for them outside. Tensae started shrieking before she even got out the front door. The breeder was waiting outside with the puppy. Tensae was so overwhelmed, she fainted. Shelby named the mutt Edna, after the salty old aunt from *National Lampoon's Vacation* who dies mid-road trip and gets strapped to the roof. I had massive anxiety about having a dog in the house but I'm not going to lie, it did make for a magical Christmas for the kids.

—

In 2019, I ran the Boston Marathon and finished with a time of 2:35, a full two minutes slower than my fastest marathon in Tucson in 2017. I began to feel that I'd gotten as fast as I was going to get on my own. I had the drive, but my strategy was lacking. I didn't know what I didn't know . . . but I knew someone who did. In Boston after the race, one of my closest friends had introduced me to a coach named Mario Fraioli. Mario was from Worcester, another crumbling ruin of a city in Massachusetts to rival Somerville. He'd wound up in California, too, and he'd coached some very elite runners. From our very first meeting, I felt like Mario could see who I was and what was driving me. I reached out to him via email late that summer and he agreed to coach me for the California International Marathon taking place in Sacramento later that year.

"So Ken, what does your training look like?"

"Every day I go out in Temescal Canyon behind my house and run ten miles. When I'm training for a marathon, I throw in some long runs."

"Do you do any track work? Pacing?"

"Nah. I just run as fast as I can."

"Ken, I . . . wow. Well, it's remarkable what you've accomplished so far. Looking at your race splits, you've been going out too fast and then barely hanging on those last six miles. You need to be able to race those last six miles. Let's try something with a little more structure."

Mario drew me up a plan and we got to work. I figured he'd have me running more, but my workload only increased slightly, if at all. He got me running repeat track workouts at a specific pace, and running intervals during my long runs. I'd never bothered with crap like this, but I forced myself to listen to Mario and act on his advice.

Sure enough, when the California International Marathon rolled around on December 8, my time was 2:28:25, shaving more than five minutes off my previous best time, and I finished sub-2:30 for the first time. Still, it irked me that I'd come so close to running sub-2:28 and hadn't pulled it off.

"Ken," Mario said at the finish line, "cheer up, buddy! We did it. You did it. Your first marathon under two-thirty is a big deal. This is a win, a big win. Take a minute to enjoy it."

As much as I tried to follow Mario's directions to the letter, this was one thing I just couldn't do.

In 2020, I ran the Pasadena Half. Half marathons don't get a lot of attention, but it was a deep field, nearly nine thousand runners with a televised finish in the Rose Bowl Stadium. I was probably going to get my ass kicked.

I woke up the morning of the race the same way I woke up for every race, drenched in dread and doom. People talk about prerace jitters as if the person is about to go on a date with someone who could be "the one," but that ain't it at all. I felt as if I was about to go take the bar exam: I'd done every bit of preparation I could, but I knew it might still eat me alive.

I understood that pain was coming. I might eke out a podium finish or I might blow up and leave on a stretcher halfway through, but the one thing I knew for certain was that I was about to subject myself to tremendous mental, physical, and emotional suffering. I wasn't a naturally gifted runner, and I didn't have a distance runner's thin, lithe physique. If you looked at me and ten other normal people, you'd never pick me as the marathoner. I knew that for me to win this race, I'd have to do everything perfectly, I'd have to wring everything out of myself, I'd have to run the well dry.

My mind started to eat itself. *Why are you doing this? You've put so much pressure on yourself, and for what? No one gives a shit about your results.*

And then, in my head, it all clicked into place. *No one cares about it except you. But you're the only person who needs to care. And you care deeply.*

I got my shit together and hauled ass to the starting line.

I took off fast. It was a risky move but if I was going to almost kill myself, I might as well swing for the fences. Five miles into the race, it was just me and this kid—a big guy, but young, running in a T-shirt. I fell into conversation with the kid. Not a full-on conversation because we were breathing hard, but small talk. This kid was fucking moving.

"You in college? Who you run for?"

"High school. Senior."

"Oh yeah? What's your distance?"

"The mile. I'm number one in the state."

I looked at the kid. He was long and lean, moving easily, effortlessly eating up the road, like a coyote. I had to be thirty years older than him with some hard wear, inside and out. But I had some fire left in me.

"Well, buddy," I said, "if you're the state champ in the mile, I'm not gonna hang around long enough for us to get into a sprint with one mile left to go. Let's fucking do this."

I put the hammer down. The kid couldn't keep up.

The race route wound through Pasadena, not much of a city, more like a high-end residential neighborhood. Not totally unlike Beverly Hills. A little past the halfway point, I saw a friend of mine, Mike Buchanan. He was the Deputy CIO at Western Asset Management, a huge player in the finance markets. Bucky was unmistakable with his pair of massive, attack-trained German shepherds.

"Yo, what the Buck?" I called out to him, a corny dad joke I used at every opportunity.

"Hey, Ken, all right, let's go!"

"I'm winning," I yelled back.

Man, the look on his face, like I'd smacked him on the ass or something. He was just flabbergasted. He'd probably been waiting for me to come rolling through with the pack. He knew I ran, everyone knew I ran. But I don't think he knew I ran 5:34 for thirteen miles.

With maybe a mile to go, and still no one on my heels, I considered my position. Everything had just clicked. I was at my absolute limit, but I hadn't felt in distress the entire race. For the first time, I thought to myself, *You can win this.*

The course wound around to the tunnel leading into the Rose Bowl, the same tunnel that the UCLA Bruins emerged from for football games. Sprinting into that tunnel as fast as I could, I felt like an ancient gladiator running into the emperor's arena. When I emerged from the tunnel into the Rose Bowl, a roar went up from the people in the stands. I saw the news cameras trained on me like I was some red-carpet celebrity, and I heard the announcer go into his spiel.

"And here he comes, folks, your 2020 Pasadena Half Marathon

race winner from Pacific Palisades, Ken Rideout. Here he comes! Ken's also an incredible Ironman competitor. Oh my goodness, forty-eight years old, this man is one tough customer! Give it up for our Pasadena Half Marathon winner, Ken Rrrrrrrrideout!"

I crossed the line, my heart just singing. I was ecstatic but also in shock. I'd done it, I'd really done it, I'd beat out nearly nine thousand other runners to break the tape at the finish in the Rose Bowl on live TV. The minute I finished, the news crews were there with the cameras in my face.

"And here he is, the winner! What's your name?" a female news anchor from KTLA said.

I walked over, still wiping the sweat out of my beard.

"I'm Ken. Ken Rideout."

"Ken, what was it like out there?"

"When an old man is winning by this much, it doesn't say much about the competition."

—

I felt like I was walking on air in the days following Pasadena. Here it was, proof that I could do something massive. This was going to be my year and nothing but nothing could derail me.

A month and a half later, the world shut down. On March 11, the WHO declared Covid-19 a global pandemic. The NBA suspended the rest of its season, and the president announced a travel ban from Europe to the United States. The Dow plummeted 20 percent from its peak in February. Every major road race around the world was canceled in short order. So much for my big year.

CHAPTER TEN

MARATHON MAN

IT FELT WEIRD TO BENEFIT FROM THE PANDEMIC WHEN SO MANY PEOPLE WERE dying, suffering, or losing their shirts, but the "time out" proved to be what our family needed. We were living in a relatively small house in the Pacific Palisades at the top of Palisades Drive in the Highlands neighborhood. It was a pretty radical departure from Westchester, to say nothing of Manhattan. With no live-in nanny, we had to rely on ourselves, our family unit. Which meant I didn't just have to man up for Shelby, I had to dad up and be the parent my kids deserved.

There were parts of lockdown that I liked. Even though I regretted the kids' losing so much school, it was nice just to spend some time with them. And Shelby rose to the academic challenge like a champ. She set up MIT Academy in the garage—Mom Is Teaching. She got the whole place kitted out. The floor was covered with brightly colored interlocking foam tiles, and we got desks for each of the kids.

She had different lesson plans prepared for every single day, with field trips and science experiments and everything. She often taught with the garage door open. I'm never not proud of my wife, but the way she handled lockdown made my entire chest ache with love for her.

One day, she invited me to do hydro-dipping with them. I'd never heard of it before. Shelby told me it involved spraying paint in a big Tupperware bin and just from that, I knew I wanted nothing to do with it. Little kids and spray paint in an enclosed space is a great way to make sure Dad has a rotten day. But she twisted my arm, so okay, fine.

She filled a big plastic bin with water, then sprayed a thin, multi-colored layer of paint on the surface. Then she carefully took one of the kids' water bottles and slowly twisted it in the paint as she pushed it into the water. The thermos came out with this unique swirly design, full of vivid colors. The kids were delighted. I'm not going to lie, it was pretty incredible. My wife was full of miracles, and once again, I'd very nearly missed it.

In that period when much of the world was on the couch, the Rideout family was all about activities: We had a crappy little basketball hoop for the kids at the foot of the drive, the kind where you fill the base with water. We set up a slackline in the backyard so the kids could learn how to do that. I played Wiffle ball with them every single day. They loved it. They had no conception that they were missing out on anything.

Obviously, the lockdown wasn't entirely a pleasure cruise. Some days were heavenly. Some were stressful. Some days I felt as if I was going to kill someone. It gave me plenty of opportunity to recall times my father had seemed overwhelmed or impatient and wonder if I'd been too hard on him.

As the pandemic appeared to wind down and things started opening back up in the spring of 2021, I started shopping for a marathon I thought I could win. I knew I wasn't going to win Boston, but I wanted to find a legit marathon that had some name recognition, a race where if I had a good day and ran fast, I'd have a chance at winning. Winning the Rumpelstiltskin Marathon with six other people in it just wasn't going to cut it. It was time to run a real race competing against more than just weekend warriors.

The more I read about the May 1, 2021, Myrtle Beach Marathon in South Carolina, the more it seemed like the right opportunity. It typically drew only about a thousand marathoners, so it wasn't a massive, destination marathon, but it was a qualifying race for the World Marathon Majors, a series of the six most prestigious and competitive marathons in the world. The location looked easy to get to, so I could fly in the day before race day and fly home the next. The course was relatively flat. The organizers had been putting on the race for more than twenty years, so it had a history. I hated training in the summer, so the time of year was perfect. When I looked at the previous years' times, it seemed as if a 2:30 could win it. You never knew who was going to show up—some hotshot could come out and blow my doors off with a 2:20—but I liked my chances. And it was the day before my fiftieth birthday, so if everything came together, I'd have something to celebrate. I pulled the trigger and signed up.

On the last day of April 2021, I flew down to Myrtle Beach for the race. The city itself was the ultimate redneck Riviera—trashy dive bars and dance clubs advertising tacky drink specials, thrown-together airbrushed T-shirt kiosks, bums and hustlers shuffling along the grimy boardwalk at all hours. I always treated myself to a top-of-the-line accommodation before a big race but there was nothing decent close by, so I checked into this shithole little hotel close to the starting line. It was the kind of place that gave me mad anxiety just driving past it because I could imagine all the desperate lives coming undone inside—the stepped-on coke, the escorts, the mini bottles of Absolut and Fireball. But whatever, this was purely business, I was on a mission. I threw my stuff in my room and went down to grab my bib and race packet.

I was stressed because they'd assigned me to the third corral. To avoid congestion, large marathons usually launch runners in waves, with different categories of runners—pros, amateurs, men, women, etc.—arranged to launch in succession. In New York or Tokyo, if you're in the third corral, you're way in the back. This marathon would be tiny compared to those marquee events, which feature tens of thousands of runners. These corrals wouldn't slow me down as much, but if the Myrtle Beach organizers were super strict about the assignments, it was going to be harder to grab an early lead.

Before arriving, I'd emailed the race director, letting her know that I thought I could be competitive, and asked to be put in the first corral, but no dice. So I reached out to my friend Josh Cox, who was a pro running agent. He'd called the race director and asked them to put me in the A corral. Again, no luck—when I went to pick up my race package, there was a big C on my race bib, indicating the third corral.

Sometimes you have to make your own luck. I stopped into a CVS, bought a black Sharpie, and just wrote a big A right over the C, not even trying to fiddle-fuck it. If someone stopped me in the morning, I'd just tell them, "Yeah, they did this at check-in. Now buzz off, I'm supposed to be here."

I always tried to eat clean before a race, so I grabbed dinner at a seafood place with decent ratings. It was basically a Red Lobster in fancy dress, another disappointment. It didn't matter, none of this shit mattered. The only thing that mattered was tomorrow morning, I was going to push through anything and anyone standing in my way and crush that marathon.

I got to the race nice and early, as per usual. I warmed up and there were no problems, I was feeling good. It was a little hot and humid, with winds gusting at maybe twenty miles an hour, which I knew would affect my time a little, but everyone would be dealing with the same shit. I positioned myself perfectly at the start. When the gun went off, I went out hard.

The route ran us through downtown Myrtle Beach toward the water, then south down Route 17 to the Market Common. Around mile seven, the route took us down to the boardwalk for ten miles right on the water up to the Dunes Golf and Beach Club. At mile seventeen, we'd swing around and run inland for the next nine miles to finish in the parking lot of the Pelicans stadium. After a mile and a half, two miles, I was in the lead by a fair amount. But I knew I couldn't get too excited—there was still a shitload of running to do.

At three miles, some kid came up right behind me. I glanced back and he had on headphones. His footsteps were so loud, it sounded like Bigfoot trying to stomp out a fire behind me. That's a tactic people use sometimes. I used it myself in Pasadena, but not with such heavy stomping steps. I wasn't about to let this guy clomp behind me all day. Finally, I got irrationally angry, whipped around, and snapped at him.

"Yo, will you get off my heels, Bigfoot?"

He mumbled something in surprise, then jumped in front of me and started flying. He must have been running five-minute miles. I fell in right behind him—let's see how he liked it. No way either of us were going to be able to keep that up, but I wasn't about to let him go.

From mile three to mile seven, we wound through developments composed mostly of second-rate condos and shitty little inland strip malls. To run this fast in the first seven miles of a marathon was suicide. I knew I could run fast when I had to, but each runner only has so many matches to burn. Whether you burn them the first mile or the last, you have what you have.

The lactate threshold is the maximum pace a runner can maintain for an hour. It varies wildly from runner to runner. Tempo pace is a pace you can hold for several hours—basically, your marathon pace. When runners "bonk" in a race, it's generally because they've mismanaged their pace and gone out too fast. Marathons may seem like a sport of brute endurance, but at the elite level, it's as strategic as a game of chess.

I was trying to run smart and hold something back for later in the race when I'd need it, but I was determined not to let this galloping Bigfoot get away from me. I stayed behind him, but, importantly, I stayed *with* him. Around the seven-mile marker, we ran out of the cover of downtown Myrtle Beach and turned onto the boardwalk, running north up the beach, totally exposed. We'd been getting little gusts but the wind suddenly turned into a ferocious headwind, buffeting us constantly. A couple of times, I stepped out from behind this guy with the intention of passing but the wind was so vicious, I just fell back in line behind him.

Had he at any point said, "Come through," I'd have gone. Had I been in his shoes, I'd have said, "Dude, you got to help me. Come on, let's switch off, we'll take turns." Because it takes a lot of extra energy to run out in front, particularly with a headwind that intense. We'd run a mile apiece, even half a mile apiece, or rotate every two minutes. That's what the normal protocol would be. That'd be proper race etiquette.

But to win a marathon, you have to bluff, you have to take chances, and you need to be absolutely cutthroat. There have been big races, Olympic races, where leaders have turned around and urged the other runner trailing them to take the lead. Sometimes they do and sometimes they don't, saying literally or with their body language: "I'm not doing it. You slow down. I don't care. I'll slow down, too. If you want to let everyone else catch up by running slow, be my guest. I'm going to outkick you all at the end."

But the other runner didn't say a word to me. So after I'd yelled at him not to do it to me, I sat on his heels for ten long miles while that nonstop wind packed our teeth and eyes with sand. At times, I felt he was going way too slow. I was just chilling out back there. I could have been drinking a cup of coffee and he was working his ass off. But if he wasn't going to ask me to do the work, I wasn't doing it. I was there to win.

The minute we turned off the beach out of the wind, I took off like a bat out of hell. I ran the last nine miles completely alone. There was no roaring crowd at the finish line because of social distancing, no friends or family there to cheer me on or congratulate me, but I couldn't give a rat's ass. I'd come roaring out of the darkness and isolation of lockdown and I'd done it. I'd won a real marathon, and no one could take that away from me.

The other runner turned out to be plenty tough. As much unnecessary effort as he'd expended, I still only beat him by thirty-eight seconds. He came over to me after the race to congratulate me. We shook hands and chatted for a minute. His name was William Moore, from Latrobe, Pennsylvania. He was thirty-three, seventeen years younger than me, and had run cross-country in college. After some chitchat, I hit him with the question that was killing me.

"Dude, I got to ask . . . When we were on the beach, why didn't you wave me through to come into the wind? I'm happy to do some of the work."

"Eh, when you yelled at me when I first caught you, I was like, 'This guy's crazy. I don't want to ask him anything.'"

"I only yelled at you because we're three miles into a marathon and you're stomping behind me super loud. Bro, you were almost touching me. I don't have a problem with sharing the workload. But in that moment, you were so close that I thought you were trying to fuck with me."

"Yeah, I made a mistake. In hindsight, I shouldn't have gotten so close. I had my headphones on so I couldn't really hear how loud my footfalls were, but I knew I was a little too close for comfort."

"Dude, at three miles into a marathon, you don't need to be right behind someone. We could have worked this whole thing together and settled it in the last couple of miles."

William shook his head.

"Yeah, good point, good point."

"Bro, I think you know this, but you obviously have a lot of talent. You're a tough competitor and you're going to win races. But you need to dial up your strategy. And if someone turned around and yelled at me, I'd have just kept going. I'd never let anyone derail my race by cursing at me. You're a great runner, and I hope you never let anyone intimidate you in a race again."

—

I was happy with the win, obviously, but I felt really good about ending it on a positive note with a fierce competitor who'd battled me so hard for most of the marathon. Fausto Coppi, an Italian cyclist, once said, "Old age and treachery will always defeat youth and skill." There's a lot of truth to that, and I always used it to my advantage. But after my races, I did everything I could to share what I knew with the younger guys.

Two years before, in the Malibu Half in 2019, I'd been leading at the turnaround by maybe sixty seconds. At mile nine, this Prefontaine-looking kid with the same mustache and short shorts came right up behind me out of nowhere. In that moment, in my heart, I quit. Immediately, in my brain, I was like, *Oh well, I guess I'm going to get second*. I just waited for him to stick the knife in me and blow past me with authority. In the course of one or two seconds, all these thoughts ran through my head.

He's going to get me now. I'm already running as fast as I can. It's not like I can take off. I'm redlining. And we're still only at nine miles. I've still got four miles to go.

But the kid didn't push past me. He just fell into step beside me.

In a situation like this where you've caught the lead runner, only one of two things can happen. Either you motor by them like they're not even there because everything is clicking and you're feeling awesome. Or you've burnt too many matches trying to catch them, and you can't pass them because you're out of gas. When the kid didn't pass me, I knew I was still in it.

We were humming along, and I saw this guy up the road, a guy in his fifties on a bike, holding out a squeezable water for the kid. Must have been his coach or something. The kid grabbed the water bottle and took a big pull off it. Which was a big no-no.

In Ironman, you can't have outside assistance during a race. If they catch you taking food, clothes, beverages, anything from anyone who's not official race staff, they'll disqualify you right there on the spot. In amateur races, they're a little more low-key about it, but it's still not cool to get an advantage like that. Maybe when you're in the middle of the pack, but certainly not when you're leading.

"Hey, give me that bottle," I said.

The kid tried to tell me what was in it, but I didn't care.

"If it's good for you, man, it's good for me."

If you're taking outside assistance, we're *both* getting it. I drank as much as I could in one pull, then chucked the bottle. Did he want more? I didn't care. He wasn't getting that back from me.

Eleven miles in, I put a little surge on him, and he didn't respond. I got maybe five yards out in front. Then, for whatever reason, I decided, *Fuck it, I'm all in.* And I took off.

We had two miles left, mind you. I was already running as fast as I could and he was ranging from between twenty and only five yards behind me. At one point, I swore he could have reached out and touched me. But the next time I checked, there was a decent gap, though still nothing comfortable. We ground it out to the very end. I ended up beating him by only seventeen seconds.

After the race was over, I talked to the kid for a minute. Great guy, just out of high school, about to go to college for running.

"Listen," I said, "you want some free advice?"

"Sure."

By now the older guy on the bike had rolled over. Turned out he was the kid's dad. I could tell he was listening.

"When you caught me like that, for a split second, I mentally quit. I was like, 'Oh shit, he's got me.' All you had to do was put in a mad surge to get around me. I probably wouldn't have even tried to chase because I felt so defeated. But when you didn't break away, that gave me a second to recover mentally. I was like, 'Oh, he killed himself to get to me.' Catching me and not going past me was bad strategy. You either should have hung back and then made the move or made the move when you caught me. You could have had me."

The dad turned to his kid.

"Are you getting all this? This guy is giving you some invaluable information."

He was right. I'd just given the kid the insight he needed to come to my next race and beat me. If that were to happen, I'd be fine with it. Obsessed as I was with winning, I still valued human greatness more.

More than one person had told me that before races I was like a caged pit bull, ready to tear someone's face off. They were stunned to discover after races that I was as mild and friendly as a golden retriever. What people need to understand is that when we're lining up at the start, you are my competition. Within the confines of what's fair and what's ethical, I'm going to do everything in my power to make you fail and to make me succeed. But the instant I cross that finish line, everything turns on its head. Please know that the minute our competition is over, I am rooting for you with my entire being to have the best race of your life.

Before that gun goes off, the only thing that matters to me

is that I win. By win, I mean that I get the most out of myself, that I refuse to yield to the internal voice campaigning for self-preservation and looking for the easiest way out. The minute I cross the line, what matters to me is my community of athletes. My wife and kids—that's my team, my family, my entire heart. But every single person who dreamed big dreams and got up early and trained their asses off and tried to be better—not just the elites, not even just the finishers, every single person who got up before sunrise with dread, anxiety, and excitement in their hearts and dragged their asses down to the starting line and tried as hard as they could, even if they blew up and their race ended early . . . those people are my tribe. Every single person out there on the field competing is my brother or my sister. While the race is on, it's the theater of war. The minute the race is over, it's a support group, a workshop, a family reunion, a party.

The most genuine moment you'll ever see in professional sports is two fighters hugging after ten or twelve rounds of trying to kill each other. To an outsider, it may seem strange, but they hug because no one better understands the ordeal they've been through—the training camp, the insane pressure, the gauntlet of suffering. Though my wife and kids knew me better than anyone else in the world, those strangers out there on the racecourse understood something about my life that my family couldn't. They understood what it's like to battle this monster we call the marathon.

Of course, the marathon is just a microcosm of all our personal struggles. The quote "Be kind, for everyone you meet is fighting a hard battle" has never been truer than on the racecourse. In contesting the marathon, you aren't just fighting everyone, you're fighting everything. Yes, you're competing against all the other runners out there, but you're also continuing a gauntlet that began long before the starter's gun, a series of obstacles consisting of blisters, soreness, and muscle strains; serious injuries such as tendon and ligament pulls or stress fractures; resistance or resentment from your spouse, family, or job; and, always, mental and physical exhaustion.

Most important, by taking on the marathon, you're fighting against yourself—your weak self, your shadow self, your destructive self that wants to just say "fuck it all" and get a bottle or a bag or a mountain of pills and set your life on fire and watch it burn to the ground. I wanted to win, I wanted to beat everyone, I wanted to annihilate the competition. But that was temporary. What ran through the entire experience was overpowering respect and admiration for my fellow runners. To get out there, to compete, every single person had made an enduring decision to not give in, to stand and fight, to overcome. Runners have the hearts of warriors, and I loved every single one of them.

—

My finishing time of 2:30:57 at the Myrtle Beach Marathon put me within striking distance of the world's fastest over-fifty runners. The World Marathon Majors was a series system in which the champion male and female runners were crowned according to points accrued based on their finishes in the six majors: Tokyo, Boston, London, Berlin, Chicago, and New York. I wasn't going to win that. But within that larger competition were the World Marathon Majors Age Group World Championships for runners over forty, which came down to a single race—the London Marathon on October 3 of that year. I'd just turned fifty, which made it the perfect year to try to dominate my new age class of fifty to fifty-four.

It felt like the stars had aligned for me to be the fastest marathoner over fifty and bring home the championship. Was that goal arrogant, hubristic, unrealistic? Life is for living. If you're not going to try to be the absolute best version of yourself, what's the fucking point? I trained feverishly with the singular purpose of winning London. My coach, Mario, turned me inside out, trying to get my time down. When the race finally rolled around, I felt cautiously optimistic. Was there someone out there running a 2:20 in his fifties? One way to find out.

Every time I competed in a big race, I splurged on first-class travel and accommodation. For London, I stayed at the Four Seasons in Hyde Park. And I'd done all the homework required to understand this marathon. Due to the massive number of runners participating, London had three distinct start areas, each of which had their own corrals. These starting areas were a considerable distance from each other. Most important, from one starting area, you could not tell who was in the other starting areas. All the starting areas would merge onto the same route a few miles into the marathon.

There were a lot of different races unfolding under the umbrella of the massive London marathon. There was a college championship, the British national championship, several age-group championships. My starting area held athletes fifty and older for the World Marathon Majors Age Group World Championships—not a huge group. Forty to forty-four were off in another start, forty-five to forty-nine off in a separate start. When I went through my warm-ups, everything was perfect. We had numbers on our front and back, and our age group listed on the back, so I had my eye on every single runner in my age group. I was in great shape, ready to win. This was my moment.

When the gun went off, I was standing right on the starting line so I could clock every single one of my age-group competitors. I went out hot at 5:35 per mile. After a couple of miles, I was out in front by myself. I wasn't leading the London Marathon per se, but I was leading that start area. It was a bold move, but that way if someone passed me, I knew whom I had to chase down.

As I ran, I heard someone, a race official on the loudspeaker, announcing my name and number as the leader. I knew that there were other areas, but still, it was cool to be leading a start area of the London Marathon with the big motorbikes out in front of me. Just before we all merged around mile three, I looked back. I couldn't even see the field. It was just me, out front, leading my race in the London Marathon, and it felt fucking great. When we merged, I could see a couple hundred yards up the road. No one in my age group in sight.

No race is simple or easy, regardless of the distance. Best-case scenario, you have signed up for a day of suffering and exertion right up to the limit of what you can bear. Sometimes, it feels like every single system in your body is on the verge of failure: you are about to cramp up and throw up and shit your pants and black out and have a heart attack. But for me, to describe the singular experience of racing a marathon, I have to talk about swimming.

Racing a marathon is like kicking off one wall toward the end of your workout and trying to swim from one end of the pool to the other underwater. You've been working hard for a while so you're hyperventilating and quickly running out of oxygen. Then at some point, you think, *How much longer can I hold my breath?* You stare at the far wall and try to calculate how many more strokes it will take to reach it, how many flutter kicks. *Do I have enough oxygen left in my lungs to make it?* It seems impossible. Your arms and legs seem to slow as your heart speeds up. The far wall appears to recede. There's no way you can make it. Still, you know you can go a little longer. A few more strokes. *What then? Will I black out? Will my lungs fill with water? Will I drown? Will I die?* But still, you keep going. *How much farther can I make it before everything shuts down?*

Your brain clouds over. It's not just that your body is moving underwater, your thoughts are moving slowly and laboriously as if they, too, are underwater. In a marathon, your brain gets so starved of glycogen that it's impossible to think clearly or perform even the most basic math. You can't remember how deep you are into the race, you can't remember how much you have left. You're interrogating yourself with this one plaintive question: *Can I hold on can I hold on can I hold on?* Your brain comes back with nothing. At no point does a glamorous, explosive miracle come for you. The wall never opens and draws you in, you never start breathing underwater. But somehow, you keep going, you keep doing it. You hold on.

That day in London, all the interlocking parts fit into place. No one even tried to pass me. I crossed the line at 2:29:54. Maybe I could have run faster at the end but who cares, I fucking won! I was over the moon. I felt so good, so strong, I even jogged back to the Hyde Park Four Seasons. I grabbed my gear and got a taxi to Heathrow to grab the next flight home. I couldn't wait to touch down in the USA a fucking champion.

On the way to the airport, I called my coach to tell him I won.

"Yo, Mario! I fucking won!"

"Oh, man. Ken, you took second. Some guy finished ahead of you."

That was impossible. Someone must have cheated, someone must have cut the course. I watched every runner in my field, no one got past me.

"What? No, he definitely didn't beat me, I saw every single other competitor out there. Dude, we got a course cutter. We're going to get this guy."

"I mean, we can look into it. But it looks legit."

I felt like I'd been hit in the skull with a brick.

As it turned out, one of the other starts was the British National Championship. An over-fifty British runner had chosen his start area based on the British National Championship, a much smaller title than the World Marathon Majors. He'd hammered the first three miles around 5:00 per mile and gotten far enough out in front of me that when we merged, I couldn't see him. He then barely held on to beat me by less than a minute.

Probably 99 percent of people racing a marathon are just racing against their own time. It'd have been nice to know during the race that he was a minute up the road when the multiple start areas merged. Maybe I wouldn't have caught him, but I'd have killed myself trying had I only known he and I were competing. Nevertheless, it provided great motivation for future races.

I knew that the only two people who cared about this result were me and this other runner, but I cared about it tremendously. Could he beat me one-on-one? I'd never find out and it ate away at my soul. Still not good enough.

CHAPTER ELEVEN

NEXT WE TAKE BERLIN

LOCKDOWN HAD ACCELERATED THE SCHEDULING FOR ALL THE MARATHON majors, so as the world slowly opened back up, it made for unusual timing. Tokyo, Boston, and London were typically spring marathons, with New York, Berlin, and Chicago in the fall. But in 2021 with the calendar having been completely shuffled by Covid shutdowns, all six of the World Marathon Major races took place in only forty-two days. Some high-profile runners viewed it as a once-in-a-lifetime chance to run all six majors in less than two months, a grueling undertaking.

Though London had taken place on October 3 in 2021, the New York City Marathon was only five weeks later, on November 7. I hadn't had New York on my schedule for the year, but after my hopes were dashed in London, it looked tempting. I was trained up. I was healthy. I was sharp. My 2:29:54 hadn't won the day in London, but maybe in New York I could get the job done. I hadn't registered, but I had enough goodwill and qualifying times to call in a favor and get a bib in the "local elite" corral. I was in.

Of course, "healthy" is a transitory state for a marathon runner. I'd felt great at the end of the London Marathon, but I developed a sore calf going into New York, a spasm deep in the muscle that just wouldn't go away. I'd been getting treatment from a roster of different physical therapists and doing everything I could to iron it out right up to the day of the race, but it wouldn't budge. Part of me said punt. I'd run my ass off in London, I'd barely had time to recover . . . and if I hadn't won London when I had zero issues, I wasn't going to win with a calf that was screaming before the race began. And the other part of me said *Just shut the fuck up and run.* I got my ass down to the start.

I'd run New York enough times that I knew the drill: catch the ferry from South Street Seaport to Staten Island wearing a bunch of old clothes you don't care about, mill around in the freezing cold with a ton of other runners stretching and yapping and trying to keep warm, strip down and chuck your old clothes, run as hard as you can for as long as you can, then freeze your ass off again at the finish. But because of the time I'd run in London, I got special status and was assigned to the local elite corral, basically starting with the pros. Instead of waiting outside at the standard staging area at Fort Wadsworth at the base of the Verrazzano Bridge in Staten Island with all the other runners, we got to wait for our start indoors at the nearby Ocean Breeze Athletic Complex. The upgrade was a welcome change. The facility was beautiful, catered with fresh bagels and coffee. There was a plush indoor track so you could warm up and get loose. They even had massage therapists. As our start time approached, they drove us out to the corral in nice new coach buses instead of beat-up old school buses. It was a rare glimpse into the life of a professional runner and my heart soared just being there.

We ended up only being outside for a few minutes, but I'd prepared to wait in the cold like usual, so I was wearing an old button-down flannel shirt and a pair of crappy old cotton sweatpants. Probably looked like a farmer going out to feed the chickens. I started chatting to this tall, thin, good-looking kid.

"How you doing, buddy, you ready to do this thing?"

"I mean, I'm here so I hope so! What about you?"

The guy looked kind of familiar. I wondered whether we'd maybe run together before.

"I'm ready, baby, I'm ready to go. What are you trying to run today?"

"Oh, I don't know. What are you trying to run?"

"I'd love to run under two-thirty."

"Holy shit, really? That's so fast! I'd be stoked if I finish in under three hours."

I looked at him sideways for a second. Who in this corral was only trying to run sub-three? Finally, I connected the dots. There was a start wave for celebrities, and they started right behind the pro runners. I'd seen this kid's face before, just not in person.

"Bro. You're the host of that show *Catfish* on MTV."

He smiled.

"My name is Nev Schulman, nice to meet you."

I introduced myself and we shook hands.

"Dude, my wife is a huge fan of your show. She loved the documentary, too."

"Let's send her a message!"

"You're going to run the race carrying a phone?"

"You don't have your phone?"

He looked appalled. To be fair, few New Yorkers would ever be caught dead without their cell phones.

"Are you crazy? I'm not carrying anything I don't absolutely need. Under this crap, I got running shorts, a singlet, and one gel."

"One gel?" Nev started laughing. "Jesus, I've got all kinds of gels, I've got my phone, I've got lip balm, I've got wet wipes and hand sanitizer . . . I've got everything."

"Are you crazy? Why would you carry that here? It's like carrying sand running through a desert! There's practically a sushi bar at each aid station. They have everything. Gels, bananas, oranges, water. You could run a thousand miles on this course and never want for anything."

We were dying laughing, each of us convinced the other was out of his head. But he took out his phone and we took a selfie, and he texted the picture to Shelby. She loved it, and Nev and I have remained friends to this day.

I hadn't mentioned it to Nev because I didn't want to give my anxiety more oxygen than necessary, but I carried two other things with me as well. I had a twenty-dollar bill and a MetroCard tucked into the little pocket in the back of my shorts. I had my calf all wrapped up with that black Kinesio tape, but it was still barely holding together. I was nervous it was going to derail my race. Realistically, I might not even finish.

When they fired off the starting cannon, we took off. Some days, you run a race, and you just feel like you're floating. It feels effortless, and you're just like, *Oh my God, please let this feeling last forever.* This was not that day. Every step was labored in New York. I felt like I was carrying a piano on my back. And from the drop, my calf was howling like a banshee with every footfall. I was never going to make it.

Then somehow, three or four miles into the race, the muscle spasm in my calf just released completely. It was like my leg finally realized, "This guy's not going to stop, we may as well let go." It felt incredible. There is no better feeling during a race than when the pain finally stops. For a couple of minutes, I felt like I was flying.

Then, with the pain gone, I realized that I was completely out of gas. I'd been focused solely on the pain in my leg. With it no longer eating up all my attention, I had to deal with a bigger problem. Fit as I was, I'd just taken my body to the limits of endurance not five weeks earlier. Now, every single part of it was begging to quit.

The beta voice in my mind immediately chimed in. *Dude, just shut it down. You had a good race, and you broke two-thirty in London. That was an incredible day. No one expects you to run that fast twice in a year.* I was feeding myself every excuse under the sun. But every time I got close to convincing myself to stop or even let up, I'd force myself to recall how I felt in Kona after quitting.

When you were eight years old and those kids shoved you down in Alabama, you said you'd never surrender again. When you pulled your little diva act on the hockey team and got dropped from the roster, you said you'd never phone it in again. When you allowed yourself to get bullied at Euro Brokers, you said you'd never be anyone's bitch again. After you wussed out at Kona, you said you'd never quit again. But you let Percocets own you for a solid decade. Subutex had its boot on your neck for years. And now you're ready to quit again because you're tired? Because your little leg hurts? Do you have a tummy ache, too? Fine, just give up, tap out, go cry about it, go get high about it. And be second best for the rest of your fucking life.

It's easy to refuse to quit when things are going well. Everyone's full of inspirational bravado when they're on the internet, posting from an easy chair with a plate of nachos in one hand and a cold beer in the other. It's difficult to refuse to quit when every single muscle in your body is wailing and crying, just begging you to stop. And for me it never got easier. There wasn't a single fun thing that happened in that race. Everything sucked. I was at my absolute limit, on the verge of quitting every single second of that marathon. Every fucking step was torture.

As I was coming up on the finishing stretch in Central Park, a small cheer went up from the crowd. My online profile had started ticking up after my wins in Pasadena and Myrtle Beach and my performance in London, but when people started clapping I knew they weren't clapping for me. I glanced back, and rapidly closing in on me was Shalane Flanagan. I didn't know Shalane personally, but I absolutely knew who she was. She was a Boston gal, from Marblehead, less than an hour away from Somerville. She'd brought home a silver medal from the 2008 Olympics and in 2017, she became the first American to win the women's New York City Marathon in forty years. She was one of the brave and foolish souls running all six of the World Marathon Majors in forty-two days. New York was the last one, so she was spending everything she had left, absolutely storming her way to the finish line. Shalane was a badass competitor in every way. I should have felt honored and humbled to be sharing the same stretch of pavement with Boston's own Shalane Flanagan. Instead, a petty, insecure thought popped into my head: *I am not getting chicked.*

"Getting chicked" is a term in long-distance running that means getting beaten by a girl. I say "girl," not "woman," because it's a juvenile, schoolyard sentiment. I'd gotten beaten and beaten easily by many women over the years. No shame in it. Women marathoners are hardcore. They've had to be. In 1966, after Bobbi Gibb had been denied entry to the Boston Marathon because women weren't allowed, she showed up and ran without a number to prove that it could be done. The next year, when Kathrine Switzer covertly entered the race by writing down only her first initial on the registration so they wouldn't know she was a woman, the race director tried to tackle her off the course during the race. Female athletes are athletes, and they deserve every inch of respect, honor, and money their male counterparts get.

I loved my three boys but when I became a father, the first kind of father I became was a girl dad. No one was going to tell my daughter she couldn't do anything just because she was a girl. At every turn when we were raising her, we always made sure Tensae knew she could do anything the boys could do, and I'd fight till my last dying breath to ensure she had the same rights and opportunities as the boys around her.

But that day in New York, all that went out the window. In an instant, I devolved into a typical insecure guy. My caveman brain thought, *I am not getting beaten by a girl*, and I dug in harder. Never trust your brain when it's telling you that you're at your limit. You always have a little bit more to give.

I started sprinting like a lunatic. I probably looked crazy because my muscles were spasming and my form was horrible, but I sprinted all the way through the finish line. And as ugly as it was, that petty insecurity worked. I ended up finishing right in front of Shalane with a time of 2:33:31. She came in one second later.

The minute I got back to my hotel, I tried to look up the race results. I could see my time but for some reason—perhaps just the sheer amount of data to be logged from the biggest marathon in the world—I couldn't see where I'd finished in my age group. I tried to hack the system and look up other fast runners my age to figure out what their times were, but it was impossible for me to figure out the final standing. I went to sleep that night just hoping and praying I'd managed to win my age group.

I woke up the next morning to a text from my friend Amar Kuchinad. *Holy shit, dude, you won the entire masters division.*

Though it was significantly slower than my time in London, though I'd felt like dogshit the entire race, it turned out my time wasn't just fast enough to win my fifty-to-fifty-four age group. I'd won the entire masters division of over-forty runners. To the best of my knowledge, it was the first time anyone over fifty had won the masters division at a major marathon. I hadn't even thought that was a possibility. I'd just been praying that I won my age group. The next-closest finisher came in at 2:33:34. I'd won the masters division by three seconds. Thanks, Shalane!

By this point, I'd imagined myself to be a seasoned marathoner. I knew the distance, I knew the race, I even knew what it took to win. But the marathon is so massive and so profound, it didn't matter whether it was your first or your hundredth, it always had something new to teach you. After I'd had a moment to process it, I realized this marathon held three lessons for me.

1. **ALWAYS SHOW UP.** Before the race, I gave myself all kinds of reasons not to show up. I was exhausted from London; I hadn't given myself enough time to recover; my calf was locked up. I overcame every one of those reasons because I knew my greatest

competitor was the race itself. To run that hard and that fast for that long takes a toll on the human body—not just my body, all bodies. If you look at marathon results closely like I did, you'll see it's rare for one person to dominate race after race because injuries are so common and it's so hard to stay healthy. Yes, every marathon is a competition, but every marathon is also a gamble. My time wouldn't have won the masters division any other year. But you never know who's going to bail out, who's running sick or injured, or who's just going to have a bad day. If you bail, it's 100 percent certain that you lose. If you show up, you just might win.

2. **FIGHT TO THE DEATH.** During the race, I gave myself all kinds of reasons to give up. I'd done well enough in London that New York didn't really matter; if I hadn't won London fresh, I wasn't going to win New York tired; I just felt bad and hurt and wasn't having any fun. I overcame every one of those reasons because I knew my greatest competitor was that beta voice in my head. I'd fed my body, I'd trained my body, I trusted my body to do the work I knew it could do. When 49 percent of my spirit wanted to stop running, drop out, and catch a cab back to my hotel, the other 51 percent of my spirit pinned my weaker self to the wall with a forearm across the throat and told it to shut the fuck up.

3. **FUEL IS FUEL.** When I glanced back and saw Shalane Flanagan on my heels and sprinting like a cheetah, I could have just rolled over. She was a world-class athlete. She'd won New York in 2017 with a time of 2:26:53, which I knew I couldn't beat on

my best day. She was a legit running celebrity, and I could have just reveled in her company and gotten my ass over the line. But seeing her gaining on me tapped into my insecurity, my vulnerability, my misogyny. Fifty years old, proud husband, proud father of a daughter, a true believer of equality for everyone across the board . . . and I couldn't bear the thought of being beaten by a girl. It was an ugly feeling in a weak moment, and I'm not proud of it. But that shitty chauvinistic knee-jerk response compelled me to dig a little deeper and kick like I never had before in that last two hundred meters. Without Shalane and, specifically, without my insecure response to Shalane, I'd never have won. A win is a win is a win. Whether it's love or hate or hope or fear that drives you, it doesn't matter. It's all fuel. If it makes you faster, lean into it.

At the time, winning the masters division in the New York City Marathon was my proudest athletic accomplishment. I even got a cut of the prize money. A month after the race, they mailed me a check for $3,000. It was nothing compared to the thousands and thousands of dollars I'd spent over the years to enter races and pay for airfare and hotels. Still, I had that check framed, and it hangs over my desk to this day.

That unexpected masters win catapulted me into the company of my heroes. Meb Keflezighi is a marathon hall of famer. He won silver at the 2004 Olympics in the marathon. He won the New York City Marathon in 2009, becoming the first American to win it since 1982. In 2014, he won the Boston Marathon, the first American to win it since 1983. And in 2015, he won the masters division at the New York City Marathon. Just like me. Somewhere in the universe was a list of New York City Marathon masters winners, and our names were on that list together. It was too cool.

In 2011, I'd run the New York City Half Marathon with a time of 1:21:48 and thought I was hot shit. We'd only brought Tensae home three months earlier, but I insisted that Shelby bring her out in the freezing cold because I knew Gebregziabher Gebremariam, the defending champion of the previous year's New York City Marathon, would be there. He was Ethiopian, so we had to get a picture of her wrapped in an Ethiopian flag next to him. We'd also snagged a picture of Tensae and me with another elite runner, Abdi Abdirahman. He'd had an insane career, competing in five Olympic Games spanning twenty years. Imagine for a minute the amount of talent and sacrifice it takes to run at Olympic caliber for two decades. At thirty-nine, he became the oldest runner to make it to the podium at the New York City Marathon. At forty-three, he became the oldest American runner to make it to the Olympics. In 2017, he won the masters division, edging out Meb Keflezighi for the top spot.

Abdi and I had become friends and had kept in touch. The day after the marathon when the results were announced, I got a text from him: *Congrats, champion! Welcome to the club, my brother.*

It blew my mind. Ten years earlier, I'd just been some random blowhard, wanting a picture with an elite runner. Now that elite runner was messaging me, welcoming me as an equal. I was walking on air.

But soon enough, we had to get back to real life. The day after the race, I had to fly to Portland, Oregon, for a work meeting. As soon as I got on the plane, I noticed that sitting behind me was the pride of Boston, Shalane Flanagan.

"You're right behind me again? I can't get rid of you!"

She gave me a funny look, and I told her the whole story. When I finished, she held out her hand for a knuckle bump.

"Glad I could help," she said with a grin.

The Boston Marathon—the longest-running marathon in the world—was scheduled for April 18 in 2022. Growing up in Somerville, I don't remember ever learning about it, I just always knew it existed. Running the race felt like some kind of homecoming, and I was determined to bring home a win. But I knew every step would be a battle, even before the gun went off.

Everyone knows getting to the starting line in Boston is a clusterfuck. Boston is a point-to-point marathon, so though you finish in the heart of downtown, you start twenty-five miles out in the sticks in Hopkinton. Normally, it's this sleepy little unassuming town. But every April, thirty thousand runners show up to start the world's most famous marathon on a tiny two-lane road. Everyone is kept waiting in corrals until their wave, at which point event staff will frantically begin funneling runners toward the starting line. It means you have to be out there three or four hours before the race. In the Northeast in April, that can mean hours milling around in the cold or rain before what could be the race of your life.

In running, there's a distinction between amateurs, elites, and pros. The amateur class includes everyone from people running their first 5K to trained marathoners who just can't make it onto the podium. Elite runners place near the front in local, national, or even international races. They train rigorously, but their perks are limited to some comped race entries and maybe free gear. Pros compete at the highest level: national championships, World Marathon Majors, the Olympics. Running is their singular calling, and they earn their living from races, appearance fees, sponsorships, and endorsements. Pros live, eat, and breathe running, and they reap the rewards for their drive.

But in running, as it is in everything else, it's all about whom you know. In 2018, my friend Des Linden had won the women's Boston Marathon, the first American to do so in thirty-three years. Pro runners were allowed a "plus one" on the pro bus to the starting line to accommodate a coach or an agent. When I'd arrived for the Boston race in 2019, Des reached out and offered up her guest spot on the bus. Thank God she did because she had the whole thing figured out.

Through Des, I'd met Mary Kate Shea, the senior director of Professional Athletes. She reminded me of so many women I'd known growing up—tough, honest, hardworking Irish women who weren't particularly warm and fuzzy. MK was sarcastic and outspoken, constantly busting your balls to try to cover up that she had a heart of gold. I liked her from the minute I met her.

I'd been a hanger-on in 2019, but winning the masters division in New York opened up a lot of doors for me. I reached out to MK, and though she grumbled about it as I knew she would, she got me into the race. There was no elite amateur class or "local elites," as we were called in New York. Boston was just the pros and then everybody else. I hit Des up and, once again, she got me on the pro bus with her. Those connections made a world of difference.

On the morning of the race I met Des early and because of her experience, we had it dialed. We grabbed seats in the very front of the bus so we'd be the first ones off. It got us to the start an hour or two before the race and dropped us off at the Korean Presbyterian Church in Greater Boston. The church was as much a community center as a house of worship. For years, it had offered itself as a staging area for professional runners before the race. Behind the church, there was a little side street that only the pros had access to. It was probably less than a quarter of a mile, but you could at least run back and forth and get loose. Inside the auditorium, organizers had yoga mats laid out for runners to stretch and basically just hang out and stay warm till the start. And the church was right next to the starting line, so you didn't have to shuffle a mile in the cold from the outdoor staging area, a field at Hopkinton High School. There was nothing plush or showy about it, but having all those little conveniences, those little advantages—well, the cumulative difference was night and day. But if you work hard, you get the spoils of hard work.

When the race officials announced the pros, I walked out with them at the very back of the pack. The pros were in the first corral with just a rope separating them from the top amateur qualifiers directly behind. Because I'd walked out with the pros, I was in the pro corral, in the very back. As the pros started, I just stepped back. After a few minutes, they dropped the rope and I joined all the local and elite amateurs and we walked up to the starting line. I was right at the front of the race—exactly where I wanted to be.

Pros were all business. The vibe in the church auditorium had been muted and serious, like the locker room before a big fight. There'd been no chitchat or fooling around, everyone full of nervous energy but ruthlessly focused on their own prerace routine. Only difference was that we were all going out there to do battle with ourselves. The amateur corral was much looser: people talking and joking, taking pictures, checking their pedometers, and so on. They were there to have fun, maybe bring home a personal best. Not me. I was there with a singular purpose: to suffer enough to win.

A photo surfaced a couple of days later that captured the moment perfectly. That year, two C-130 Hercules military transport aircraft from nearby Bradley Air National Guard Base were scheduled to do a flyover of the marathon route. They passed overhead just before the amateur start. A photographer snapped a picture of us seconds before the gun went off. Virtually every runner in the photo was looking in a different direction: watching the planes overhead, smiling at the photographer, looking at the crowd, looking at their shoes. I was out front and center, game face on, the only runner staring right down that course to the finish line.

To win a marathon, you must do two things. First, you must accurately gauge the disparity between when your mind tells you you're done and when your body tells you you're done. When your mind says "Oh, I'm done," you're nowhere near done. I've quit many races in my mind and then forced my body to keep going till it broke the tape.

Second, you need to time your body's collapse perfectly. Running out of gas at mile twenty-two is as bad as cruising through the finish ready to run another four miles. To win, you've got to get it right on the nose. You must spend everything you have—not just your calories or your energy or your strength but all your frustration, your anger, your hope, your joy, everything—and you need all your reserves to expire with that last footfall.

That day in Boston, it all came together. I crossed the line at 2:30:21, a full three minutes faster than the next-fastest runner my age. I'd done exactly what I'd come to do. I won my age group at the legendary Boston Marathon, and won it pretty handily, too. Still, that twenty-one seconds ate at me. "I ran Boston sub-2:30" was such a great, tidy story. But I couldn't say that. Somehow, I could win and still not be good enough.

My performance in the previous majors won me access to the pro start in Berlin in 2022 and all the accoutrements that went with that level of elite marathoning. Instead of standing around in a cold field with all the other humps, I got to hang out in a posh heated tent. I'd picked up a great sponsorship from the athletic clothing company Saysky, so I had my whole matching kit on, my name on all my gear like a pro. I walked in there with all the confidence in the world. I looked like a champion, I felt like a champion, I was fit and ready to go to war.

When I walked into the men's pro tent, all the different national teams were sitting together—the Chinese in one spot, the Japanese in another, the Americans in the back. I was probably the worst runner in the tent but somehow, people knew who I was. One of the Americans greeted me with, "Yo, Ken, what's up, man?" It was shocking to me that some of the top American runners knew who I was. I felt like a legit professional runner, and it felt fucking amazing.

All the seats were taken except for one with the Kenyans, right next to Eliud Kipchoge, the greatest runner in marathon history. I wasn't about to let this moment slip by. I walked right over there, knuckle-bumped them all.

"Hey, what's up, guys? You mind if I sit?"

"Sure, sure, have a seat."

I sat right next to Kipchoge, smiled, and said hello.

"How you doing, brother?"

We started talking like it was nothing. It was insane. Kipchoge is the greatest of all time, the only runner in recorded human history to ever run a sub-two-hour marathon. Here we were, chatting away, just two dudes hanging out. I felt like a little kid in the locker room with Tom Brady before the Super Bowl. I started to organize my shit, put on my shoes. Right next to me, Kipchoge stripped completely naked and started putting on his race uniform . . . because why wouldn't he? We're just a couple of fellow marathoners, comrades getting ready to do battle against this heroic, timeless event on one of the largest stages in the world.

I walked out of the tent with all the pros to the starting line. All the other runners were backed up in the corrals for half a mile, but we walked to the front of the race, right in front of the historic Brandenburg Gate. There's a causeway there so we started loosening up. I'd jog a mile, then do four or five ten-second sprints to get everything loose and warmed up, get the blood pumping. There were people crowding the viewing area, not even trying to see the pros race, just trying to catch a glimpse of them warming up.

Two or three years before, I absolutely would've been one of those rabid running fans, busting their asses just to see one of their heroes in the flesh. Now here I was, in with my heroes, warming up with the Kenyan pros. Talk about surreal. I thought to myself, *I'm here. This is it. Regardless of what happens, I made it here.* No one could take this away from me.

And because of all these things, I was telling myself, *All right, I'm fit, I'm ready, I'm going to go for it.* This was a huge mistake.

In the marathon, you have to be patient. You have to ease into it, no matter how good you feel. You always run a little fast right at the beginning when the race takes off just to get a little separation, kind of find your groove and avoid elbowing it out with others. I liked to get out front and let others worry about me, rather than run around other people. But after that clusterfuck in the beginning, you've got to lay off the gas, you've got to be a little conservative.

After the start, the pro men quickly took off. Then the first group of pro women slowly got away from me. About twenty or thirty seconds per mile behind them was the second group of pro women, probably the fifteenth- to thirtieth-place finishers. They were running almost exactly 5:30 per mile. The fastest I'd ever run a marathon was 5:39 per mile.

I quickly did the math in my head. A 5:30 pace would get me in there around 2:26, way faster than I'd ever run. Probably too fast. But I was still feeling buoyant from my masters division win in New York. I'd outrun the mighty Shalane Flanagan in the final seconds, hadn't I? I was just like, *Fuck it. I'm just going to tuck in with this group of girls and see how long I can go.*

The answer to that question was sixteen miles and change, because by seventeen miles, I was at death's door. I was seeing stars and people were passing me like I was standing still. Jesus, I felt like I was going in reverse, like I was going to drop dead. Though I was running incredibly slowly by this point, I kept running as fast as I could, just holding on for dear life.

The second I crossed the finish line, I whispered "medic" to a race official. I was panicking. I got off to the side and collapsed, convinced that death was a possibility. "Win or die trying" feels like a badass mantra until you get to the "die trying" part. The people who were assigned to help the finishers came and threw me on something that looked like a World War II stretcher, with two big wheels on it, and carted my carcass into the medical tent. They gave me an IV, maybe two, but I was so delirious, I can't even remember it.

I'd hoped to run 2:27. I came in at 2:35:48. A disastrous day. I went out too fast like an asshole and blew up my entire race. As soon as I got medically cleared to leave the site and got back to my hotel room, I called my wife, devastated, trying to choke back tears and failing.

"Ken, Ken, honey, what's wrong?"

"I just feel so humiliated."

"In front of who? Nobody there cares that you had a bad day."

"Just in front of myself, I guess. I just feel so ashamed that I fucked it all up."

"Ken, listen to me. This does no good for anyone. You have got to ease up on yourself."

But, as it turned out, only one guy in my age group ran faster than me. I'd fucked myself by going out too fast . . . but because I was determined to empty the tank, to give it my all, I still got second in my age group. I didn't know how to feel about it.

Sometimes, moments of great emotional importance take a while to settle. A week after Berlin, I still hadn't gotten my head right. I felt the stink of shame on me from finishing second when bad strategy was the only thing that'd held me back from winning. Shelby wasn't having any of it.

"Ken, you got to let it go. Knowing how bad you were suffering, I'm prouder of you for finishing than I'd have been if you'd won. You win a lot. But showing that kind of toughness and wherewithal and staying power is far more impressive than winning another one. You could have quit—and I'd love you exactly the same if you had—but because you had the internal fortitude to hang in there, you got second in your age group, and that counts, damn it. You showed that you have the determination to stay in the fight even when you're on the edge of breaking down. That's heart. It shows you're not just a winner, you're a champion. It's an incredible lesson for the kids. That's not something I can teach them."

As usual, what Shelby had said made sense. Maybe my heart wasn't singing like it did after a win, but the more I thought on it, the more I realized she had a great point.

Any race I enter, every race I enter, I'm there to win. When I don't win, it eats at me. Though it took me a minute to get there, blowing up in Berlin does not eat at me at all. If anything, Berlin is a loss I am proud of. I may be prouder of losing Berlin than I'd have been of winning.

People say "I did my best" when they fail at something. Bullshit. Ninety-nine times out of a hundred, they did *not* do their best. Me, I'm leaving a race with a gold medal on my chest or I'm leaving in an ambulance. If I blow up, if I leave on a stretcher, I may not feel as good as I would have if I'd won, but I will have clarity. And I will have peace. Maybe the event beat me, maybe another runner beat me, maybe just the day beat me. But if I give up on myself, if I give in to that weaker voice, if I don't spend it all, then I know that *I beat me*. The other guy wasn't better, I destroyed my race by not giving it my all. I can't live with that. You've got to do your best. Empty the tank. Spend it all. Fight to the bitter end. The race is worth it, the day is worth it, you are worth it.

—

Fourteen days after nearly dying in Berlin, I ran 2:29 in the Chicago Marathon and took second in my age group. I got fooled in London and I screwed up in Berlin, but I'd still had a massive year. More important, I was learning from my mistakes, still clawing my way forward. The World Championship had been tantalizingly close, but still just out of reach.

Poring over it obsessively, I tried to divine what the future held. Did my big wins mean I was ramping up for a World Championship the next year? Or did my dumb mistakes mean that I'd never make it? I couldn't tell, and it chewed me up inside.

CHAPTER TWELVE

ONWARD, UPWARD, INWARD

IN JANUARY 2023, I FOUND MYSELF AT THE BOTTOM OF THE WELL. ON THE surface, everything looked great. I was making great money. I was winning races and garnering respect from my heroes. I was getting recognized online and in the media as a good runner. I had my dream family: a pack of kids, both adopted and biological, and a beautiful, razor-sharp wife. We'd relocated to Nashville in 2021 and we were living in a beautiful new house—another slice of heaven, this time southern style. My father had even stepped it up and built a relationship with our kids. Given all my successes, I should have felt totally fulfilled. But somehow happiness just wasn't happening.

After a big race, it was normal for me to go into a bit of a depression. Having a big goal kept me laser-focused on making progress and prevented me from being alone with my thoughts. But after the goal's completion, it was easy to get mired in mundane, day-to-day shit.

This emotional plunge was different, though. I'd wrapped up the most intense stretch of my athletic life—performing for the first time on a global stage, running all six World Marathon Majors in eighteen months—and the comedown was savage. It all cascaded into intense anxiety. I wasn't being as good a parent as I knew I could be. My relationship with my wife had become so icy and strained that it bled over and negatively affected my relationships with my children. If I'm honest about it, my marriage was dangling by a thread.

Shelby and I had a bad argument one night—a spat that left her in tears. For the life of me, I can't recall what it had been about, but I remember her final entreaty.

"Ken, when you act crazy, you make me feel like I'm teaching kindergarten again and there's this little boy who keeps going out on the playground and picking fistfights. Just fight after fight after fight. And then he comes in, his face all banged up, and he's picked me this little bouquet of dandelions. And he's like 'Here, Mrs. Rideout, I picked these for you.' And he's just the sweet little kid who doesn't know how to handle himself. Ken, the dandelions—they're beautiful, they're so sweet. But they don't erase the constant battles. Why's it got to be war all the time? Everyone loves the dandelion guy—what's stopping you from just being the dandelion guy?"

My inability to be at peace with myself pissed me off. This wasn't the way it was supposed to be. I thought if I got sober and did all these things—build a career, settle down and get married, have kids—that it'd transform who I was, how I felt inside. But I was still dealing with the feelings of worthlessness, insecurity, and anxiety. I started having irrational suicidal ideations. I didn't want to kill myself, but I often thought that if a car ran me over while I was running, that'd be okay. That scared the shit out of me.

The races I won, the work I did, the money I made—it was never enough. I ran every single morning but that wasn't enough. So I lifted weights in the afternoon but that wasn't enough. When I wasn't training, I spent 90 percent of my waking hours shut up in my office, staring at my computer for ten or twelve hours because I always felt like I had to do more. I was hyperaware of what I was doing but felt powerless to stop it. I knew I had to find an answer. I was desperate.

I was friends with Chris Spencer, an offensive lineman in the NFL for ten years. When I confided in him that I'd been struggling, he mentioned Onsite, a four-day intensive inpatient trauma healing program in rural Tennessee. I rapidly clicked through the website, anxiety mounting in me. It looked like they were selling Cialis and horseback rides and sunsets—how was this going to help me? I called Chris.

"Yo, Ken, what's up, bro?"

"Chris, listen. This program at Onsite. What do you think? Just yes or no. Very simple."

"Yes. Most important thing I've ever done."

"Thanks, I'll call you back."

I trusted Chris. So, before I lost my nerve, I called them up, right then and there. Ten thousand dollars. Cash up front, no cancellations, no refunds. For ten thousand dollars, it better be a fucking magic miracle. I signed up.

Whenever I sign up for a race, I learn every possible thing about it beforehand. I research the weather, the altitude, the elevation change, the winning times, who's putting it on . . . everything. It's like a military strike—I want to know every bit of information, every single possible detail before I even get on the plane. I did the opposite for Onsite. I wrote down the most basic details on my calendar and then I tried to push Onsite out of my head completely. I knew nothing about it, and I didn't want to know anything about it. I knew there'd be rules and regulations and daily schedules, things you had to do and things you couldn't do, details about food and lodging. But I was so anxious about going, I couldn't force myself to look it up. I kept thinking *I really need to call them*, and then I'd do everything to avoid calling them.

Finally, the day rolled around. I drove the hour and change out to Cumberland Furnace on the verge of tears. I felt like I was reporting for a stretch in prison. Cumberland Furnace wasn't a city, it wasn't even a town. It was an "unincorporated township"—just a post office and a few houses and that's it. It'd have been easy to just turn around and bail. I didn't have the dealer network in Tennessee that I'd had in New York, but money opened doors—why not just buy a hundred Percs and spend the next four days in a blissful opiate haze in some opulent, anonymous hotel room in downtown Nashville?

But I'd committed to do it. I knew I had to be a better father for my kids, a better husband to my wife, and a better man for my family. After I quit in Kona, I'd promised myself that I'd never give up on myself again. *Win or die trying* didn't just apply to races. I told myself that it covered everything. But in that moment, I'd have happily run a hundred miles if it meant I didn't have to go and talk to strangers about my stupid fucking feelings. In the end, I didn't turn around for one reason: the only thing that scared me more than going to Onsite was *not* going to Onsite and returning to my unraveling life with my head still full of hornets.

I suppose the campus was nice enough. Onsite itself was a small cluster of buildings on an old homestead. There was a stately manor house still decorated like it would have been a hundred years ago, very elegant and elevated. There was a newer barndominium, which was clearly the main headquarters, surrounded by six or eight cottages. The buildings were tucked into rolling hills and big open horse pastures surrounded by thick forests. I sure wasn't in a mood to appreciate it. Some people were walking around outside, not just aimlessly strolling but clearly engaged and focused, deep in thought. There was a unique vibe in the air, chill but serious. It filled my heart with dread. I hadn't even started, and I couldn't fucking wait for this shit to be over.

Sure enough, as soon as I checked in, they asked for my phone and laptop.

Ah shit.

"When do we get it back?"

"Monday, at the conclusion of the program."

Fuck me. It was Thursday afternoon.

"Oh my God, I haven't told anyone I'm here. I haven't put an out-of-office message on my emails. I should have changed my outgoing voicemail."

The woman looked at me coolly, without saying a word, like she'd been through this a million times before.

"You know what? Fuck it. We're here. Let's do this."

I took my laptop out of my backpack and pushed it and my phone across the desk.

Someone gave me a little tour of the facility: a modern, higher-end dining hall; the music room; the meeting rooms. It certainly wasn't posh, but it wasn't a dump either. It was just basic, functional, minimalist. We were here because we had work to do, and they weren't going to make any effort to disguise that.

At the end of the tour, they pointed me toward the little cottage I'd be staying in for the next four nights. When I walked in, it was just one big room with basic furnishings and three double beds. They were giving me roommates, like I was back in the fucking dorms at Framingham State? No way. I'd hated it when I was nineteen and I certainly wasn't going to stand for it now. I went back to the reception area.

"I think there's been a mistake, you guys accidentally put me in a room with roommates."

The woman behind the counter smiled at me and nodded.

"That's no accident. That's your room and those are your roommates."

"Listen, I can dig out the emails and stuff but I'm pretty sure I signed up and paid for a private room."

"We don't offer private rooms here so it's unlikely you were promised one. I can pull up the welcome email on my computer here if you'd like."

"No, that's fine, that's . . . I mean, I feel like that's something you should make people aware of when they're signing up but okay, that's fine, whatever."

I walked back to the room, all pissy. I guess the good news was that, since I was there first, I got first pick of beds. I nabbed the one farthest from the bathroom so I wouldn't have to deal with anyone's bullshit. After I put all my stuff away, I just sat on my bed with no idea what to do with myself. I hadn't read any of the welcome emails they'd sent, so I hadn't even thought to bring a book. Thank God there was a little bookstore next to the reception desk. But of course, it was all self-help books. I bought a copy of *Atomic Habits* and then stalked back to my room.

I was sitting on my bed when another guy walked in. He was a tall, athletic, handsome dude in his thirties with a beard. He nabbed the bed closest to the bathroom—no one wanted to be stuck in the middle. Neither of us were very upbeat to say the least, but he was friendly enough.

"Hey, how you doing, I'm Eric."

"I'm Ken, nice to meet you. You get in okay?"

"Yeah, not too bad. Guess we'll see how this goes, huh?"

"Right? I guess we'll find out. Hey, did, uh, did you play sports? I mean . . . you don't need to answer that."

They'd been real clear at check-in that it was first names only. We weren't supposed to know who the other people were in their real lives.

"Yeah, I played sports."

"Did you play in college?"

"Yep."

"What'd you play?"

"Football and baseball."

"Did you play after college?"

He grinned at my interrogation, probably not the first time he'd been through it.

"Yeah. I played for Denver and the New York Jets."

"Oh shit, you're Eric Decker. Man, it's really nice to meet you."

He put his hands up and smiled sheepishly.

"Got me dead to rights."

"Hey, fair's fair. My last name is Rideout. Ken Rideout."

"Mum's the word, Ken Rideout," he said with a slow, sad smile, and we bumped knuckles.

Decker was a regular, down-to-earth dude. We hit it off, so we ended up spending a lot of our time there together. An older guy showed up to grab the middle bed, a banking consultant. He seemed a bit uncomfortable but quickly revealed himself to be a very smart and kind person. Decker and I were both in the individual intensive course. There'd be group events in the morning and evening, but for the bulk of the program we'd be one-on-one with our individual therapists. Our first group therapy session was that night.

The group meetings were kind of like NA or AA, mostly support meetings for people to share their experiences and feelings. There were maybe forty of us there. When we got settled in and I could feel the anxiety emanating from other people, it finally occurred to me that everyone felt like I did, and I relaxed a little. When people started sharing their stories, I immediately went into protector mode and stopped worrying about my own anxiety.

One woman had survived a horribly abusive ex-husband. He'd tried to kill her, then got arrested and went to prison and died shortly thereafter. She started crying when talking about her feelings.

"What he did to me is fucking inexcusable. He went to prison as a result of it. So why do I still miss him so terribly? I feel like I'm going insane."

A couple of the women there tried to comfort her in low voices. Without thinking, I just stood up, walked over to her, and gave her a big hug.

"You can't control what other people do," I said, "and you can't control how you feel about certain people. Bad things happen, but you're here now, and it's going to get better. No one's going to die. You're going to leave here in a better place."

I didn't know her from a fucking hole in the wall. And who was I to be giving out advice at this thing? But it was innate for me to be the protector. Somehow, it worked.

I think the therapist actually liked having me there because I wasn't shy about trying to be helpful. But I also knew that when I was telling that woman "Yo, everything's going to be all right," I was trying to reassure myself of that, too.

There was another guy, heavyset, probably sixty years old, from Louisiana. A guy's guy, real no-nonsense character.

"Yeah, I'm here because I'm a fucking drunk. I've been through rehab and detox more times than I can count. I know I'm almost out of chances. I've hurt so many people . . . and I've hurt myself. I know if I don't fix this, it's going to be lights-out."

He was getting a little bit choked up, but he was a hard dude, you know what I mean? An old guy from the Louisiana swamps, so he was fighting it back. After he was done, I went over and gave the guy a hug. He didn't hug me back.

"Hey, man, keep fighting. Keep throwing punches, and keep getting up when you get knocked down. This fight ain't over until you win."

I could feel him relax a bit. I kept going.

"You ain't alone, man. You ain't doing anything that other people haven't done. Just remember that: you're not special. Many people have done this, and you can do it, too."

"I like that, man. I like that," he said.

Finally, he hugged me back.

―

Lying in bed that night, I knew my suffering was coming. I didn't know whether they were going to fiddle-fuck around or just go straight for it, but I knew at some point, my therapist was going to want to talk at length about my childhood. I was afraid I was going to start crying the minute we went into it. Why had I paid so much fucking money to come out here and cry in front of a stranger? What I was feeling was the epitome of discomfort. I felt more vulnerable than when I'd had to get a colonoscopy. I felt the same thing then that I did now: just knock me out already and let's get this over with.

We had to be at therapy at eight thirty each morning. But I still had to get in my ten miles—I wasn't going to destroy my physical health in pursuit of mental health. So each day, I got up at four thirty, turning off my alarm as quickly and quietly as I could to avoid disturbing my roommates. We were in Tennessee, not Minnesota, but it was still the depths of winter and bitterly cold. I'd get dressed quietly in the dark in my full snow gear—pants, shirt, jacket, hat, gloves—then head over to the main building, where the kitchen, auditorium, and meeting rooms were. I'd make myself some herbal tea and sit alone there in the dark, trying to wake up enough to face what was ahead of me. No phone, no TV, no newspaper, nothing. Finally, I'd get up to run, not because I felt ready or even awake, just because I was running out of time.

You weren't supposed to leave the facility, so the only place to run was up and down the tree-lined driveway, a steep slope of less than a quarter mile. I ran down the hill, up the hill, down the hill, anything to make up my miles. Since I didn't have my phone, I couldn't listen to podcasts or music while I ran. It was just me alone with my thoughts for ten miles. Fucking great.

It was the dead of winter and there was no ambient light, so I was just laboring out there, alone in the dark. Occasionally, to spice things up a bit, at the bottom of the street I'd run a quarter mile up the street, then turn around and run back . . . I felt like I was going nuts. That routine seemed like a metaphor for my life: just running and running and running, and never arriving.

Finally, I'd run back to our cottage, rinse off all my running clothes in the shower, get cleaned up, grab breakfast, then start going to meetings. My roommates found my morning rituals hilarious. But each cold, wet morning meant one fewer night before I could get the fuck out of there and go home.

My therapist was this young woman with dark hair named Jess, from Alabama, a mother of two. She was welcoming but not overly friendly, very professional.

"Hello, Ken. How are you doing today?"

I was nervous, but I tried to be positive.

"I'm doing good. I'm drinking this jasmine tea from the dining hall, got some honey in it. It's good stuff, makes me feel super healthy. Every time I see the name, it reminds me of that easy-listening song, 'Summer breeze makes me feel fine, blowing through the jasmine in my mind.'"

She smiled, then explained that their program was based around trying to help clients process childhood trauma. And then she asked me to run down any trauma I'd suffered as a child, like I was reading off a damn résumé.

"Listen," I told her, "I really don't feel like I have trauma. There are so many people out there who've had real trauma, and my life really hasn't been that bad. I just feel like I should be so much happier. Given the success I've had, I should be happy as a motherfu—"

I caught myself before I cursed in front of Jess on my first day of therapy.

"I should be obnoxiously happy. I have everything I've ever dreamed of. So why does suicide keep popping into my head like it's some destination vacation?"

"Well, let's start at the beginning. What's your earliest childhood memory."

"I don't know."

"Really, Ken?"

"I mean, I vaguely remember my childhood in little glimpses, I guess. Little bits and flashes. My memories as a kid are super sporadic. I know I've blocked out a ton."

"Who was your favorite teacher?"

"I'm sorry, I mean this sincerely. I can't remember the name of a single teacher I had."

She didn't say anything, just wrote on her pad.

"Why would I lie to you? I'm going to try to tell you everything. My earliest memory . . . it's not like a concrete memory per se, more of just a feeling. I always felt so incredibly vulnerable that, as a child, from my earliest moments of awareness, I remember thinking, 'God, just get me to the finish line. I know I'm getting out of here. I know this is going to end.' And that's why I think, to a certain extent, I can't remember a lot of things. I mean, I'm sure I had some pleasant experiences. But my recollections of my early life are very sad."

"Okay. How about we start with a couple of interactive exercises?"

Jess got me playing with rocks and fucking crayons. I was super uncomfortable. I hated every bit of it. But I told myself, *You are not here to be in charge. Just trust that they know what they're doing. You bought the ticket, now take the ride. Just fucking go for it.*

She broke out a deck of cards with different images on them. She had me do this exercise where I had to assign different cards to different people from my early life and identify what they represented. The first three images I chose were the fire-breathing dragon, the troll, and the wicked witch.

"Ken, these images that you've chosen to represent your closest family members . . . they're all very negative. These were the people who were charged with taking care of you. Can you expand on why you chose these specific images for these specific people?"

I told her some of the stories from my childhood. Getting slapped around by my mother and my stepfather. Getting sent to my room for several days. Being abandoned at some stranger's trailer in Alabama with Keith while my mother and stepfather went off to do who knows what. Getting whipped with a belt. Shit that if you read about it in the newspaper, you'd be like, "Whoa, these people are fucking savages."

"Jess, you have kids, right? Can you imagine hitting your children? And not just hitting your children, but beating them with a belt? Like you're smacking the shit out of some little kid and you think, *Nah, this ain't enough, I need to use an actual weapon?*

"Even as a kid, I understood that it was sadistic to whip a child. As a parent, you're charged with teaching a child the ways of the world . . . and when children make a mistake or behave in a manner you don't approve of, you beat them with a weapon?"

"Ken, these things that you endured . . . you don't think that's trauma?"

"It's just how we were brought up. Lots of people had it worse than I did."

"How would you feel if any of this happened to your kids?"

I felt myself starting to spin out.

"I'd lay my life down to prevent any one of my kids from ever having to experience a single thing that I had to deal with," I said, my voice shaking.

"Why do you think that you could handle it, but they couldn't?"

"It's my job to protect them. Over and above any other responsibility I have in my life, my first, last, and overarching responsibility is to protect my children."

"Yes," said Jess. "Your children should be protected because they're people. You're a person, too. It was your parents' first, last, and overarching responsibility to protect *you*. And they didn't. No one protected you. What they did to you is unacceptable. Someone should have protected you."

And I just lost it.

When I walked into Jess's office the next day, she wasn't there. There were no phones allowed at Onsite, but there on her desk was her cell phone, playing "Summer Breeze" by Seals and Crofts. It touched me that she'd remembered that from our session the day before and thought to cue it up. Not really my jam—I was still blasting 50 Cent in my earbuds on my runs. But I sat in my chair with my jasmine tea and tried to chill out to it.

I'd been hearing this song my entire life but had never once stopped to soak it in. But in that moment, I was open and had my guard down, and it hit me like a ton of bricks. The song was about peace, a moment of internal and external peace. It was so uncomplicated. It captured the feeling of completion, of connection, of satisfaction—a person coming home from a long day's work and having someone there who'd put their arms around them and appreciate them for what they'd done. It was a feeling I'd been chasing my entire life.

My life hadn't been entirely without peace. I'd obtained brief glimpses of it here and there. But working against me was this compulsion I felt to be like a Formula One driver, screaming through everything at top speed, even the pit stops. I should have been in therapy from the minute I hit New York—but here I was, trying to cram a lifetime of healing into four days. It had come to this because nothing was enough. Never enough money, never enough nice clothes, never enough drugs, never enough *performance*. I'd built a life in which it was impossible to sit and drink a cup of tea and listen to a song and breathe and just *be*.

I was almost done crying by the time Jess walked in. And then I dried my eyes and blew my nose, and we got to work.

It was eye-opening to be in one-on-one psychotherapy for four straight days. Every single day there felt like the longest day of my life. Decker and I would hang out at meals and between meetings, both of us with our heads down, working our programs, doing our time. I knew I was in good hands. Jess stunned me daily with her insight, and I quickly became convinced that she was a psychological genius. But it was still very difficult, very emotional therapy. It's just one of those things: having the best surgeon in the world still doesn't make surgery fun. It was humiliating and terrifying and painful and it sucked in every way. But I knew that when the pain was over, I wouldn't just feel better, I'd *function* better.

From the very first day, every time the subject of my childhood family came up, I'd melt down. I'd get emotional and weepy, but also very angry. If certain members of my family had been in front of me, I might have knocked them out.

"Jess, the way I feel . . . I want fucking vengeance on these people. I have so much resentment toward them, I can't stand it. I know being this angry at someone is not good. I know that the opposite of love is indifference, and I want to be indifferent toward them. By carrying this anger, I feel like I'm still letting them fuck with me."

Jess gave me a thin smile. "What would revenge accomplish if you can't learn to forget them? It takes so much out of you. Look at all the energy you're wasting hating them. Wouldn't it be easier for you if you just tried to find a way to forgive them and let them go do their own thing?"

"You think they deserve forgiveness?"

"I want to be clear about what I'm suggesting here, Ken. You're not writing to them or telling them 'Hey, I forgive you.' You're not letting them off the hook. You're writing off bad debt so you can move forward. You're forgiving them in your head and your heart as a means of forgetting them. Look at what holding on to this is doing to you. You're visibly tense, sitting on the edge of your chair, your leg bouncing up and down. None of that hurts *them*. All of that hurts *you*. You're drinking poison and hoping they die."

It blew my mind that I'd wandered into a trauma center convinced that I had no childhood trauma, only to discover that I was made almost entirely of trauma. I told Jess about how much I'd hated my childhood home, how it still haunted me. It hadn't been filthy, but it had been disorganized and chaotic and unstable. Shit could pop off at any time. And even when things were relatively quiet, I still felt the danger. I told her about the puke-yellow carpet and the soft spot in the living room floor.

"It felt like you could fall through the floor into the next apartment downstairs. It was one of my biggest fears of my childhood, this huge sagging menace in our living room. When I look back at it now, the amount of anxiety it caused me is insane. My throat starts to close just thinking about it. I was just a little kid and I became obsessed with thoughts of *How can we fix this?* Even though it was never within my control to fix it."

Jess nodded. "Even as a child, you were trying to be the father, the protector. That soft floor, it's really a perfect analogy. You were a child with parents who failed to protect you."

Finally, we talked about Shelby. Jess broke down for me what she understood to be at the root of all my troubles. A child needs to feel unconditional love from their parents. I'd gotten some of that from Granny, but never from my parents. I'd tried to fill that wound with hockey, with cocaine, with money, with luxury, with pills, and finally, with running. When I met Shelby, she was the first person since Granny who'd made me feel unconditional love. That connection was incredibly powerful. She didn't just make me feel like I was the only man for her, she made me feel like I was the only man in the world. She made me feel special, she made me feel secure, she made me feel loved completely.

For me, our love had been a vehicle of massive transformation. Without Shelby as a beacon of hope, I'd never have gotten off Subutex and Percs. But over a decade of drug abuse, I'd trained my body and brain to only feel pleasure from pills. With that gone, my only source of pleasure was physical intimacy. I'd made Shelby into my mom, and I'd made her into my drug.

That was too much of a burden for any person. Shelby wasn't charged with healing my psychic pain. My validation couldn't come from her, or my job, or my races. It was *my* job to tell myself that I was enough, it was *my* job to hear it, it was *my* job to internalize it and carry it with me. Shelby was my wife, and that's it. And as a wife and the mother of our children, she already had her hands full without my emotional neediness.

Shelby had told me time and again exactly what she wanted: a husband, a partner, a present and engaged father to our children. And I'd responded by working harder and making more money and winning more races—none of which she'd asked for. The answer had been right there in front of me the whole time, and I'd done everything I could to avoid seeing it: if I wanted a better marriage, I had to be a better husband.

I walked out the front door of Onsite feeling transformed. I glanced back at the campus as I was getting into my car. When I'd arrived, it had looked like a prison. Now it looked welcoming, homey, not a place of confinement but, rather, a ticket to freedom. I felt incredibly optimistic.

I called Shelby the instant I got in the car. I was crying and talking super fast, trying to tell her all the things I'd learned. I acknowledged letting her down and taking her for granted. I told her how much I loved her and all the ways I planned on being a better husband and partner as well as a better father to our kids. I could hear her getting excited, then laughing, then matching my tears with tears of her own.

"It's so good to hear you happy and excited again!" said Shelby. "I was so concerned that you were going to come back from there not having gotten what you needed. I couldn't help thinking if this doesn't work, if he doesn't get some clarity out of this, I don't know where we go from here. But you sound so good, you sound great! I can't wait to hear all about everything. The kids and I can't wait to have you home again."

I cried the entire drive home. In my head, I'd savaged everything I'd seen on the drive in. Now, on the journey back I reveled in it—the ancient crumbling barns, the cozy farmhouses, the occasional cow placidly chewing its cud. This was all part of my story, part of my journey, and I felt grateful for every single frosted blade of grass. I kept thinking, *I am finally seeing the truth for the first time.* I couldn't wait to see Shelby and the kids, to show them how much I'd learned and how I'd transformed. Finally, I felt comfortable in my skin.

When I pulled into the driveway, I was greeted by giant cardboard signs the kids had made to welcome me, like I was returning from winning the Olympics or some other monumental achievement. Before I'd gone to Onsite, I'd have let my embarrassment rule my actions and minimized what the kids had done, maybe even have groused at them to put the signs away. But now I was able to allow my elation to overcome my embarrassment.

They were right, I *had* done something remarkable. I'd asked for help when I needed it, and I'd accepted the help that was provided. It was a rare time in my life when I felt genuinely proud of myself. I'd identified a problem and faced it head-on. I felt thankful for

Onsite for the change they'd sparked in me, for the friends who'd guided me to Onsite, and for the friends I'd made there. (In the weeks and months that followed, whenever anyone asked me how I knew Eric Decker, I'd say, "We were roommates in the psych ward.") And I felt crushed with gratitude for my wife and children, who loved me and supported me unconditionally—whatever I was going through. My heart was so full, it hurt.

—

Onsite didn't fix *everything*, of course—nothing can fix everything. But it gave me a North Star. I finally knew which way was up, and which way was down. When I got lost—and I still got lost from time to time—I had the tools I needed to navigate back to where I needed to be. The hardest part was watching for backslides and trying to catch them early, but each time I caught myself slipping, I came back from the experience more enlightened.

I threw myself back into training not with fury, resentment, and self-loathing, but with love, gratitude, and joy. *How fucking lucky am I to be here?* I ran the Clearwater Half Marathon down in Florida and won by a full five minutes. I ran the Tokyo Marathon and won my age group. I felt like the last obstacle to greatness had been erased.

CHAPTER THIRTEEN

THE HARDEST RACE IN THE WORLD

WHEN THE GOBI MARCH SHOWED UP ON MY RADAR IN THE SPRING OF 2023, it scared me shitless. Considered one of the world's toughest endurance races, it was a 155-mile-long, self-supported, multistage ultramarathon that followed the historical footsteps of Genghis Khan. In 2010, it'd claimed the life of a competitor, an American businessman based in Shanghai named Nicholas Kruse. He'd gotten heatstroke on the dunes and had to be taken off the course by camel because trucks were unable to get in to retrieve him. He died in the hospital three days later. He was thirty-one. I was fifty-two, more than twenty years older. I was in good shape, but I knew I wasn't immortal. Part of me wondered whether this was where I'd finally enact the "die trying" part of my mantra.

I'd have to carry everything I needed in a backpack and run roughly a marathon a day for six days across one of the world's hottest deserts in the blazing heat of summer, totally self-supported.

As some people around me warned, I was mulling a race that, from any rational perspective, seemed completely over my head. I'd never done an ultramarathon before. I'd never run with a pack before. I'd never even slept in a tent before. And I had no desire to—if I have any choice, I'm going to sleep in a real bed in a real building like an actual human being. But the idea of that race stuck in my head.

I initially heard about the Gobi March during a conversation with my friend Scott DeRue, who was running the race. At the time, Scott was the president of Equinox and he would go on to become CEO of Ironman. He'd called to ask my advice about training and explained that he was doing an adventure race in Mongolia. Out of nowhere, without knowing anything about the event, I just blurted out, "Scott, I think I can win that race."

Scott chuckled.

"Ken, don't get me wrong, but . . . it's considered one of the toughest races in the world. If you could squeak out a finish in the top ten, that'd be one hell of an accomplishment."

I remember feeling irrationally insulted. While I understood exactly where he was coming from, the insecure part of my brain sprang to life and I convinced myself that he was doubting me. Top ten, are you fucking kidding me, bro? How could you disrespect me like that? Now I *had* to do it. And I had to win. I had to convince myself that nobody believed in me, that it was me against everybody. I dialed up my friend Rich Roll.

Rich is a legendary ultra-triathlon competitor, Stanford-educated attorney, and wildly popular podcast host. He is well-connected and very knowledgeable about all things ultra-endurance. Our call lasted about five minutes. I asked Rich what he knew about the Gobi March.

"Oh man. That race has taken down many a seasoned ultra-athlete. It's known to be pretty treacherous."

Though I know it wasn't his intention, all I heard was, "Ken, that's a crazy-hard and potentially dangerous race. You're not ready for it. It's over your head." I immediately hung up and went online to sign up.

But the race was sold out, with a waiting list till 2024. I emailed the race director with some of my running accolades and the media I'd done recently and said I'd love to have a crack at the race if they'd let me. A day later, I was in. I looked at the calendar. The race started in four weeks. What the hell had I done?

How do you train yourself to run a marathon a day for six days with a twenty-pound pack in less than a month? Sure, I'd done some training on the trails in the Pacific Palisades when we lived in California, but I was a road runner. The Gobi March website promised every possible type of terrain except road: jeep trails, single track, grassy plains, soft sand, gravel, dry riverbeds, water crossings, rocky climbs, and steep descents. It was impossible to get in shape for an event like that because the number of training miles a competitor needed to log, and attempts to duplicate the challenges of the terrain, would inevitably cause injury. And besides, I was still obsessed with winning the World Marathon Majors Age Group World Championships, which would be taking place in Chicago in October that year. This Gobi throw-down was just a side quest—a dumb, *dangerous* side quest. Still, I threw everything I had into training and preparation.

So important was it for a marathoner to discard inessential weight that I didn't even carry water when I ran. Now I started running with a twenty-pound backpack every single day in Nashville in June. The backpack held bottled water for weight and towels for cushioning. I sweat so much every day that when I came in, the towels inside my pack were drenched with sweat. I was killing myself, losing five to ten pounds in water weight every run. I prayed it was enough.

Going into the Gobi March, I knew I'd have to rely heavily on the fact that I'd trained so consistently over the years. Other people trained to perform. They trained to run a specific marathon or ultra-marathon or Ironman on a specific date. But since getting sober, I'd never really let myself get out of shape. By grinding consistently day after day, week after week, month after month, year after year, I'd trained my ability to recover. To wake up one day and not run would be like forgetting how to breathe. I knew in my heart that I wasn't different from everyone else in being able to trick my brain into thinking there was no option other than to get up and run. But if anyone was going to be able to absorb the punishment of a marathon-a-day, multistage event and bounce back day after day, it was me.

I knew from racing marathons that there were a thousand little things that could happen in a race this long, and 999 of them were bad. One of the reasons I'd excelled at marathons was that I prepared for each race like an NFL coach preparing for the Super Bowl. I did my research, I mapped out every possible detail of the entire procedure front to back, I knew which tools I'd use and when, and I had contingency plans if something went awry. This race across Mongolia would be entirely guesswork, though. I worried about the experience I didn't have and the questions I couldn't answer, but I worried most about the unknown unknowns—surprises that I'd be completely physically, mentally, and emotionally unprepared for. This would be the longest, hardest race I'd ever undertaken. The blunt fact was: I wasn't ready, and there was no way to get ready.

The race organizers would supply us with water and tents to sleep in. Everything else I needed for the week would have to fit in my pack. I didn't just have to plan what gear I needed or what I was going to wear, I had to anticipate every single little thing I'd need to perform at the highest level, day after day. How much toilet paper would I require? A whole roll? Did it make sense to take the cardboard out in the middle and compress it down to save space and weight? How many shits would I take a day while running through the desert on the other side of the world? How many sheets per shit?

I had to strategize every single calorie I was going to eat for seven days of peak performance. How much electrolyte drink mix was I going to bring? Only two a day was still fourteen packets of powder. I needed to be light but still be able to go all day long. Should I bring recovery powder? Or should I bring real calories? Because this wasn't just about getting the right amount of creatine and protein. This was about survival.

I drove myself nuts trying to prepare for every possible scenario, including scenarios I couldn't even imagine. I wrapped my water bottles in a couple of strips of duct tape. For what, I couldn't tell you, but if I needed it, I'd have it. Finally, it dawned on me that it was impossible to get ready for the Gobi March. I could prepare for it for years and still not be ready for what might be out there. I had to yield to the fact that I was going into the longest race of my life mostly blind. Best-case scenario, I'd suffer greatly for a long time. After that, I might *still* leave the course on a stretcher.

Driving to the airport with Shelby, I felt like I was headed to the

Roman Colosseum to fight real gladiators with no sword or shield. I was scared of everything. I might lose. I might not even finish. I might fucking die. I didn't want to go camping, I didn't want to go *glamping*, I didn't want anything to do with sleeping on the ground, I wanted to bunk at the Four Seasons. We could have a fight to the death if the race organizers wanted, I didn't give a fuck—but I didn't feel the need to prove to anyone I was tough by sleeping outside. But I'd pestered the race director to let me in and publicly committed to doing it. I had all these brands sponsoring me, and I felt an overwhelming sense of responsibility to go out there and get it done. And, of course, in the Rideout dictionary, "get it done" meant "win." There was no other option.

As I was walking out to the plane, my wife called out, "Pops, cheer up! You signed up for this! You're going to Mongolia! There's something exciting about that."

"I don't give a fuck about Mongolia," I said morosely. "I'm not interested. Yeah, I'd like to see it, but from horseback or something."

Shelby rolled her eyes, then pulled me in close and kissed me. "Ken, you got this." And then she flashed that billion-dollar smile.

I adored her and felt another wash of gratitude that I'd gone and suffered at Onsite to save our relationship. But I felt the same way I'd felt decades before when my mother had dropped me off on Boston Common to go to summer camp at Agassiz Village in Maine—abandoned. I had no idea what was coming, and that was terrifying.

Despite the fact that I'd never competed in an ultramarathon before, once I walked onto that plane, I convinced myself that I was unbeatable. I had complete confidence that, regardless of what the Gobi March had in store, my mental and physical fitness would be superior to that of every other competitor. No one had worked as hard as I had for as long as I had. As unprepared as I felt for the experience, I knew I was ready. Other competitors had been trying to get ready, but for the last five years, I'd stayed ready. Yes, when Shelby left me at the airport, I'd felt like I had when my mother left me at summer camp, but I needed to play that tape all the way through. I needed to remember how that one ended—with my winning Camper of the Year. I suddenly felt a surge of aggression. *No sense in going all the way over there and not kicking ass. Let's fucking do this.*

Getting to the race was the first battle. I flew from Nashville to Atlanta to South Korea to Ulaanbaatar, the capital city of Mongolia: more than twenty-four hours in transit. As soon as we landed on a Friday afternoon, the race staff, volunteers, and racers were clucking and cooing about the beauty of the city and the ancient Buddhist temples with roofs tiled in gold right next to sweeping, ultramodern skyscrapers. I was so fried and riddled with anxiety, I couldn't enjoy it. I just wanted to find my hotel and take a shower.

Just my luck, the room I'd booked wasn't ready. However, they did have one room available due to a last-minute cancellation for a wedding party. Nearly cross-eyed with jet lag, I stumbled into a room full of red heart-shaped balloons, the bed all done up in red satin. Of course, the bathroom was a mess, with mildew in the grout and tiles peeling off in the shower. But the bed was the last real bed I'd sleep in for a week, and the garish decor was the cherry on top of what was already a wildly absurd adventure.

I linked up with Scott DeRue in the lobby of the hotel where we were staying, and we went to grab some lunch. One of the race photographers dropped by, an American guy. He knew who Scott was and he knew the lay of the land, but he didn't know me from a hole in the wall.

"Hey, buddy," I chimed in at one point, "are there any people at this race who've won these adventure races before?"

He looked at me coolly.

"This your first time?"

"Yup."

"There are a couple of guys here this year who are truly awesome. Reinhold Hugo is here. He's from Switzerland, a real trail beast. The race organization does other adventure races like this around the globe, and Hugo's won in Namibia and Georgia. David Dano is here, we call him Dudu. Ex–Israeli special forces, another incredibly tough competitor. Jason Yoo from South Korea is a fitness influencer, which, yeah, I know . . . but he's only twenty-six, has an incredibly positive attitude, and is in dynamite shape. Nobody's beating those guys. Your first time out, just be happy if you can finish."

I nodded like I agreed with him and kept my mouth shut, but my mind was screaming. *Bro, you have no idea how much motivation you just gave me. Happy to finish? We'll fucking see about that!*

At six the next morning, they packed us all on some noisy old buses for a six-hour journey out to the middle of the desert where the race would begin. The other racers were gabbing and laughing, delighted to be in Mongolia—some seemed delighted to be *back* in Mongolia. The race hadn't taken place since 2019, so some of these dudes had been waiting four years to do it. It made me wonder who was crazier, me or them.

I knew I had to get fired up to win, and I knew I had to create imaginary enemies to get myself fired up. So on that long bus ride into the desert, I told myself that all these runners were teaming up against me. I know it sounds outright crazy, but I literally convinced myself that everyone in the race was trying to get me, that their only goal was to make sure I didn't win. My objective was to prove them all wrong.

When we got to the site, the organizers had a couple of big cream-colored yurts set up for the race staff, and smaller green canvas tents for the racers. The temperature was in the mid-eighties, but it cooled off at night. Once again I had to get used to having roommates, but this time there was a twist. The staff had me bunking with three women—one from Hong Kong, a second from Thailand, and a third from Ireland. Initially, the women weren't wild about sharing space with me because a few years before, they'd had a German guy in the tent with them. Every time he'd come into the tent, he was naked. But the real deal-breaker was that when he had to piss, he'd just piss in his water bottle in the tent—day or night—and he was dehydrated enough that it stunk. I assured them that they'd never have to deal with disgusting, unsanitary bullshit like that from me, not in a million years.

I threw down my thin sleeping pad and sleeping bag and tried to get as much rest as possible. But in the middle of the night, it started pouring, with winds so strong that the rain was coming down almost sideways. Oh, for those relatively plush accommodations at Onsite that I'd failed to appreciate . . .

Of course, in the middle of the night, I had to piss. No way was I going out in that rain and getting drenched. Rolling my eyes and silently shaking my head and cursing myself, I very, *very* quietly pissed in my water bottle, then dumped it out the tent flap. I'd rinse it out in the morning. This was already a nightmare, and we hadn't yet run a single step.

That first morning, the guys took it out super hard. It was a short day, just twenty-one miles—piece of cake, right? We started on a fire trail, basically a couple of dusty ruts in the grass where a truck had driven through a couple of times. You had to be conservative on these long races. But right from the gun, we were running as fast as we could. The minute we started racing, all the doubts I'd had went out the window. I'd trained like I couldn't win. Time to race like I couldn't lose.

I ran right through the first aid station like a lunatic. It was completely irrational. But the leaders had no choice but to follow me. After running through several rivers with only four or five miles left to go, I came to the side of a mountain with Dudu and Reinhold right behind me. It was straight up. I didn't have poles, but they did. They left me choking on their dust, sputtering with frustration. Was I the only person who hadn't brought poles? That was a major oversight.

We were running along this ridgeline—the spine of a mountain—that looked like something you might see in a viral video and think, *That guy is going to die if he falls*. After a while, the trail carried us straight down toward a valley and we could see the camp off in the distance. But first, we had to run through a dry riverbed about a half mile wide. Well, it looked like a dry riverbed, but it was actually a thin, dry layer of clay covering wet, sucking, ankle-deep mud. The shit was like quicksand and there was no way around but through. I fell a couple of times, so I was cursing and yelling, pissed off because I hate getting dirty and I was covered in mud. Two miles out from the finish, I got passed by a guy for third place. Really nice Italian guy but what the fuck, he hadn't been in sniffing distance of me the entire rest of the day. The first day and, already, I was falling apart.

I finished fourth on that stage, feeling sorely disappointed and exhausted. By the time I got cleaned up and back to camp, I was really doubting myself. But I hadn't fared as badly as some others. Many people came in looking like they'd been buried in mud, and a couple dropped out on the spot, having only logged a single day.

That night, for the first time, I talked with some of the other runners beyond just basic niceties. I connected with this group of Italians—two of them journalists, three of them runners, and one runner's adult son who was volunteering for the race, traveling stage to stage with us, helping break down and set up camp each day. Technically, you were supposed to carry everything with you, but somehow every night, the Italians had these incredible feasts. They looked out for me from that night on.

"Hey, Ken, you want some mozzarella? Some prosciutto? How about some parmigiano?"

"Dude, you guys carrying an entire wheel of parmesan with you?"

"Ken, the parmesan, it's good for you," they said with a sly chuckle.

I suspect the son may have been muling some food for them, but the Italians were just looking to complete the event, not to compete, so everyone turned a blind eye. I met another guy that night whom I hit it off with, an Irish guy named Cillian Ryan. He was a big, muscular dude with a beard, huge personality, super funny. He was sober, but I could tell that back in the day, he'd have turned the place into complete drunken chaos. He shared some crucial information with me.

"Mate, those guys who beat you today, they know you're a marathon runner. Maybe they don't know who you are, but they know of you. They think they're going to wear you down a little every day, just keep putting time on you."

That made sense. Since I had four age-group wins in the World Marathon Majors, my online following had been creeping up and up. I wasn't getting recognized on the street, but I'd been getting recognized at races more.

"Do with that information what you will," he said, "but just know that they're gunning for you."

I knew Reinhold and Dudu felt super confident. When I'd rolled into camp that evening, I definitely got the feeling that they were like, "Yeah, we showed him a lesson." It'd burned me up. But now the game was on.

A quote that people who have never boxed love to recite is Mike Tyson's infamous "Everyone has a plan till they get punched in the mouth." But every boxer knows the fight doesn't start when the bell rings, it starts when punches start landing. Many great fighters don't really wake up till they've caught a punch that'd knock out a lesser fighter. Dudu and Reinhold had caught me in a mistake, they'd spanked me, and it stung. But now my head was in the fight. I went to sleep that night determined to come back a thousand times harder.

The second day was twenty-eight miles of pain and suffering, farther than I'd ever run in my life. I fell into step with a British guy named Paul, a real runner. He'd run a 1:08 half and a 2:20 marathon and I was sure he was going to beat me. But I was starting to form a strategy to take down the current leaders, Dudu and Reinhold.

"You know what, Paul? I have got to ease into this. I can't go hard with these guys. If they go hard, I'm just gonna let them go, then try to come back on them and sit with a negative split."

Dudu and Reinhold pushed for the lead, and we let them have it. They got away from us, but not so far that I couldn't see them.

But I forced myself to just run even and methodically and not pay any attention to them.

Ten or fifteen miles into it, Paul started fading and let me go. I started gaining on the leaders without really trying. I was just steady. I slowly rolled up on them, ran with them for a minute, then just rolled away from them.

These guys are setting a trap. They're watching me, waiting to see what I'm going to do.

I gradually started turning the screws on them. Any time I'd drop down behind a hill or go around a bend, I'd open it up for a few minutes while out of sight so that when I popped back into their view, they'd notice that they'd dramatically lost ground. As they say, out of sight, out of mind. This is absolutely the case in distance racing. Finally, with ten miles to go, I couldn't see them behind me. I started hammering it like my life depended on it.

With five or six miles left, I tripped and went down hard. I busted my elbow open and ripped the stitching out of the strap on my backpack at the bottom where it connected to the bag. I tied the broken strap to the other strap and managed to get over the line, carrying the bag over my shoulder. I won the stage by twelve minutes and went from fourth overall to second. But that progress came with a price.

Though I'd given Nev Schulman shit for running a marathon with his phone, and though I was doing a much longer race where every ounce counted, I'd made the decision to carry my phone with me, both for my own safety and to document some of the run. I captured some great moments: running with sheep, running with cattle, running with nothing and no one, surrounded at all angles by a barren, desolate landscape and an unforgiving sky. At the end of that second stage, I turned the camera on myself and recorded a little postrace wrap-up.

Watching it now, eighteen months removed from that weeklong gulag, confirms that when I felt like I was in hell, I wasn't wrong. In the video, I look less like an athlete and more like a hostage. I'm unshaven, my cheeks hollowed out, eyes narrowed to slits from the sun. My black running shirt is starched white from sweat—what kind of idiot packs a black shirt to race across the desert? Dried blood is splashed across my nose and cheek, with a longer, thick trail of dried blood descending from a gash on my elbow down to my wrist.

"All right, end of stage two. Twenty-eight miles. I won the stage, but I may have paid the price. I'm all fucked up. I fell down, my pack busted, and the shoulder strap broke. So for the last six miles, I was running holding this twenty-pound bag on my shoulder. I'm as tired as I've ever been. I can't imagine running twenty-four miles tomorrow and fifty the next day. Something's got to change. I either have to slow down or I'll probably die."

I hung my head and cried. But no tears came—I was too dehydrated.

"I'm in fucking hell. I don't know what the fuck I'm doing. I'm so tired. I'm fucking destroyed. But I'm going to keep trying to win. Or die trying."

The mood around the camp that night was far more subdued than it'd been the first night. Exhausted, filthy runners lay on their backs under a shade tent, stretching their legs and elevating their feet, trying to steel themselves for what lay ahead. I worked on my cursed backpack, a $500 endurance running pack that'd shit the bed on the second day of the race. I got some sutures from the doctor and spent two hours stitching it up. The second I got it on my back for a trial run, the stitches blew out. Then I cut small holes and zip-tied it all together. I peeled the strips of duct tape off my water bottles and wrapped the zip ties where I'd cut them so the sharp bits wouldn't be poking me all day long. It recalled for me so many conversations I'd had with combat military friends about their being out in the field and having to make do with whatever was at hand—just MacGyver it and hope it worked. Maybe my repair would hold. It *had* to hold.

That third morning when I woke up, I told myself that each day was a new race, and I wasn't letting anyone win anything. This stage was only twenty-four miles. I could hold anyone off for twenty-four miles as long as my pack held up. They started us out by sending us straight up a rock wall. Looking at it, I thought to myself, *There's no way all these people are going to be able to climb up that. Someone's gonna die.*

Almost immediately, Reinhold and Dudu got away from me. They had those mountaineer soldier skills while I had only . . . tenacity. After we got up and over the rocks, we plunged down into the sand dunes. Up till this point, I'd understood us to be in the desert, but we'd mostly been running on trails and dirt roads. The dunes were something else entirely. The sand was so fine, it swallowed half your shoe with each footfall. It was like trying to run underwater while wearing overalls. Even so, I managed to catch up to Dudu and fell into stride next to him.

With no warning, the strap on my pack ripped again with probably twenty miles left that day. The way it ripped, I was left with a short end and a longer end. I tied them together in a weird way and kept going. I couldn't believe it worked. The bag held up, but I knew there was no way I could start the next day's fifty-mile stage with a bag like this. If I couldn't find a new bag somewhere, I was out of the race.

I ended up spending most of the day's twenty-four miles carrying my twenty-pound pack like it was a football. Reinhold won the stage again, which left me in second place overall, only eight minutes behind. Victory was still within reach. But if I couldn't get my pack sorted out, I'd never make it far enough to find out whether I had what it took to win.

I've always been super meticulous about keeping my gear organized and getting all my stuff dialed in perfectly. One of the benefits of finishing at the front was that when I got back to the camp each night, I was able to set everything up exactly how I wanted it. I'd put my thin little sleeping pad and ultralight sleeping bag and pack right inside the door, in the corner of the tent. The tents were already set up by volunteers when we rolled in, but they weren't sleeping in them, so there were always rocks and sticks under the tent. I'd reach around under there and make sure my sleeping spot was perfect. But I also went out of my way to climb under the tent a few times and take rocks out to make sure that the girls were comfortable, because they'd quickly become my friends. Especially after the first day or two when they were saying things like, "Holy shit, you're in second overall? Oh my God, you could win this!" It quickly became a team effort, and we looked out for each other.

At home, I was obsessively clean. I'd shower once in the morning after my run and once at night before I went to sleep. I was fucking filthy the entire time I was in Mongolia. I'd wanted to get out of my comfort zone, but I didn't realize I'd be plunging myself up to my eyeballs into my discomfort zone. Still, I did what I could. You could easily just not wash your clothes and race in them for a week . . . and risk getting a rash or skin infection, to say nothing about feeling disgusting all week. I'd brought a tiny bit of super-concentrated camp soap and a drop went a long way. I'd get my body a little bit wet, then lather the shit out of myself with a drop of soap. Other people would rib me, saying things like, "Dude, you're carrying soap? That's crazy." I thought *they* were crazy for not bringing soap. I had a little tiny shammy towel that I'd use to dry myself. Then I'd rinse the towel out and dry it in the sun, so it was clean for the next day. Each night, I washed out my running kit. Since we had to carry everything, I had one change of underwear and one change of socks. I'd wash them in my water bottle with a drop of soap, so I'd have a clean set each day.

I was doing my best to keep my game face on and keep telling myself that all the other runners were conspiring to make me fail, but it was hard to not like them . . . a lot. I'd wildly underestimated the food I'd need and had only budgeted twenty-five hundred calories a day. My Whoop fitness tracker showed I was expending close to ten thousand, so I was starving. Night after night, I'd scavenge any food that people were going to discard—rice and beans, noodles, a pack of sardines. I hated sardines, but at that point I was so desperate for calories, I'd have eaten a leather shoe. Point is, it's hard to keep telling yourself people hate you when they're sharing their food with you. Almost every single person I encountered at Gobi March, from the runners to the race organizers to the local Mongolian staff, was incredibly kind and supportive. Even Dudu and Reinhold. Especially Dudu and Reinhold.

I'd told myself that they were my mortal enemies, that I had to bury them before they buried me. But I wasn't just running against them, day after day, I was running *with* them. And then we'd roll into camp together, hours before everyone else, and end up stretching and doing our laundry together, chatting and shooting the shit. It was impossible to compete against these men again and again at the utmost level of exertion and not develop tremendous respect for them as athletes and human beings. I kept hammering away in my mind, telling myself that I was tougher and in better shape and at any moment they'd fold up and quit, but the truth was that we were incredibly closely matched. Reinhold was only a couple of years younger than I was and he effortlessly ran up and down the sheerest cliff walls like a billy goat. Dudu was quiet, intense, and devout, saying his prayers every afternoon and evening with his leather prayer straps wrapped around his arms. They were good men, and the toughest competitors I could have imagined. Even when we were trying to run each other into the ground, it still felt like we were all in this together.

Attrition was setting in now, and people were dropping like flies. There was no way home for people who dropped, so they'd still have to go stage to stage with the volunteers till the race ended. I asked one of the guys who was quitting whether I could use his bag; he was an older Belgian guy who lived in Vietnam and was the CEO of a chocolate factory there. He said no. I told him I'd give it back to him after the race, I offered to buy it off him for full price, I offered to have Amazon send him a replacement, I offered to give it back at the end *and* give him $500. Still no. *Are you fucking kidding me?* His obstinacy made me insane. His race was over, I could win this . . . and he wasn't going to help me? Finally, a woman who was dropping out was kind enough to give me her pack. If I finished, I'd do it in a too-small silver women's backpack with pink accents.

The medical tent had little basins into which you could put some soap and wash your feet, because we were all taking damage each day. I stayed on top of taking care of my body because I knew if I neglected something and tried to just power through, it'd be worse the next day. I'd wash everything I could reach and put new bandages and tape on my rashes and chafing and road rash. Nobody made it through unscathed—it was like being in battle—but I was able to manage it. A blister here, a blister there, but nothing that really required special assistance. Some other folks, by the second day, it looked like they'd been walking on hot coals. It made me wonder: if their feet turned to hamburger after a couple of days, what kind of training had they been doing?

I was standing outside the med tent after the third day when we saw a rain squall approaching. You could see it heading in our direction across the desert. It looked so cool, like a herd of approaching animals. Finally, I snapped out of it and realized it was going to clobber us. Just like in a movie, the squall rolled in and began to dump rain on us. When the wind hit our tents, it looked like the hand of God plucking a few of them up and chucking them effortlessly a half mile into the dunes.

All the workers started scrambling around, trying to retrieve the tents. They had this huge box truck with all the supplies, so a bunch of them piled in that and headed out to grab the tents. Of course, they got that truck stuck so deeply, even the frame was buried in the sand. It felt ominous, just another reminder that human beings were not in charge out here. If we were still alive and moving, it was just because the desert hadn't bothered to kill us yet. I went to sleep that night with sand stuck in every crevice, dreading the fifty-mile stage the next day.

We headed out in the morning, Dudu and Reinhold and I in a loose cluster. I was running with only one AirPod in at a time so I could charge the other one and never be without music. After blasting Rage Against the Machine all morning, I ran up beside Dudu, feeling good.

"Hey, David, did I ever mention to you that I never get tired?" I said with a grin.

He looked at me and I could see the life drain from his face. A moment later, he started walking. Two minutes after that, he was gone. Now it was down to me and Reinhold.

For the first time in my life, I got to fully appreciate just how far fifty miles actually was. We went up and over mountain ranges, wove through winding pastures, ran in and out of tiny little villages where old women wearing Adidas slides were milking goats and young men on 1970s Honda street bikes were herding horses. On a stage this long, this deep into the race, it was a fool's errand to try to run the steep, rocky inclines. We ran all the downhills and all the flats and power-hiked all the uphills.

At thirty-five miles, we rolled into a little village, and they surprised us with an aid station. They had Coca-Cola there—not Diet Coke, not Coke Zero, old-school liquid diabetes Coca-Cola, packed with sugar and caffeine. I probably drank an entire two-liter bottle myself and I walked out of there grinning and almost dancing, feeling like I'd gotten a snout full of donkey dust.

I was on cloud nine. But as soon as the town disappeared from view and we got back into the shifting sands of the dunes, Reinhold started struggling.

"Ken, I need to walk a little bit."

"All right, I'll walk with you."

We still had an incredibly long way to go, and I wasn't overly concerned with getting into a shootout with him now. If I took the initiative here and dropped him, I'd have to be looking over my shoulder while running the next fifteen miles alone. Reinhold was good company and I wasn't in a hurry to ditch him. It wasn't long before he spoke again.

"I gotta take a break."

He stopped suddenly and just stood there, swaying on his feet. I stopped with him.

"I gotta sit down."

"Nope. Brother, I'm sorry, we can stop to breathe for a second, but we can't sit down. It's like a thousand degrees out, there's no shade, and we're in the middle of nowhere. Let's get to the next aid station, then you can get first aid. It's got to be just over the next rise."

I pushed and pulled and cajoled him probably another two miles, over the next big rise. No aid station.

"I can't, Ken. I can't go."

"Come on, buddy, hang in there. I swear, it's just gotta be over the next rise, it can't be far now."

"I can't."

"Here, let me carry your pack."

But he wouldn't, because if I carried his pack, he could get disqualified. Respect to him—he was falling apart, but he still wasn't giving up.

Finally, he sank down into the soft sand of one of the dunes and refused to get up. I stood over him, shielding him from the sun with my body, and looked around. There was no trace of civilization, only sand, sun, and sky. We could have been standing on the surface of Mars.

I started giving him some of my water because I figured at this point, it was better for me to run out than for him. We were just sitting there, not moving, watching the time tick by: ten minutes, twenty minutes, thirty minutes. My mind started chewing on itself.

The entire time we were sitting there with our thumbs up our bums, the other competitors were closing the distance. Maybe Dudu had rallied and was just over the last rise, feeling good and moving well. Jason was a ways back but he was young and in great shape, with an indomitable spirit—it'd be stupid to count him out yet.

But those guys were still only a distant threat. My greatest competitor, the only man standing between me and first place was right here, stretched out on the ground. Instead of blowing the commanding lead we'd built up, I should've been taking this opportunity to seal the deal, leave my toughest competitor in the dirt, and let the race staff deal with him. He wasn't my responsibility. My only responsibility was to win.

You don't even know this motherfucker. You're never going to see him again. You're only here to win.

But this was the exact same situation that'd claimed the life of Nicholas Kruse. He was only thirty-one when he died. What could he have done with his life if he'd lived? I thought about where I'd been when I was thirty-one: lost, miserable, all the way down the well of addiction. Had I tapped out then, there'd be no sobriety, no Ironman, no running podiums. But fuck all that shit. Dying at thirty-one also meant no Shelby, no Tensae, no Jack, no Luke, no Cameron. Standing there in the blazing sun in the godless desert, I watched my entire family vanish from my life in a second. Reinhold was my age—whom did he love in his life, who loved him? A wife, kids, friends . . . how many people would grieve him if he died? Hundreds? A thousand? Thousands?

No fucking way was I leaving him. "Win or die trying" was my mantra, and I stood by it. It was my life to do with what I chose, up to and including losing it doing dumb shit like this in the far-off corners of the globe. But "win or die trying" did not mean abandoning others, it didn't mean letting other people die. I'd stay with Reinhold all day if I had to. I'd stay with him through the night if I had to. If it meant I came in dead last, it didn't matter. I'd stay with him till he was safe.

Finally, finally, finally, a big new Ford Raptor 4x4 came growling over a distant dune. As soon as it was clear that he was in good hands and the situation was stable, I took off. And because I'd been walking and resting while trying to help him, I'd had a ton of time to recover. When they cleared me to leave, I flew. I probably ran my fastest six miles of the race that day, hauling ass to get into camp.

I made it in around six that evening. The race organizers allowed people two days to cover this stage as it was fifty miles, so people kept trickling in all night, some even late the next morning, staggering like zombies. My first-place finish in the fifty-mile stage put me in first overall and meant I had an entire day off to rest and recover. Thirty-six hours to kill in the middle of nowhere? I wanted to just keep hammering.

There was a gorgeous little stream behind our campsite, so I thought I might treat my tired body to a real wash. I jumped in wearing my clothes and stripped down, ready to give everything a thorough washing. My back screamed as soon as I hit the water, as it was all torn up from the too-small, ill-fitting backpack, but the water was cool and soothing. As soon as I got out, I immediately broke out in hives. The water looked clean, but it must have been full of bacteria from nearby livestock. Every day in Mongolia was a fresh, new nightmare.

The second-to-last stage was exactly 26.2 miles. I could tell that we were finally getting toward the end of it. Reinhold had rallied after his crisis in the dunes, and we ran together most of the day. After an endless sea of dunes the previous day, the landscape transformed in front of our eyes again and again. We ran across broad grassy plains, maybe fifty feet from huge herds of wild horses, to the foothills of a steep mountain range. It was an overcast day but the minute we reached the mountains, the sky yawned open into this perfect, irrepressible blue. There was long, plush grass and tall pine trees . . . it looked like we were running in the Swiss Alps. My soul filled with gratitude, something I didn't think would have been possible before Onsite.

With about three miles to go, Reinhold ran away from me on a steep technical downhill. *You motherfucker, this is how you pay me back for saving your ass in the desert?* But had he tried to wait for me, I'd have yelled at him to keep going, to give it his all. This was a race, damn it, a race I was fixated on winning, and not because someone else was phoning it in.

We ran along a gravelly ridgeline with a faint trace of a trail, which then plunged down into a valley glowing green with a big river running through it. I could see Reinhold slowly making his way across the river, then crossing the finish, maybe a minute ahead of me. Had to hand it to him, he beat me fair and square that day. It was one hell of a comeback.

When I got to the river crossing, there was a thick rope bridging it. Really, people needed a rope to cross? Well, yes, and I needed it, too—the water was waist-deep, freezing cold, and flowing quickly. One stumble and it would've been easy to get washed away. In the deepest part, I stripped my backpack off, held it over my head with one hand, and dunked my entire body underwater so I wouldn't have to wash my clothes that night.

When I got to the end of the water crossing, one of the course designers, a Spanish dude named Carlos, yelled out to me.

"Rideout! How'd you like that course?"

"Dude, that was crazy-hard. You better call an ambulance."

He looked at me with instant concern.

"But not for me," I shouted with a grin, and blew past him to cross the line. I had nearly a ninety-minute lead by that point, and the next stage was only six miles, basically just a victory lap.

That night, the final night of the race, camp was a little more festive. The vibe was high—we could all taste the finish. The organizers had brought along some native Mongolians in traditional garb and they entertained us with trained eagles. Then the race staff made us a big bonfire . . . but of course, still no food, only what we'd carried. The next morning, when we were lining up, my friend Cillian sidled up to me.

"Mate, you won. You're up by almost an hour and a half. Only six miles today. You could practically hike it in."

We bumped knuckles. We were almost home.

"You going to let someone else win this stage?" he said with a smile.

Cillian was a great dude. His company over the last week had made my life so much brighter. Still, I looked at him with all the disdain and contempt I could muster.

"Bro, are you serious? I'd never disrespect any race by letting someone win. You think in the Tour de France, the yellow jersey winner is going to let a guy win a stage just so he can have a win? Look at me, look at yourself, look at everyone standing here. Every single one of us has suffered beyond comprehension over the last week, even those at the back of the pack. You think I'm going to cheapen their experience? No, man. Even on a six-mile stretch, I don't give a fuck. You want to beat me, you'll have to kill me. We're racing to the death."

And we raced to the death. Reinhold and I were in a mad sprint from the very beginning. We had only the most minimal equipment in our backpacks now, just water and calories and the mandatory safety equipment. We bombed up and over a hill, through a little wooded trail, then came to a tiny village with cobbled streets, the first paving of any kind we'd seen in days. Not a word passed between us—we were flying. Finally, he dropped off and I sprinted across the finish line. It was over. I'd done it.

And the win meant nothing. There were no reporters or cameras or screaming crowds. All that had happened was I'd made a promise to myself and then kept that promise. That alone proved I wasn't worthless. I forced myself to take a moment just to let that soak in.

They had soda and pizza at the finish line. I probably ate two large pizzas myself and drank a six-pack of soda. The race organizers had gone all out and made sure that at the finish every racer's country was represented with a full-size flag on display. When Reinhold and Dudu came in, I grabbed the old Stars and Stripes and had them grab the flags for Israel and Switzerland and we got some pictures together. They were great guys off the course, absolute warriors on the course, and had done their countries proud. Though I'd come into the race wanting to believe they were enemies, I felt tremendous gratitude for them. They were more than just worthy adversaries. Dudu was an excellent technical runner and had left me choking on his dust more than once. Four out of five trail races, Reinhold would have beat me. Had he not fallen apart during the fifty-mile stage, the Gobi March victory would have been his. It'd been a tremendous honor to slug it out day after day with such relentless competitors.

The race directors came over and shook my hand, congratulated me, invited me back the next year, and immediately started pitching me other races they were putting on that I should enter. I looked at them, dumbfounded.

"Bro, are you kidding? One and done, man."

To underscore that I was saying goodbye to this experience *completely*, I beckoned over a group of local Mongolians who'd traveled with us the entire way. They'd been incredibly kind, friendly, and hardworking, and I wanted to acknowledge it, so I started giving away my gear: not just my busted pack but my ultralight sleeping bag, my sleeping pad, my waterproof bag, my water bottles . . . a big pile of top-notch camping gear.

Then I grinned at the race directors and pointed at my face: sunburned and unshaven, cheeks sunken in from the weight I'd lost, eyes bloodshot and half-closed from fatigue.

"Thank you so much for the experience of a lifetime. Now get a good look at this face. You'll never see it again."

CHAPTER FOURTEEN

SHOWDOWN IN CHICAGO

GRANNY PASSED ON APRIL 28, 2023. SHE WAS EIGHTY-NINE YEARS OLD. HER obituary listed her name as Margaret Barnett, but all her relatives had called her Auntie Hutsie. I'd never known where that nickname came from, and I guess I'll never find out. To me, she was always Granny, from when I was very little right up until she died. I felt happy for her because eighty-nine is a great run, especially when you drank like Granny did. She was one of the kindest people I'd ever met, and I was grateful that she'd been so loved by her friends and family.

Still, I felt incredibly sad. Until I met Shelby, Granny was the one person who'd shown me unconditional love. I grieved her like a child might grieve losing their mother. She'd certainly shown me more kindness, affection, and support than both of my parents put together. Much as I hate to cop to it, under my sadness was a slight twinge of relief. I felt no connection to my mother. I felt little connection to my father. Granny was the last psychic anchor tying me to Somerville and so much of my past that I wanted to bury.

—

That year, the World Marathon Majors Age Group World Championships took place at the Chicago Marathon on Sunday, October 8. I felt tremendous pressure to dominate my age group, not just because it was a dream I'd been chasing for two years, but because there were so many more eyes on me now. In August 2022, I'd joined Rich Roll on his massively popular *Rich Roll Podcast*. Rich and I had many points of connection. I felt immediately that he wasn't just a professional contact or a friend but a true brother, and I'd bared my soul during our lengthy conversation. The response had been overwhelming. Overnight, my social media profiles blew up with thousands of new followers. It was incredible, and I'll always be grateful to Rich for shining a light on my journey, but all those new followers did mean more pressure to dominate my races.

I realized that most people who tracked the marathon only track the elites and that age-group titles only draw a tiny fraction of the world's eyes. But I realized, too, that there are lots of other folks out there like me—ex-drunks, ex-druggies, middle-aged people striving to set one more personal best before old age kicks in, people of all ages who've neglected a dream till later in life and are now determined to see it through. More of those people were tracking my races than ever before, and I was determined to not let them down.

As it happened, the spotlight was shining even brighter because the *Wall Street Journal* had run a profile of me in February 2023 with the headline "How One of the World's Top Over-50 Runners Got Faster Every Year." Again, a fantastic development . . . but to me, it meant not just that I had to podium every single race, but I had to keep getting faster. If I'm being honest, though, the greatest damage had already been done. In June 2022, the *New York Times* had run a profile of me entitled "How a Former Boxer and Opioid Addict Became the World's Best Marathoner Over 50." That title left me no wiggle room—I had to be number one. When I later got beat in London, it made me feel like a phony. Odd that being dubbed the "best marathoner over fifty" by a legendary newspaper made me feel like a fraud, but that's how my mind worked.

But the one good thing about treating every single race like it was the Boston Marathon even if it was the Palisades Turkey Trot was that it got me used to pressure. Going into Chicago, I was all keyed up—but then I was *always* keyed up. That familiar discomfort felt comfortable to me.

I didn't feel overly confident, but I knew I was ready. There'd been races where I was sure I was going to destroy my competition. Somehow, that always seemed to backfire. Other races I'd gone into feeling as if I'd already lost and had managed to come out on top. For Chicago, I felt somewhere in the middle, an unusual mental space for me to inhabit. I was in good shape coming out of Mongolia after all the novel ways that ordeal had challenged me. I'd emerged from that crucible healthy and had just spent the previous eight weeks tuning up. But in Chicago, I was going up against the best of the best, guys who'd been serious runners for decades, guys with vastly more experience.

Well, you can prepare for something your entire life but if you don't have the guts to take the plunge and go for it, that sacred moment will pass you by. I was ready because I'd stayed ready, because I was always ready. If not now, when?

I rolled into Chicago the night before the big race. Mario was there—he'd come to see me race. He had a few choice words for me, too.

"Ken, listen to what I'm telling you. If you go out too fast, you're going to blow this race. I'm going to stand at the halfway point. If you come through before one-fourteen, I'm walking off the course. I'm gone. You go through at one-twelve, even one-thirteen, your day is done and I'm not going to wait around for another hour and a half to see you stumble through on fumes."

I checked into my room at the St. Regis, picked up my race packet, grabbed dinner, and hit the hay. Like with any other race, I wanted to make sure I had everything I needed exactly how I needed it and to eliminate every variable I could. I was probably way too meticulous, but it was the way I had to do things.

I woke up early the next morning to go through my normal pre-race routine. I'd called down the night before and ordered a large pot of coffee and oatmeal with brown sugar, raisins, and peanut butter. I ate as much as I could, but it was a struggle to get any calories down. I never had much of an appetite before a race because I was so nervous. I drank some coffee and tried to move around a little bit in my room to get the blood flowing because it was relatively cold outside.

The defending masters champion at the World Marathon Majors in Chicago in October 2023 was a Belgian guy, Tom Van Ongeval. He'd run a 2:25 in London the year prior. Sipping my coffee and looking out my hotel window, I knew I wasn't running 2:25. If this guy had his best day, he was going to beat me. I didn't know this at the time, but another guy in our age group, an Aussie named Wayne Spies, had also run 2:25 that year. So much for doing my research and eliminating all the variables.

I bundled up in some old clothes against the chill and made my way to the "local elite" tent. It wasn't quite the posh professional tent that they'd had in Berlin or in New York, but it was nicer than being out in the cold. A couple of people recognized me and said hello, then I went and sat in a corner by myself. I'd really recognized during the Gobi March how anxious and on edge I was when I was in race mode, so it felt safer and easier to just sequester myself away from other runners. Inevitably, I watched a couple of people recognize me, come over as if they didn't see me, and sit nearby. I could see them strategizing internally, and eventually they'd slide over and awkwardly strike up a conversation. As stressed as I was, it still made me smile a little. Five years prior, when I was just another schlub in the crowd trying to prove to the world that I was special, I wanted to talk to any runner, every runner. I'd busted my ass and gotten to a point where I maybe felt half-special on my best day, and now I just wanted to get in and quietly do my job, then get out. So it goes.

I excused myself and went outside and did my warm-up. We were in a tiny park maybe the size of a football field with no track, just a maze of trails. I got running right away, not just to warm up but also to get away from other people, to stay busy and to stay by myself. Today was a big day, maybe the biggest of my life, and I had to make sure my head was in order.

I tried to get loose without sweating too much because it was freezing and I knew I'd get chilled standing on the starting line. Finally, there was an announcement over the loudspeakers and the organizers started funneling us toward the start. It was crazy: you'd go from being alone in your head, in your own private bubble, to being surrounded by hundreds, even thousands of other runners on all sides, everyone talking and jostling and making last-minute adjustments. You'd see guys taking a knee and pissing into Gatorade bottles in the middle of the crowd, then capping the bottle and chucking it to the side for some volunteer to pick up afterward. It wasn't pretty, but that was the game we'd chosen.

When we were lining up for the gun and everyone started jockeying for position, I bullied my way to the front, as close to the start line as possible without being on top of it, maybe two or three people back. We had our numbers on our front and back so you could see everyone in the race who was in your age group. Some guys wanted to be right at the very front, and time had taught me it was better to be a couple of people back and off to the side. That way, once we got rolling, I could create a little space for myself and protect that space. Experience had shown me that I had to.

In Tokyo the year before, I saw a guy get toppled a few people in front of me. I watched one hand shoot up as he lost his balance and flailed, trying to regain it. And then I saw his head and shoulders go down. Immediately, other people spilled over the top of him, literally head over heels, falling and catching other people in the process till you could see a rapidly expanding clot in the crowd as a steamroller of thirty thousand other runners bore down. As I scrambled to give the throng a wide berth, I could hear the painful thuds of knees, elbows, and skulls hitting the pavement, occasionally the dull whoosh of someone getting the wind knocked out of them, and cries of alarm and dismay. It reminded me of watching a surfer caught in the whitewash, getting spun and pummeled and dumped on their head as wave after wave hammered down. It'd made me hyperconscious of the dangers of a packed starting line. I just wanted to get out of that packed scrum without tripping over anyone and falling down or running anyone else over.

The gun went off and I went out hard. Once I was clear of that starting crush, I let off the gas a little bit. I knew I was in first place in my age group because there were no 50–54s in front of me. Anyone who was going to beat me had to pass me, and I had my head on a swivel.

Three or four miles into the race, the Aussie Wayne Spies passed me like I was standing still. I had no idea who he was, but I knew he wasn't Van Ongeval because I made sure I knew what Van Ongeval looked like. My heart sank. In theory, I should have gone with him. I was there to win. But I knew going too fast too early could blow up my entire race. *Just be patient, don't freak out. Focus on running a 2:28 and getting a new personal best at fifty-two. There's still a long way to go, anything can happen.*

Around the ten-mile mark, I could hear someone coming up on me fast: Van Ongeval.

As Tom caught me, he said, "Hey, Ken."

"Nice work, brother," I said between breaths. "There's a guy in our age group up the road. Go get him!"

If Van Ongeval was going to beat me, I wanted him to win it. He glanced over at me and gave me a quick thumbs-up before dashing past.

I wanted to win this race more than anything else in the fucking world, but not at the cost of my conscience. I knew almost nothing of Van Ongeval's experience on this earth, but I knew that to be running this fast at this age, he'd made sacrifices, he'd suffered, and he'd persevered. I wanted to win, I needed to win, I absolutely had to win . . . but Van Ongeval had earned some sportsmanship. "Win or die trying" had served me well for a long time, but maybe it was time to let that go? Winning was great, but after Onsite, I was no longer ready to risk death trying. I wanted to live—for my wife, for my kids, even, finally, for myself. Today, I would focus on running my best race. That had to be enough.

But shit, now I was in third place! Giving up on myself or settling for a podium finish was not an option. *I'm going to empty the tank. These next sixteen miles, I'm going to run faster than I ever have in my life. I'm going to run my best race. That will be enough. I will be enough.*

At the halfway point, I saw Mario in the crowd and he lit up and howled my name. I glanced down at my GPS: 1:14:08. My current personal record was 2:28:20.

"I'm doing it, Mario, I'm doing it!" I yelled as I ran past.

This was a promising omen. This just might work. *Stay honest and keep grinding.* I allowed my mind to retreat into the fog of marathon exertion and let my body do what I'd been training it for five years to do.

Around mile twenty-one, whom did I see on the side of the road stretching his hamstring? It was Van Ongeval. Back in business, baby! I was miraculously now in second place. The other guy had been going so hard and looked so strong, there was no way I was going to catch him. Well, I certainly wasn't going to catch him if I didn't try. *Let's fucking go.*

There was a little out and back at twenty-four miles. As I made the turn, I said to myself, *Is that the guy?* He wasn't falling apart, he was still moving at a good clip, but I was definitely gaining on him. Unfortunately, I was closing the gap so slowly that the distance between us was giving me mad anxiety. I'd been running as fast as I could for fourteen miles to get a new personal record. Now this race was coming down to a sprint and I was already destroyed. I could maybe sprint a little bit farther, but there was a good chance that if I tried, I'd blow up completely and find myself literally crawling to the finish line. It was going to be a dogfight to the end, and that scared me to death. But I stayed steady on the gas.

When I finally caught Wayne Spies, I felt completely spent. Still, I forced myself to give it a little more juice and hammer past him with confidence. I wanted so badly to look back, but I knew I couldn't allow him to see me do that because then it'd be like I was running scared. I was listening for his feet and his breath behind me when every part of my body—my legs, my lungs, my heart—wanted to seize up and burst into flames, like a race car engine run dry of oil.

Finally, finally, finally, I realized he wasn't right on my heels. He'd have gone with me if he could. He was at his limit. *You got this*, I thought over the pounding in my head, *you can fucking win this.* It gave me this insane burst of energy. I just kept sprinting to the very finish, giving everything I had left.

Somehow, everything held together, and I got over the line without Ongeval or Spies getting past me. Could it be? Had I done it? Ever since London, I always second-guessed myself at the finish.

Finally, a race official confirmed it. I'd run 2:29:06 for first place in my age group. I'd beaten Spies by only forty-eight seconds and Van Ongeval by only sixty-five seconds. The World Championship was mine. I was the fastest marathoner over fifty *in the world.*

At my lowest, I could have never even dreamed of something like this. When I'd started running ten miles a day every day five years earlier, I had no idea of what I was running toward. Once the crazy idea of winning the World Marathon Majors Age Group World Championship came to me, I obsessed every single day for two fucking years to get here. No one could diminish what I felt, this feeling was mine forever. All the pills I'd choked down, all the coke I'd hoovered up my raw nostrils—nothing compared to the high of being number one. I felt proud . . . and, yes, relieved. I'd turned myself inside out to achieve this honor. I'd come into this world with something to prove. Finally, I'd proved it. I couldn't wait to call my wife.

"Shelby, I did it. I won my age group."

"That's so great, Pops! Another medal to hang on the wall with your other ones."

"No, Shel, this is it. This was the big one, the Age Group World Championships. I'm the World Champion."

"What? Oh my God, Ken, I had no idea this race was that big! How did I not know that? Did you tell me and I just spaced? Congratulations, that is such a massive accomplishment."

"I don't know, I guess maybe I *didn't* tell you? I think I tried to minimize it in my head by not talking about it or thinking about it in those terms. I didn't mean to keep it a secret, Shel, I was just really focused. This one was really important to me and I just didn't want to fuck it up. But it's over, and I did it. I won."

Shelby could hear my excitement and fanned the flames. "The kids are going to freak out. It sounds like you couldn't be happier."

"I don't know, mostly I'm just relieved. Relieved that I did it, that I don't have to worry about this anymore. This has been *the* item on my list for the last two fucking years. I do feel happy, but my relief outweighs the happiness tenfold."

"Well, get happy, Pops. This is it. You did it. You're the best. I mean, you've always been the best but now you're really, *absolutely* the best."

She was right. The suffering was over. Time to get happy. Time to take a moment to rest, relax, and enjoy the incredibly cool thing I'd done. But two minutes later, I'd forgotten about the anxiety, the pressure, the cramps, the feeling that my heart was going to burst. I was already wondering what hard thing I'd do next. Not because I had anything left to prove, but because it's who I am, I guess. Competition is what has always kept my motor running. When I'm exhausted and sprinting, totally redlining, that's when I feel most myself. Though it makes no sense, inside that tunnel of pain is where I feel most alive.

—

In the five years leading up to the World Championships, I ran approximately twenty thousand miles. That's nothing compared to the distance I've traveled in my head. From vulnerable, unsupported child to insecure dreamer to relentless druggie to manic head case to finally, hopefully, a settled, secure—or at least less insecure—husband and father. To escape myself, I needed coke, pills, more money, more power, more VIP treatment, better clothes, faster cars, everything and anything—until nothing worked anymore. I was running away.

Ironically, running was what finally gave me the strength to turn and fight instead of running away. Running—and yes, therapy, lots and lots of overdue therapy—gave me the courage to slow down and confront what I'd been running from, to throw down with my demons, and move forward.

I've been blessed to race against some incredible competitors, and I feel overwhelming gratitude for them. Each time, I did them a disservice by painting targets on their backs and making them villains in my mind to get the most out of my athletic performance on race day. But it has always been clear to me that these people are my brothers and sisters. In my head, I talked about ruining them, destroying them, crushing their will to live—but I always knew that even if they were strangers, I probably had more in common with them than with my closest friends.

Many of my running rivalries have blossomed into friendships that will last a lifetime. Months after the Gobi March, I saw one of Dudu's posts on Instagram where he was wearing a traditional Jewish linen sudra. I messaged him and asked him whether he could send me one. Several days later, a package arrived in Nashville from Israel. Most ultrarunners would think nothing of sharing gear with a pal during a race. But to go out and buy something, pack it up, and actually send it to a guy in another country whom you met once—that's a commitment.

I don't want to come off as arrogant and put too much emphasis on this World Championship. I'm not going to lie—I love being able to say I'm the World Champion, and it's awesome having people introduce me as the fastest marathoner in the world over fifty. But it's not like I won the Olympics. To the rest of the world, it is what it is—a niche win at best, picking up the blue ribbon in a category of old-timers and has-beens, if you're uncharitable. But to me, it absolutely was the Olympics.

In the depths of my addiction, I didn't have any goal but survival. *Let me get through this meeting so I can take some pills. Let me get through this day so I can buy more pills. Let me get through tonight without running out of pills. Please, God, I beg of you, let me never, ever run out of pills.*

I've found that chasing audacious goals is the opposite of addiction.

You don't have to set out to win a heavyweight title in boxing. You can set your sights on winning a Golden Gloves tournament, or even just a single amateur boxing match. What matters is that you choose a goal that's important to you, that seems at the outer limits of what you may be able to achieve—something for you that's nearly impossible. Choose a goal that feels audacious, then go out and do it. For the rest of my life, I'll be seeking out nearly impossible things to do, and doing them.

Age-group wins don't mean much . . . unless you're a competitor, in which case they mean the entire world. Mostly, you're trying to best yourself. In every race on my way to the World Championship, I was competing against other runners, and I was certainly racing against the distance itself, because the marathon loves nothing more than to watch you crumple. But at the end of the day, it was just *let me see if I can run faster than I did before.*

For all the targets I painted on the backs of my competitors, for all the ways I shit-talked them in my head, there was only ever one person I was fighting with, one person who was my nemesis, one person I was determined to run into the ground. That person was me—the *old* me. Through trauma, weakness, self-loathing, and fear, I became an addict. More than anyone else in my life, that guy has been my enemy. He's the one who held me down for ten years. He was the one with his foot on my neck.

And I finally beat him.

In my mind's eye, I see an anxious, insecure little eight-year-old, his head full of dreams and his heart full of dread, firing slap shot after slap shot into the gray chain-link fence outside a dilapidated duplex in Somerville. I'd give anything to go back in time and just have five minutes with that kid. I know now how to be a dad, how to be a dad to boys, how to give him what he needed and didn't get. I'd just walk over to him, squat down, put my hand on his shoulder, look him in the eye, and say, "Kid, I love you. I believe in you. What you've got ahead of you isn't going to be easy. But if you can just get to the other side of hard, it will have been worth the journey."

Piia Wirsu was always going to be a storyteller – her love of stories was forged around campfires on weekend and holiday adventures. A journalist and producer of ten years, Piia has interviewed, written about, and told the stories of people from all walks of life – from politicians to refugees to community heroes. The host and senior producer of *Expanse*, one of the ABC's top performing and award-winning podcasts, Piia Wirsu has turned her storytelling nous to creating longform narrative podcasts including *Dig: Saving the Franklin*, which won the Asia-Pacific Broadcasting Union's Best Radio Documentary. She lives in Tasmania.

Mick Doleman is an Australian maritime worker and trade union official who started work as a 16-year-old deck boy. At age 18, Mick was a crew member of the MV *Blythe Star* which sank in the Southern Ocean off Tasmania and was among the remaining crew found almost two weeks later on a remote peninsula. He gave evidence at the inquiry into the sinking, which led to significant changes in maritime practice, and he continued a high-profile domestic and international maritime career. He lives in Victoria.

ABOUT THE AUTHOR

KEN RIDEOUT is the fastest marathoner in the world over fifty and a former prison guard, Wall Street trader, and opioid addict. His life story has been chronicled in such publications as *The New York Times*, *The Wall Street Journal*, and *Outside*. Since getting sober more than a decade ago, he has won some of the world's toughest races, including, at age fifty-two, the Gobi March—a 155-mile self-supported race across the sweltering Gobi Desert in Mongolia—and a few months later, the Masters (50+) Marathon World Championships. In addition to his many running victories, he has completed more than ten Ironman triathlons. In 2018, Ken founded the capital solutions firm Camrock Advisors. More recently, he founded the talent agency Rideout Sports and Entertainment. He lives in Nashville with his wife, Shelby, and their four children.